Attachment Theory in Mental Health

MW00654853

In the fifty years since its inception, John Bowlby's attachment theory has been a powerful influence on developmental psychology and, more recently, mental health. Bringing together the experience of a diverse range of mental health practitioners and researchers who routinely use attachment theory in their own work, *Attachment Theory in Adult Mental Health* provides a guide to using attachment theory in everyday practice.

Adam N. Danquah and Katherine Berry present a wide-ranging and practical approach to the topic that includes studies on clinical practice, the provision of mental health services and accommodating intercultural perspectives. Section One covers the basics of attachment theory and practice. Section Two presents clinical problems and presentations, including the treatment of depression, anxiety disorders, psychosis, personality disorder and eating disorders. Section Three addresses the needs of specific populations, discussing the influence of sociocultural factors such as gender, ethnicity and age. Finally, Section Four examines the organisation and the practitioner, including using the theory to organise services and how individual therapists can integrate their own attachment histories into their approach.

Including the most up-to-date theories and practice in the field, *Attachment Theory in Adult Mental Health* is an ideal resource for psychologists and psychological therapists, counsellors, psychiatrists, occupational therapists, social workers and mental health service managers and commissioners.

Adam N. Danquah is a clinical psychologist in Pennine Care NHS Foundation Trust, where he works in secondary care adult mental health with adults across the age range with complex and longstanding mental health problems. He is co-founder and associate editor of the *Ghana International Journal of Mental Health*.

Katherine Berry is a postdoctoral research fellow at the University of Manchester, funded by the National Institute of Health Research, and a clinical psychologist. Her main area of expertise is interpersonal relationships in people with a diagnosis of psychosis.

Attachment Theory in Adult Mental Health

A guide to clinical practice

Edited by Adam N. Danquah and Katherine Berry

Routledge
Taylor & Francis Group

LONDON AND NEW YORK

First published 2014
by Routledge
2 Park Square, Milton Park, Abingdon, Oxon OX14 4RN

and by Routledge
711 Third Avenue, New York, NY 10017

Routledge is an imprint of the Taylor & Francis Group, an informa business

© 2014 Adam N. Danquah and Katherine Berry

The right of the editors to be identified as the authors of the
editorial material, and of the authors for their individual chapters, has
been asserted in accordance with sections 77 and 78 of the
Copyright, Designs and Patents Act 1988.

All rights reserved. No part of this book may be reprinted or
reproduced or utilised in any form or by any electronic, mechanical,
or other means, now known or hereafter invented, including
photocopying and recording, or in any information storage or
retrieval system, without permission in writing from the publishers.

Trademark notice: Product or corporate names may be trademarks or
registered trademarks, and are used only for identification and
explanation without intent to infringe.

British Library Cataloguing in Publication Data
A catalogue record for this book is available from the British Library

Library of Congress Cataloging in Publication Data
Attachment theory in adult mental health : a guide to clinical
practice / edited by Adam N. Danquah and Katherine Berry.
p. ; cm.
Includes bibliographical references.
I. Danquah, Adam N. II. Berry, Katherine.
[DNLM: 1. Object Attachment. 2. Adult. 3. Mental Disorders--
therapy. 4. Psychotherapy--methods. WM 460.5.O2]
RC480.5
616.89'14--dc23
2013016224

ISBN: 978-0-415-68740-9 (hbk)
ISBN: 978-0-415-68741-6 (pbk)
ISBN: 978-1-315-88349-6 (ebk)

Typeset in Times and Gill Sans
by Saxon Graphics Ltd, Derby

MIX
Paper from
responsible sources
FSC
www.fsc.org   FSC® C013604

Printed and bound by CPI Group (UK) Ltd, Croydon, CR0 4YY

Adam – For my family
Katherine – For Jacob and Ethan

Contents

SECTION 3
Specific populations

SECTION 4
The organisation and the individual practitioner

Figures

The editors

Adam N. Danquah is a clinical psychologist in Pennine Care NHS Foundation Trust, where he works in secondary care adult mental health in Stockport, Greater Manchester. Clinically he works with adults across the age range with complex and usually longstanding mental health problems. His research interests include attachment processes both in therapy and in mental health service provision more generally. He is currently training in psychodynamic psychotherapy with the Tavistock & Portman NHS Foundation Trust at the Northern School of Child and Adolescent Psychotherapy, Leeds. He is associate editor of the *Ghana International Journal of Mental Health*, which he co-founded whilst working as a clinical psychologist and lecturer in Ghana.

Katherine Berry is a postdoctoral research fellow at the University of Manchester, funded by the National Institute of Health Research, and a clinical psychologist. Her main area of expertise is interpersonal relationships in people with a diagnosis of psychosis. After completing her PhD, which explored the relevance of attachment theory in psychosis, she obtained a fellowship to develop and evaluate an intervention to improve staff–patient relationships in inpatient psychiatric settings.

Contributors

Gwen Adshead is a forensic psychiatrist and psychotherapist. She trained at St George's Hospital, the Institute of Psychiatry and the Institute of Group Analysis. For the last ten years she has worked as a consultant forensic psychotherapist at Broadmoor Hospital, where she runs psychotherapeutic groups for offenders and works with staff and organisational dynamics. Gwen also has a Master's Degree in Medical Law and Ethics and a research interest in moral reasoning and how this links with 'bad' behaviour. Gwen has published a number of books and over 100 papers, book chapters and commissioned articles on forensic psychotherapy, ethics in psychiatry and attachment theory as applied to medicine and forensic psychiatry.

Anne Aiyegbusi is Interim Director of Nursing and Patient Experience at West London Mental Health NHS Trust and visiting Fellow at Buckinghamshire New University. She previously led and developed nursing practice within forensic mental health services, with a particular focus on integrating forensic psychotherapy with the nursing role. She has a special interest in psychological trauma and how it can reverberate throughout mental health services. Anne is a strong advocate of the clinical value of attachment theory as a framework for understanding and supporting people with traumatic histories and complex mental health needs.

Rudi Dallos is Professor of Clinical Psychology and research director on the D Clin Psychol training programme at the University of Plymouth. He is also a family therapist and has utilised his research and clinical experience to incorporate attachment theory into systemic therapy. He has published a number of books, including *Attachment Narrative Therapy* and *Systemic Therapy and Attachment Narratives*.

Paul Gilbert OBE is Professor of Clinical Psychology at the University of Derby and consultant clinical psychologist at the Derbyshire Health Care Foundation Trust. He has researched evolutionary approaches to psychopathology for over 35 years, with a special focus on shame and the treatment of shame-based difficulties – for which compassion-focused therapy was developed. In 2003 he was president of the BABCP and a member of the group that produced the first NICE guidelines for depression. He has written or edited 20 books and over 150 papers. In 2006 he established the Compassionate Mind Foundation, a charity with the mission statement 'To promote wellbeing through the scientific understanding and application of compassion' (www.compassionatemind.co.uk). He was awarded an OBE in March 2011.

Andrew Gumley is a clinical psychologist and Professor of Psychological Therapy based in the Institute of Health and Wellbeing within the University of Glasgow. Andrew's research spans the trajectory of psychosis, from those at risk to individuals with established psychosis that is unresponsive to existing treatments. Andrew is interested in the application of psychological theory to the understanding of mechanisms of recovery; the development and evaluation of psychological therapies, from feasibility, through piloting, to definitive randomised controlled trials; and finally, the design and evaluation of service systems to promote engagement, autonomy and psychological wellbeing.

Jeremy Holmes worked for 35 years as a consultant psychiatrist and psychotherapist in the NHS, first at University College London, and then providing a district psychotherapy service in North Devon, focusing especially on people with borderline personality disorder. He was Chair of the Psychotherapy Faculty of the Royal College of Psychiatrists 1998–2002. Now partially retired, he has a part-time private practice; has set up and co-runs a Masters and Doctoral psychoanalytic psychotherapy training and research programme at Exeter University, where he is visiting Professor; and lectures nationally and internationally. He has written more than 150 peer reviewed papers and chapters in the field of attachment theory and psychoanalytic psychotherapy. His many books, translated into nine languages, include *The Oxford Textbook of Psychotherapy* (2005, co-editors Glen Gabbard and Judy Beck), *Storr's The Art of Psychotherapy* (Taylor & Francis 2012) and *Exploring in Security: Towards an Attachment-informed Psychoanalytic Psychotherapy* (Routledge), which won the 2010 Canadian Psychological Association Goethe Award. With Arietta Slade he is currently preparing a six-volume compendium of the most important papers in attachment theory (*Benchmarks in Psychology: Attachment Theory*, SAGE). *Literature and the Therapeutic Imagination* and *John Bowlby and Attachment Theory*, 2nd Edition (both Routledge) are due in 2013. He was the recipient of the 2009 New York Attachment Consortium Bowlby–Ainsworth Founders Award.

Jonathan J. Hunter is an associate professor at the University of Toronto, where he heads the Division of Consultation-Liaison Psychiatry, which addresses the psychiatric needs of medically and surgically ill patients. He is a founding member of a network of Family Physicians, which links family practitioners in the community with mental health care mentors for advice about managing psychiatric concerns in a timely fashion. He participates in grants funded by NCIC, NIH,

CIHR, and the Change Foundation. His clinical practice centres on the psychiatric and psychotherapeutic care of cancer patients. Research interests include psychological management of chemotherapy side-effects, group psychotherapy in women at high risk for breast cancer, the role of early life experience and attachment in adaptation to disease, and the importance of mentalising in treatment.

Kenneth N. Levy is a tenured associate professor in the Department of Psychology at the Pennsylvania State University, where he directs the Laboratory for Research on Personality, Psychopathology and Psychotherapy. He is also the Associate Director of Research at the Personality Disorders Institute (PDI) at the Joan and Sanford I. Weill Medical College of Cornell University. His main research interests are attachment theory, borderline personality disorder, and psychotherapy process and outcome. He was a founding member of the NIMH Think Tank on the Treatment of Borderline Personality Disorder and is the associate editor of the *Journal of Psychotherapy Integration*. He has published more than 150 articles and chapters. He maintains a part-time private practice in State College, PA.

Giovanni Liotti is a psychiatrist and psychotherapist who currently teaches at the APC Postgraduate School of Psychotherapy in Rome. His interest in the clinical applications of attachment theory was first expressed in a book co-authored with V.F. Guidano (*Cognitive Processes and Emotional Disorders*, Guilford Press, 1983). His work over the past 20 years has focused on the links between trauma, dissociation and attachment disorganisation. In 2005 he received the Pierre Janet's Writing Award of The International Society for the Study of Trauma and Dissociation, and in 2006 the International Mind and Brain Award of the University of Turin. His latest book, co-authored with Benedetto Farina, is *Sviluppi traumatici: Eziopatogenesi, clinica e terapia della dimensione dissociativa* (*Traumatic Development: etiology, clinical features and therapy of the dissociative dimension,* Cortina Editore, 2011).

Brent Mallinckrodt is a professor in the Department of Psychology at the University of Tennessee. He is former editor of the *Journal of Counseling Psychology*, and director of Graduate Studies in Counseling Psychology, where he has helped develop the first programme accredited by the American Psychological Association with a scientist–practitioner–advocate training model, emphasising social justice advocacy. He is author of over 90 articles and book chapters, many on the topics of adult attachment and the psychotherapy relationship.

Robert G. Maunder is associate professor in the Department of Psychiatry at the University of Toronto and Head of Research in the Department of Psychiatry at Mount Sinai Hospital. His research, often done in collaboration with Jon Hunter, focuses on issues at the interface of psychology, psychiatry and physical health, especially the impact of interpersonal relationships on health. Since the 2003 SARS outbreak, he has also studied the impact of extraordinary stress on healthcare workers and how to build resilience.

Kevin B. Meehan is an assistant professor in the Department of Psychology and the Clinical Psychology Doctoral Program at Long Island University, Brooklyn. He is also an adjunct clinical assistant professor of psychology in the Department of Psychiatry at Weill Cornell Medical College, where he collaborates with his colleagues at the Personality Disorders Institute (PDI) in evaluating a manualised treatment for borderline personality disorder called Transference Focused Psychotherapy (TFP). His clinical research evaluates attachment and reflective functioning as mechanisms of change in psychodynamic and interpersonal psychotherapies, as well as the process of change in patients with personality disorders and post-traumatic stress disorder. His research also evaluates deficits in social and regulatory processes in both college-age and personality disordered populations. He also maintains a private practice in downtown Brooklyn.

Gail Myhr is an associate professor of psychiatry at McGill University, Canada. She is a psychiatrist and a cognitive therapist and Director of the Cognitive Behavioural Therapy Unit of the McGill University Health Centre, a university research and teaching unit which trains mental health professionals in basic and advanced cognitive behavioural therapy skills. Her clinical and research interests include suitability for short-term CBT, CBT for psychosis, attachment-related interventions in CBT, and the cost-effectiveness of CBT in the treatment of mental disorders. She is a fellow of the Royal College of Physicians and Surgeons of Canada, a diplomate of the Academy of Cognitive Therapy, and Membership Chair and Founding Member of the Canadian Association of Cognitive and Behavioural Therapies (l'Association Canadienne des Thérapies Cognitives et Comportementales).

Susie Orbach is a psychoanalyst and writer whose interests have centred around feminism and psychoanalysis, the construction of femininity and gender, globalisation and body image, emotional literacy, and psychoanalysis and the public sphere. She co-founded The Women's Therapy Centre in London in 1976 and The Women's Therapy Centre Institute, New York in 1981. Her numerous publications include the classic *Fat is a Feminist Issue*, along with similarly influential texts such as *Hunger Strike*, *What Do Women Want* (with Luise Eichenbaum), *The Impossibility of Sex* and her latest book, *Bodies*. Susie is currently co-editing *Fifty Shades of Feminism*, which will be published in Spring 2013. Susie has been a consultant to the World Bank, the NHS and Unilever. She is a founder member of ANTIDOTE (working for emotional literacy) and Psychotherapists and Counsellors for Social Responsibility, and is convenor of Endangered Bodies (www.london.endangeredbodies.org), the organisation campaigning against body hatred. She is also an expert member of the steering group of the British government's Campaign for Body Confidence. Susie is currently chair of the Relational School in the UK and has a clinical practice seeing individuals and couples.

Cecilia Yee Man Poon is a postdoctoral fellow in clinical health psychology at the Nebraska Medical Center. She grew up in Hong Kong and received her Ph.D. in clinical psychology (ageing track) at the University of Southern California. Her clinical and research interests are in ageing and mental health, particularly caregiving and coping with chronic illness. Her published work has focused on the influence of adverse parent–child relationships on health and wellbeing across the lifespan.

Matthias Schwannauer, MA, MSc, DPsych, Ph.D, CPsychol, AFBPsS, is a professor of clinical psychology who graduated in clinical and applied psychology from the University of Marburg in 1998. His first position as a clinical psychologist was in the Adolescent Mental Health Services in Glasgow. He moved to NHS Lothian and the University of Edinburgh in 2000. During this time he was able to carry out his Ph.D research into psychological interventions for bipolar disorders. This research involved the implementation of a randomised controlled trial of Cognitive Interpersonal Therapy and an investigation of the role of interpersonal and cognitive factors in the recovery process. He is currently Head of the Section of Clinical and Health Psychology at the University of Edinburgh. He is a consultant clinical psychologist in the Early Psychosis Support Service at CAMHS Lothian. His current research interests include the application of attachment theory and affect regulation to understanding the development, adaptation to and recovery from psychosis and recurrent mood disorders.

Martin Seager is a clinician, lecturer, campaigner, broadcaster and activist on mental health issues. He studied at Oxford University, Edinburgh University and the Tavistock Clinic and has worked in the NHS for nearly 30 years. He had a regular mental health slot on BBC Radio 5 Live from 2007–9. He is currently working part-time with the South West Yorkshire Partnership NHS Foundation Trust and in private practice. He is also an honorary consultant psychologist with the Central London Samaritans and a member of the Mental Health Advisory Board of the College of Medicine.

Kathy Steele, MN, CS, is clinical director of Metropolitan Counselling Services, a psychotherapy and training centre. She is also a psychotherapist in private practice in Atlanta, Georgia. She offers therapists training and consultation on psychological trauma, dissociation, attachment issues and many other related topics. Kathy has written extensively on the topics of trauma, dissociation, attachment and stabilisation. Her publications include two award-winning books: *Coping with Trauma-related Dissociation: skills training for patients and therapists* and *The Haunted Self: structural dissociation and the treatment of* *chronic traumatization.* She is past president of the International Society for the Study of Trauma and Dissociation.

Christina M. Temes is a graduate student in clinical psychology at the Pennsylvania State University, working with Dr Kenneth N. Levy. Her research interests include the etiology and treatment of personality disorders and the influence of attachment on personality pathology, as well as psychotherapy process and outcome.

Lennox K. Thomas trained in clinical social work, child and family psychotherapy and psychoanalytic psychotherapy. He was clinical director of Nafsiyat Intercultural Therapy Centre, and Co-Director of the University College London MSc in Intercultural Psychotherapy. He is a consultant psychotherapist at the Refugee Therapy Centre, a training therapist and supervisor. A member of the British Psychoanalytic Council, he has been elected as an Honorary Fellow of the United Kingdom Council for Psychotherapy. Influenced by his early work with children and parents in hospitals, he has an interest in attachment and relational psychotherapy.

Onno van der Hart is Emeritus Professor of the Psychopathology of Chronic Traumatization at Utrecht University, and until recently a psychologist/ psychotherapist at the Sinai Center for Mental Health, Amstelveen, the Netherlands.

David Wallin is a clinical psychologist in private practice in Albany and Mill Valley, California. A magna cum laude graduate of Harvard who received his doctorate from the Wright Institute in Berkeley, he has been practising, teaching and writing about psychotherapy for nearly three decades. *Attachment in Psychotherapy*, his most recent book, is presently being translated into nine languages. He is also co-author of *Mapping the Terrain of the Heart: passion, tenderness, and the capacity to love.* He has lectured on attachment and psychotherapy in Australia, Europe, Canada and throughout the United States. For further information, please visit www.attachmentinpsychotherapy.com.

Foreword

In the preface to *A Secure Base* (1988), John Bowlby acknowledged the growing body of research that attachment theory had prompted in developmental psychology; but he also noted that despite the theory's roots in his own experience as a clinician, 'it is none the less disappointing that clinicians have been so slow to test its uses'. These words bring a little sorrow to me, because in this passage I hear something of a lament. In this valedictory book, published just before his death in 1990, I find myself wishing Bowlby had been able to gain a stronger sense of satisfaction that his seminal theory had more completely fulfilled its promise for clinical practice. Ironically, because *A Secure Base* brought an influential series of Bowlby's papers and lectures to a wider audience, the book that began with this specific regret sparked a new generation of researchers to begin applying attachment theory to understand psychotherapy with adults.

I was a member of that wider audience in 1992, when I first read *A Secure Base*. I had just become a tenured Associate Professor, a licensed psychologist, and director of my programme's research and training clinic. I was strongly influenced by Bowlby's thinking about the psychotherapy working alliance as a secure attachment. Fortunately, with so many adult outpatients available to me at the University of Oregon's DeBusk Center, I could observe the unfolding struggle of many therapists-in-training and clients to forge a secure attachment – and thereby an effective working alliance. I began a programme of research into how clients' memories of emotional bonds with parents were associated with the working alliances they were able to develop. Fortunately, I was in the right place at the DeBusk Center clinic and at the right time, inspired by the burgeoning research on adult attachment that followed Bowlby's *A Secure Base* from scholars like Shaver, Mikulincer, Fonagy, Bartholomew, Holmes, Feeney, their colleagues and others. I also began a part-time private practice in which I could directly test some of my developing ideas, and I was able to gather a research team of very bright graduate students. Both became sources of continuing inspiration. In 1995, this work led to development of the Client Attachment to Therapist Scale (CATS), a 36-item self-report measure that has since been translated into five languages and cited nearly 200 times.

More recently, our qualitative interviews with expert therapists who use attachment theory to guide their work helped to refine a model of managing therapeutic distance, which underscores the importance of creating different corrective emotional experiences, depending on whether a client exhibits tendencies toward attachment anxiety or avoidance. The optimal amount of distance versus engagement appears to vary by type of client and phase of the work. Effective therapists manage therapeutic distance in different ways to engage clients who tend to be hyperactive versus deactivate in initial bids for attachment to the therapist; and then therapists gradually alter this initial stance in the working and termination phases, differently for each type of client, to foster a corrective psychotherapy attachment. Our preliminary work with the Therapeutic Distance Scale suggests that clients with anxious attachments benefit from a growing sense of autonomy, and clients with avoidant attachments benefit from a growing sense of engagement when their therapists skilfully manage distance in the psychotherapy relationship.

Dr Adam Danquah and Dr Katherine Berry have travelled a remarkably similar path to combine clinical experience with research in the application of attachment theory to understand patients and the psychotherapy process. Dr Berry has worked as a clinical psychologist in the National Health Service and conducted research on the role of attachment in the treatment of psychosis. Currently she has a postdoctoral fellowship with the National Institute of Health Research, where she is working to develop and evaluate an intervention to improve staff–patient relationships in mental health services for people with schizophrenia and related psychoses. Dr Danquah has worked as a clinician in a children's hospital, and in West Africa with former child soldiers. In Ghana he contributed to the continuing synthesis of Western psychotherapy and traditional oral healing methods. After returning to the UK, Adam accepted a position as a clinical psychologist in secondary care adult mental health, where he works to broaden the application of attachment theory to assessment and intervention. Both Dr Berry and Dr Danquah are accomplished researchers with a growing list of publications to their credit. Given their solid grounding, both as practising clinicians and as skilled researchers at the forefront of applying attachment theory in clinical settings, perhaps it is not surprising that they have edited a book so useful and so accessible for practising clinicians.

The editors' rich personal and clinical experiences and perspectives have guided them in assembling this superb and timely book. The chapters of *Attachment Theory in Adult Mental Health* are authored by an international roster of expert clinician-researchers. Thus readers will find a synthesis of the latest research in adult attachment, thoughtfully considered from the perspective of direct application to clinical work. For example, some chapters address attachment in connection with specific presenting problems such as anxiety, depression, dissociation, eating disorders, psychosis, medically unexplained symptoms and personality disorders. Clinicians working with these issues will find a wealth of practical suggestions. Other chapters address specific challenges from the perspective of attachment theory, such as working in forensic settings, bridging cultural and ethnic differences, working with older adults, or the impact of socially proscribed concepts of gender and gender roles. Further chapters take a very broad perspective, for example by considering how attachment theory can inform challenges in the delivery of mental health services. Finally, two chapters with special relevance for psychotherapy process consider the impact of a therapist's own attachment history and the importance of attachment theory for understanding the psychotherapy relationship.

Thus this book will appeal to a wide range of readers – graduate students in training, researchers, and practising clinicians. I was especially impressed by the wealth of practical advice, offered refreshingly unfettered by the 'tyranny of the .05 level'. I certainly do not mean to suggest that this book rejects the importance of evidence based practice. Indeed, the chapters are informed by the best available research findings. However, I write from the perspective of a former journal editor who rejected 80 per cent of the psychotherapy manuscripts we received, and also from the perspective of a psychologist faced with the necessity of making clinical decisions in the moment. I fear that too many of the well-controlled studies I accepted for publication in the *Journal of Counseling Psychology* were not sufficiently helpful for practising therapists. The therapist who must decide whether the specific inpatient in her care is ready to be discharged, or whether the specific client he has just assessed is appropriate for referral to group therapy, usually cannot wait for the jury of statistical significance to render a verdict 'beyond a reasonable doubt'. Instead, clinical decisions must be made based on a preponderance of the best evidence applied in that particular moment to a specific case. Of course, with time decisions like these are increasingly guided by clinical wisdom. Readers seeking this type of hard-earned practical guidance will find this book to be a superb contribution.

I am confident that Bowlby would be quite pleased to see that, soon after publication of *A Secure Base*, attachment theory expanded into such a wide range of clinical applications with both children and adults, and that the theory he developed is now a central foundation of work with a great variety of clients and in many settings. In fact, given the disappointment that Bowlby expressed in his last book on attachment, its title has now acquired a second, poignant meaning. In addition to the secure base construct that is central to attachment theory, the theory itself has now become an established 'secure base' for the application of clinical practice – as exemplified by Danquah and Berry's wonderful contribution to this developing literature.

Brent Mallinckrodt

Acknowledgements

First of all we would like to thank the authors, who somehow found time within very busy schedules to write excellent chapters. We would like to thank the editorial team at Routledge for their guidance and support over the course of the book's development. A number of people we know personally and professionally helped us – usually indirectly and unknowingly – to get the book together with their wisdom, ways of being and support. From among these, Adam would like to give special mention to Mary Hopper for setting him the professional challenge that played a part in the book's conception, and to Joel Harvey for his encouragement and generosity with insights gleaned from similar experience. Katherine would also like to acknowledge the hard work of Isabelle Butcher, Jasmine Elwheshi and Danielle Verity in helping us to polish the manuscript.

Figure from p. 24 of *The Compassionate Mind* by Paul Gilbert (Constable & Robinson, London, 2010) is reproduced by kind permission of the author and publisher.

The chapter entitled 'Working from the inside out: the therapist's attachment history as a source of impasse, inspiration and change' by David Wallin (original title 'From the inside out: the therapist's attachment patterns as sources of insight and impasse') is reproduced from *Clinical Pearls of Wisdom: 21 leading therapists offer their key insights*, edited by Michael Kerman. Copyright © 2010 by Michael Kerman. Used by permission of W. W. Norton & Company, Inc.

Section 1

Attachment theory and practice – the basics

Chapter 1

Introduction

Katherine Berry, Adam N. Danquah and David Wallin

Background

In the fifty years since its inception, John Bowlby's attachment theory has become 'the most powerful contemporary account of social and emotional development available to science' (Steele 2002: 518). Although the theory's influence has been most obvious in developmental psychology, it was originally conceived in a clinical context and the last 20 years have witnessed a dramatic surge of interest in attachment from within the mental health field (Fonagy 2001; Holmes 2001; Obegi and Berant 2009; Wallin 2007). A growing body of theory and research now links attachment to adult psychopathology and interpersonal problems. Meanwhile there is increasing consensus that attachment theory is well placed to provide the overarching framework for interventions in mental health (see Obegi and Berant 2009).

These developments notwithstanding, practitioners often find it difficult to know exactly how the concepts of attachment can be put to effective use in the clinical setting. Those who would translate attachment theory into practice have had to draw inferences from either the mainly nonclinical adult attachment literature or from the comparatively sparse and narrowly focused literature on the implications of attachment theory for single schools of psychotherapy (Obegi and Berant 2009). The present volume aims to address this gap in the literature. By inviting expert practitioners and researchers from a variety of therapeutic backgrounds to spell out how they apply attachment theory to a range of mental health problems and clinical issues we hope to make the theory an accessible resource for the broad spectrum of mental health practitioners, including those in training. We trust that the book will also be of use to service managers and commissioners responsible for the design, delivery and organisation of mental health services, as well as researchers testing key hypotheses relating to the clinical applications of the theory. In this introductory chapter we review some of the basic concepts of attachment theory, in order to provide a context for the chapters that follow.

Basic concepts

John Bowlby was a psychoanalyst who drew on psychoanalysis, evolutionary theory, ethology, developmental psychology and cognitive psychology to develop attachment theory. The theory aimed to explain 'the propensity of human beings to make strong affectional bonds to particular others ... and the many forms of emotional distress and personality disturbance ... to which unwilling separation and loss give rise' (Bowlby 1977a: 201). Attachment is defined as an affectional bond that a person forms with a 'differentiated and preferred individual' or attachment figure who is approached in times of distress (Bowlby 1979). The attachment bond is conceptualised as persistent and emotionally significant, and is associated with a desire for close proximity to, and distress following involuntary separation from, the attachment figure (Bowlby 1969, 1973, 1980). The attachment figure is hypothesised to represent both a secure base around which the individual is able to engage in exploration, developing and gaining independence (Ainsworth *et al.* 1978), and a safe haven to which the individual can retreat, seeking reassurance in situations of danger and moments of alarm (Bowlby 1969).

Attachment behaviours (crying, calling out, clinging, searching and the like) are motivated by the urge to retain or regain contact with the attachment figure in the face of environmental threat, distress, illness or fatigue. As such, the 'attachment behaviour system' is not in constant operation, but rather only when the individual senses threat. In evolutionary terms, caregiver proximity is vital because it increases the infant's chances of survival when confronted with danger. That the development of attachment bonds during infancy is originally survival-driven explains their ongoing and fundamental importance as well as their influence – not only during childhood but throughout the life cycle (Bowlby 1980). Whether in childhood or beyond, we turn when threatened to those upon whom we depend. Moreover, because the internal representations of attachment develop in a survival-critical context, their quality will largely be determined on the basis of what does and does not 'work' in the infant's relationship with the attachment figure. What works in that relationship can be integrated into the developing self; what does not work – what threatens the survival-critical relationship – will be defensively excluded (Bowlby 1980).

Bowlby (1969, 1973, 1980) asserted that as a result of their interactions with caregivers during infancy individuals develop mental representations of the self in relation to significant others and expectations about how others will behave in social relationships. These internal working models are hypothesised to be largely unconscious and to guide attention, interpretation, memory and predictions about future interpersonal interactions (Maier *et al.* 2004; Pietromonaco and Feldman Barrett 2000). They are characterised in terms of cognitive elements, which reflect beliefs about whether the individual is worthy of attention and whether other people are reliable. They also represent emotions associated with interpersonal experiences, such as happiness, fear and anger (Pietromonaco and Feldman

Barrett 2000). An internal working model, then, is the mental representation of the quality of an individual's attachment.

Empirical support for Bowlby's theory comes from laboratory-based observations of the infant's behavioural response to two brief separations from his or her caregiver in the context of a procedure referred to as the 'strange situation' (Ainsworth *et al.* 1978). Responses to the strange situation appeared to take three distinct forms which are attributed to different underlying working models and methods of regulating distress. Infants are classified as secure or insecure, with the insecure category subdivided into ambivalent or avoidant categories (Ainsworth *et al.* 1978). Infants classified as secure are able to use the caregiver as a secure base, exploring the room in an interactive way; they are distressed by the separation but willingly approach the caregiver and are easily comforted upon reunion. Infants classified as ambivalent (or 'resistant') seem less able to use the caregiver as a secure base for exploration, staying close by in his or her presence. Upon separation they are likely to show much distress and to be difficult to soothe upon reunion, seeking contact with the caregiver while also resisting angrily or with upset. Infants classified as avoidant are unlikely to show affectional sharing with the caregiver during exploratory play and upon separation they are unlikely to show distress. Upon reunion, despite some acknowledgement of the caregiver's return, they may ignore or even move away from the caregiver (Ainsworth *et al.* 1978).

The three attachment patterns described above seem to arise largely in response to the nature of the caregiver's sensitivity to the infant's nonverbal cues and signals (Weinfield *et al.* 1999). A pattern of secure attachment is generally the outcome when caregivers are sensitive and responsive to the infant's needs. As development proceeds beyond infancy, the secure pattern is associated with the emergence of a positive self-image, a capacity to manage distress, comfort with autonomy and in forming relationships with others. Conversely, when caregivers are insensitive or unresponsive to the infant's nonverbal signals, then he or she must develop alternative means by which to elicit caregiving and regulate distress. Infants classified as ambivalent are usually raised by caregivers who are unpredictably responsive – at times they tune into the infant's needs but more often they do not. The offspring of such unpredictable attachment figures appear to adapt by escalating their displays of distress, as if to heighten the probability of meeting attachment needs by making them too conspicuous for their caregivers to ignore. This defensive strategy is referred to as hyperactivation and as development proceeds is associated with a negative self-image, a fear of abandonment, an inhibition of autonomy and a tendency to be overwhelmed by emotions. Infants classified as avoidant tend to be the offspring of rejecting and/or controlling caregivers who are predictably unresponsive. These infants learn to deactivate their attachment system to avoid the pain and disappointment that have come to be associated with their unsuccessful bids for physical and emotional closeness. In the course of ongoing development, the deactivating strategy is associated with compulsive self-reliance, an estrangement from emotion and an avoidance of close relationships (Shaver and Mikulincer 2002).

Subsequent to the pioneering identification by Ainsworth, Blehar, Salter, Waters and Wall (1978) of the three 'organised' attachment patterns of infancy, a fourth, 'disorganised' pattern was recognised by Main and Solomon (1986, 1990). These researchers saw that in the context of the strange situation there were infants – whom they described as 'disorganised-disoriented' – who displayed behaviours in response to separation and reunion that appeared bizarre, contradictory and/or incomprehensible. Such behaviours have come to be understood as expressions of fear. This fear has been seen to arise in response not only to frank maltreatment and neglect, but also to what Hesse and Main (1999) call the 'second generation effects of trauma'. These effects occur when caregivers respond to their infants not with explicit abuse, but rather with frightened withdrawal or dissociation. In sum, disorganisation appears to be the outcome of interactions in which the infant experiences the attachment figure as frightening, frightened or dissociated. In all three instances, the infant is thought to experience 'fright without solution' at being placed in an untenable position – confronted with the biological paradox that the attachment figure is not only the genetically programmed 'safe haven' but also the source of the infant's alarm (Main and Hesse 1990). The bizarre or contradictory behaviour of disorganised infants thus reflects a breakdown in attachment organisation, as a result of their profoundly disturbing and fundamentally irresolvable conflict about whether to approach or avoid the attachment figure (Fraley and Shaver 2000).

The initial research sparked by Bowlby's theorising led to the identification of the attachment classifications of infancy, as summarised above. Subsequent research has led to the classifications of attachment in adulthood. This research has been carried out by two distinct groups of investigators – developmental psychologists (among whom the most prominent is Mary Main) and social psychologists (including Phillip Shaver). The work of these two groups appears to be organised by two related but distinct paradigms.

The approach of the first group – Main, Fonagy, Sroufe and others with a developmental or psychoanalytic orientation – rests on findings that suggest that individual differences in attachment relate to the organisation of mental representations of earlier attachment figures. The researchers in this tradition have conducted longitudinal studies, focused on infant–parent interactions and their sequelae, and investigated the development of 'mentalising' – the capacity that permits us to 'read' our own minds and those of others on the basis of underlying mental states. Main and colleagues developed the Adult Attachment Interview (AAI), which measures adults' 'states of mind with respect to attachment' on the basis of the coherence of the narrative that emerges when they are asked to recall and reflect upon their own attachment relationships (Main, Kaplan and Cassidy 1985). The AAI classifies adults as secure-autonomous, dismissing (the adult version of the infant's avoidant attachment), or preoccupied (the adult version of the infant's ambivalent attachment). Corresponding to disorganised attachment in infancy is an unresolved state of mind in the adult. This category is associated with reports of traumatic loss or abuse, as well as confusion and disorganisation when discussing such traumas (Hesse 1999). Main (2010) has suggested that secure parents tend to raise and resemble their secure offspring, that dismissing parents raise and resemble their avoidant infants, that preoccupied parents raise and resemble their ambivalent infants, and that unresolved parents raise and resemble their disorganised infants.

The social psychological approach of the second group grew out of Hazan and Shaver's (1987) conceptualisation of romantic love as an attachment process. Their fundamental assumption (and that of the social psychologists that followed them) was that attachment patterns exert a profound and ongoing influence on multiple aspects of the adult's psychology and behaviour. Hazan and Shaver translated the attachment categories of Ainsworth and Main (secure, avoidant/ dismissing and ambivalent/preoccupied) into prototypical adult 'attachment styles' (secure, avoidant and anxious, respectively). Their research methodology classified adults on the basis of self-sort and self-report measures of attachment. Later, Bartholomew (1990) argued that Main, Kaplan and Cassidy (1985) and Hazan and Shaver (1987) were measuring different types of avoidance, which were respectively motivated by defensive self-sufficiency and avoidance of rejection. Bartholomew's (1990, 1997) model incorporates both types of avoidance and describes four attachment prototypes: secure, preoccupied, avoidant-dismissing and avoidant-fearful – the latter, it has been suggested, maps onto Main's 'unresolved' state of mind with respect to attachment. Several multi-item continuous self-report measures have been developed to measure attachment styles in romantic and other relationships (Collins and Read 1990; Simpson and Rholes 1998). Factor analyses have suggested that the two dimensions of attachment anxiety and attachment avoidance underlie self-report measures, which can also be conceptualised in terms of model of self and model of others (Brennan, Clark and Shaver 1998). This dimensional approach to conceptualising attachment avoids the inherent problem of categorising individuals into discrete groups, although attachment prototypes are easier to formulate clinically (Slade 2000).

In the clinical context, attachment theory can contribute to our understanding of the development of psychopathology and psychotherapy. According to attachment theory, insecure attachment is originally an adaptation to suboptimal caregiving environments. Insecure attachment per se is not pathological. However, it can have an adverse effect on adjustment in later relationships and can increase the risk of psychopathology by rendering the individual more vulnerable to the effects of stress (Goodwin 2003). Research has found that among individuals diagnosed with mental health problems or personality disorders a high proportion are insecurely attached, while disorganised attachment is the classification most strongly associated with later psychopathology – including borderline personality disorder, dissociative disorders and PTSD (Dozier, Stovall and Albus 1999; Goodwin 2003). Bowlby (1969, 1973, 1980) proposed that although internal working models and the attachment patterns they encode tend to persist relatively unchanged throughout the lifespan, due to their influence on the quality of engagement in new relationships, they may be revised under certain conditions (Bowlby 1973). 'History is not destiny' (Fraiberg, Adelson and Shapiro 1975: 389) and there is evidence that individuals may become either more or less securely attached, depending upon the life stressors they encounter and changes in their key relationships (Waters *et al.* 2000; Weinfield *et al.* 2000). One such key relationship, of course, is that which develops in psychotherapy. Bowlby held the view that the therapeutic relationship had the potential to function as a new attachment relationship that could repair early attachment failures. He saw the therapist's role as 'analogous to that of a mother who provides her child with a secure base from which to explore the world' (Bowlby 1988: 140). For Bowlby, the world to be explored was, in large part, that of attachment relationships, past and present, internal and interpersonal. The aim of therapy was to foster the patient's ability to relate to others in new ways – and to engender, in the process, what Bowlby called 'earned security' (Bowlby, 1977b, 1988).

Outline of the book

Bowlby (1977a) stated that the priorities for establishing attachment theory within clinical practice were determining both the range of conditions to which the theory applied and associated variations in intervention. This book continues and extends this programme of work. In summary, the book will focus on how attachment theory can inform psychological therapy and mental health practice. It will demonstrate how attachment theory has particular relevance for understanding the therapeutic relationship and describe the application of attachment theory to assessment, formulation and intervention in therapy with adults with a range of problems and presentations, including depression, anxiety, psychosis, dissociative disorders, personality disorders, eating disorders and medically unexplained symptoms. It will also show how the theory can accommodate gender and intercultural perspectives and inform work with older adults. More broadly, it will demonstrate how attachment principles can inform the organisation of mental health services. More personally, it will be a resource for clinicians hoping to understand and make use of their own attachment histories and patterns in service of the work. Where relevant, we have asked contributors to provide case examples from their own experience. Some details have been changed to protect the confidentiality of the individual clients involved, but the details of the processes have not been altered.

The contributors are clinicians and researchers from a range of professional backgrounds, including psychology, psychiatry, nursing and psychotherapy. A variety of therapeutic orientations are represented, including psychoanalytic/ psychodynamic, cognitive-behavioural, systemic and other more integrative approaches. We believe that this diversity is a particular strength of the book, demonstrating attachment theory's relevance across the breadth of the mental health field. The chapters that follow are organised into four sections: (1) attachment theory and practice – the basics; (2) clinical problems and presentations; (3) specific populations; and (4) the organisation and the individual practitioner.

In the first section, the foundation for the rest of the book is laid out in this introductory chapter, which focuses on theory, and in the following one by Jeremy Holmes that translates theory into practice. Holmes, Bowlby's biographer and an eminent proponent of the clinical application of attachment theory, argues that although there are few specifically and overtly attachment-based psychotherapies, attachment theory as a whole has much to say about the procedural aspects of all therapies, and that these are the factors that ultimately lead to therapeutic change. Like Bowlby, he understands that therapeutic relationships are essentially attachment relationships. Conceiving of them in this way, he highlights the influence on therapy of both the client's and the therapist's pre-existing attachment patterns and explores the synergy of the therapist's efforts to foster attachment security in the client, to develop meaning and to promote change.

The second section comprises chapters focusing on clinical problems and presentations that are commonly encountered in adult mental health settings. As clinical psychologists, we do not routinely categorise people into discrete groups, favouring individualised formulations. The breakdown of chapters in terms of clinical problems reflects the fact that contributors typically have expertise in relation to specific client groups. We hope that highlighting the relevance of attachment theory to the development of, and therapy for, specific problems will provide the reader with a new perspective on problems that are anything but new.

Paul Gilbert's chapter describes the theoretical underpinnings and practice of compassion-focused therapy for depression. He describes an 'attachment loss' model of depression, arguing that disruptions in attachment and affiliative relationships are key to the development of shame, which is itself at the root not only of depression but of other mental health problems as well. He also suggests that cultivating attachment and affiliative relationships is fundamental to the treatment of shame and depression. Finally, he describes specific intervention strategies for encouraging clients' capacity for self-compassion.

Gail Myhr, writing from a cognitive-behavioural perspective, focuses on using attachment theory to inform our thinking about anxiety disorders and their treatment. She describes the conceptualisation of anxiety disorders within a cognitive framework, as well as the goals and processes that are commonly identified by cognitive-behavioural therapists. She argues that integrating attachment-informed interventions into the treatment of anxiety can not only make difficult therapeutic tasks easier, but may themselves be essential in preventing remission and relapse. These interventions include the identification of an individual's attachment style to facilitate engagement and inform treatment, and the development of a secure base to encourage both 'inner' and 'outer' exploration.

Matthias Schwannauer and Andrew Gumley present an attachment-based understanding of the formulation of psychosis and psychotherapeutic approaches that promote emotional recovery for clients in this group. They argue that attachment theory aids our understanding of key processes in the development and maintenance of psychosis. They focus on associations between attachment and interpersonal functioning and coping and the individual's capacity to seek and utilise support in times of emotional distress, including engagement with services. They describe how increasing the individual's reflective functioning (that is, capacity for mentalisation) can enhance recovery.

Kathy Steele and Onno van der Hart apply attachment theory to the understanding of dissociation in disorders involving complex developmental trauma. The chapter begins with a description of how early secure attachment supports regulation and integration in the child, and how abuse, neglect, and severe attachment disruptions can adversely affect development and result in dissociation. The authors then outline a phase-orientated treatment approach for dissociation and related attachment problems. The treatment begins with an initial phase of stabilisation, e.g. strengthening and skills-building, followed by the treatment of traumatic memory and, in the final phase, a focus on the adaptive integration of the individual's functioning across all domains.

According to Kenneth Levy, Kevin Meehan and Christina Temes, attachment theory and research provides a comprehensive framework within which personality pathology can be understood. In their chapter they review the empirical literature on attachment theory, with a focus on assessment and intervention for personality disorders. Further, utilising clinical vignettes and examples, Levy and his colleagues demonstrate the utility of attachment theory and research for conceptualising personality pathology. Specific attention is paid to explicating the patient–therapist dynamics as a function of attachment patterns and dimensions.

In applying their knowledge of attachment difficulties to psychopathology and psychotherapy, clinicians and researchers have paid particular heed to borderline personality disorder. It is perhaps the prototypical disorder of attachment trauma, yet those diagnosed are often the recipients of the most negative reactions from mental health practitioners. We therefore asked Giovanni Liotti to write a separate chapter dedicated to this personality disorder, which develops the more general discussion of attachment and personality disorder presented by Kenneth Levy and his colleagues. The first section of this chapter describes infant attachment disorganisation and how it results from early relational trauma that triggers dissociative processes. The second section describes how the presence of disorganised internal working models may help to explain the fundamental aspects of borderline personality disorder. The final section discusses helpful treatment strategies for borderline personality disorder and how their success can be understood on the basis of attachment theory and research.

Writing from a systemic family therapy perspective, Rudi Dallos highlights the ways in which disruptions in attachment can influence the development and maintenance of eating disorders. He emphasises the importance of considering 'triadic' processes in both formulations of, and treatments for, eating disorders. The chapter illustrates how attachment and systemic approaches can be combined by using attachment theory to help develop formulations about the parents' own childhood histories, and how these shape and maintain the present family dynamics. Although the focus of this chapter is on eating disorders, the integration of attachment theory into family therapy is also of relevance to the practice of this therapy with other client groups.

Robert Maunder and Jonathan Hunter describe the application of attachment theory to the understanding and management of medically unexplained symptoms, which are commonly encountered not only in mental health settings but also in general practice and other medical specialities. The authors argue that the best evidence-based treatments available (cognitive-behavioural therapy and antidepressant drugs) provide only modest benefits and that attachment theory provides a useful new window in understanding and treating the problem. They provide evidence that both dimensions of attachment insecurity – anxiety-based hyperactivation and avoidance-based deactivation – can be associated with unexplained symptoms and they describe approaches for working with these different types of attachment insecurity.

The third section of our book shows how attachment theory might be enlisted to understand and work with some of the issues that arise in our efforts to be of help with specific demographic groups.

Susie Orbach argues that attachment theory presents a perspective that is gender neutral. Missing as it is from Bowlby's work, however, she contends that a focus on gender is nonetheless resonant within an attachment paradigm. Conscious and unconscious apprehensions of gender shape both a mother's experience of herself and the ways in which she relates and 'attaches' to children of different genders. With these influences in mind, Orbach then discusses how gender issues affect the nature and focus of therapy.

Lennox Thomas describes how attachment theory informs intercultural therapy, an approach to treatment that is responsive to the cultural and ethnic variables that have impact on both patient and therapist. Such a therapeutic framework must take into account how the significance and manifestations of attachment, separation and loss are shaped by the culture(s) of each partner in the therapeutic couple. The therapist may need to consider how the meanings of the collective journeys, acculturation and patterns of child development in the patient's original cultural community are affected by the practices and injunctions of the dominant culture. Though this chapter focuses on therapeutic work with people from the Caribbean, the principles discussed are relevant to treatment across cultures. Because attachment theory itself has been documented to have relevance across cultures, it is well placed to frame intercultural work – so long as therapists take into account the differing ways in which attachment is shaped by the different communities that are its context.

Cecilia Poon applies attachment theory to work with older people. She argues that clinical work with older adults may be informed by an attachment perspective for several reasons. These include the enduring impact of attachment across the lifespan, the fact that late adulthood is filled with experiences of separation and loss, and research showing that attachment security is associated with better psychosocial adjustment among older adults. Through a synthesis of findings from attachment research and the clinical setting, Poon shows how attachment theory can help therapists to understand and more effectively respond to many of the challenges commonly faced by older people and their families, including physical decline, bereavement and dementia care.

The three chapters in the fourth section of the book explore the implications of attachment, first at the institutional level – where the focus is on forensic mental health and on the organisation and delivery of mental health services – and finally at the personal level (where the focus is on the attachment history and patterning of the individual therapist). In different ways, all three chapters address how we set ourselves up to offer attachment-informed services.

Gwen Adshead and Anne Aiyegbusi consider areas of attachment research and practice that have particular relevance in the context of forensic mental health care. Noting (as have Levy and Liotti in earlier chapters) the strikingly high incidence of personality disorders diagnosed among populations in these settings, the authors begin by explaining how personality disorder might be best understood as the adult sequelae of profound attachment disorder in childhood. They then go on to show how attachment theory can inform the assessment of risk, including consideration of individuals who engage in high-risk behaviours. The final section of this chapter emphasises the importance of attachment relationships within institutional settings and describes how attachment security and insecurity are manifest in the relationships between staff and patients.

Martin Seager's chapter argues that attachment theory should inform the design and delivery of mental health services in the most general sense. He suggests that adult mental health services are run in ways that remain blind even to the basic concept of attachment. However, as secure attachment is a core and universal factor underlying well-being for all humans, organisations that exist to foster mental health cannot afford to ignore the attachment needs of either their service users or providers. Seager makes a number of specific recommendations about how services could move to being more 'psychologically minded' and attachment-informed. These include suggestions for reducing the risk of attachment breakdown among inpatients, personalising services, promoting psychological safety, improving the availability and accessibility of the service system, de-stigmatising the concept of dependency, creating a secure family atmosphere in mental health organisations and ensuring that the attachment needs of staff members are recognised and met.

The final chapter, by David Wallin, develops a theme initially introduced in Jeremy Holmes' chapter; namely the importance of considering the impact upon treatment of the therapist's own attachment history and patterning. Wallin suggests that, as therapists, our ability to generate a secure attachment relationship will be profoundly affected by the legacy of our own attachment relationships – a legacy that is, for many of us who choose this work, marked by trauma. The chapter opens by addressing the advantages and vulnerabilities that derive from the therapist's characteristic career trajectory, with its roots in a history of trauma and adaptation to trauma. This adaptation occurs through the 'controlling–caregiving' strategy identified by attachment researchers and also described in Giovanni Liotti's chapter on borderline personality disorder. Wallin explores the ways in which clinicians can identify their own state(s) of mind with respect to attachment and the implications that flow from recognising that they are presently lodged in a state of mind that is secure, dismissing, preoccupied or unresolved. He also describes the uses of mindfulness and mentalising in recognising and working with the enactments of transference and countertransference that arise when the therapist's attachment patterns interlock with those of the patient.

This book has been put together in such a way that it can be read *in toto* from beginning to end. Alternatively, readers can select particular chapters that strike them as especially relevant to their own work or interests. In synthesising and summarising the chapters, we have noted that certain themes or motifs recur throughout the volume – most strikingly, the high level of insecure attachment in adults who present with mental health needs, the importance of the therapeutic relationship, and the necessity to consider the attachment needs and patterns not only of clients but also of the mental health practitioners who work with them. We hope that the recurrence of such themes provides an opportunity to see parallels across different presentations and that it highlights that the core, relational aspects of individuals and their problems should constitute the primary focus of intervention in adult mental health care and the organisation of services.

References

Ainsworth, M. C., Blehar, E., Salter, M. D., Waters, S. and Wall, S. (1978). *Patterns of Attachment: a psychological study of the Strange Situation.* Hillsdale, New Jersey: Lawrence Erlbaum Associates Inc.

Bartholomew, K. (1990). Avoidance of intimacy: an attachment perspective. *Journal of Social and Personal Relationships* **7**, 147–78.

——(1997). Adult attachment processes: individual and couple perspectives. *British Journal of Medical Psychology* **70**, 249–63.

Bowlby, J. (1969). *Attachment and Loss, Volume 1: Attachment.* New York: Basic Books.

——(1973). *Attachment and Loss, Volume 2: Separation: anxiety and anger.* New York: Basic Books.

——(1977a). The making and breaking of affectional bonds. I: Aetiology and psychopathology in the light of attachment theory. *British Journal of Psychiatry* **130**, 201–10.

——(1977b). The making and breaking of affectional bonds. II: Some principles of psychotherapy. *British Journal of Psychiatry* **130**, 421–31.

——(1979). *The Making and Breaking of Affectional Bonds.* London: Tavistock Publications.

——(1980). *Attachment and Loss, Volume 3: Loss: sadness and depression.* New York: Basic Books.

——(1988). *A Secure Base: clinical applications of attachment theory.* London: Routledge.

Brennan, K. A., Clark, C. L. and Shaver, P. R. (1998). Self-report measurement of adult romantic attachment: An integrative overview. In J. A. Simpson and W. S. Rholes (eds), *Attachment Theory and Close Relationships*, pp. 46–76. New York: Guilford Press.

Collins, N. L. and Read, S. J. (1990). Adult attachment, working models, and relationship quality in dating couples. *Journal of Personality and Social Psychology* **58**, 644–63.

Dozier, M., Stovall, K. C. and Albus, K. (1999). Attachment and psychopathology in adulthood. In J. Cassidy and P. R. Shaver (eds), *Handbook of Attachment Theory and Research*, pp. 497–519. New York: Guilford Press.

Fonagy, P. (2001). *Attachment Theory and Psychoanalysis.* New York: Other Press.

Fraiberg, S., Adelson, E. and Shapiro, V. (1975). Ghosts in the nursery: A psychoanalytic approach to the problems of impaired infant–mother relationships. *Journal of the American Academy of Child and Adolescent Psychiatry* **14**, 387–421.

Fraley, R. C. and Shaver, P. R. (2000). Adult attachment: Theoretical developments, emerging controversies, and unanswered questions. *Review of General Psychology* **4**, 132–54.

Goodwin, I. (2003). The relevance of attachment theory to the philosophy, organisation, and practice of adult mental health care. *Clinical Psychology Review* **23**, 35–56.

Hazan, C. and Shaver, P. (1987). Romantic Love conceptualized as an attachment process. *Journal of Personality and Social Psychology* **52**, 511–24.

Hesse, E. (1999). The Adult Attachment Interview: Historical and current perspectives. In J. Cassidy and P. R. Shaver (eds), *Handbook of Attachment: Theory, research, and clinical applications*, pp. 395–433. New York: Guilford Press.

Hesse, E. and Main, M. (1999). Second-generation effects of unresolved trauma as observed in nonmaltreating parents: Dissociated, frightened and threatening parental behavior. *Psychoanalytic Inquiry* **19**, 481–540.

Holmes, J. (2001) *The Search for the Secure Base: Attachment Theory and psychotherapy.* Hove, England: Brunner-Routledge.

Maier, M., Bernier, A., Pekrun, R. and Zimmerman, P. (2004). Attachment working models and unconscious structures: An experimental test. *International Journal of Behavioral Development* **28**, 180–9.

Main, M. (2010). Latest developments in attachment theory: A conversation with Stephen Seligman, DMH; Mary Main, PhD; and Erik Hesse, PhD. A presentation at the Annual Meeting of the International Association of Relational Psychoanalysis and Psychotherapy, San Francisco, 26 February 2010.

Main, M. and Hesse, E. (1990). Parents' unresolved traumatic experiences are related to infant disorganized attachment status: Is frightened/frightening parental behavior the linking mechanism? In M. T. Greenberg, D. Cicchetti and E. M. Cummings (eds), *Attachment in the Preschool years: theory, research, and intervention*, pp. 161–82. Chicago: University of Chicago Press.

Main, M. and Solomon, J. (1986). Discovery of an insecure-disorganized/disoriented attachment pattern: Procedures, findings and implications for the classification of behavior. In T. B. Brazelton and M. Yogman (eds), *Affective Development in Infancy*, pp. 95–124. Norwood, New Jersey: Ablex.

——(1990). Procedures for identifying infants as disorganized/disoriented during the Ainsworth strange situation. In M. Greenberg, D. Cicchetti and E. M. Cummings (eds), *Attachment During the Preschool Years: Theory, research and intervention*, pp. 121–60. Chicago: University of Chicago Press.

Main, M., Kaplan, N. and Cassidy, J. (1985). Security in infancy, childhood, and adulthood: A move to the level of representation. In I. Bretherton and E. Waters (eds), *Growing Points of Attachment Theory and Research. Monographs of the Society for Research in Child Development* **50**, 66–104. Chicago: Chicago University Press.

Obegi, J. H. and Berant, E. (2009). *Attachment Theory and Research in Clinical Work with Adults.* New York: Guilford Press.

Pietromonaco, P. R. and Feldman Barrett, L. (2000). The Internal Working Models Concept: What do we really know about the self in relation to others? *Review of General Psychology* **4**, 155–75.

Shaver, P. R. and Mikulincer, M. (2002). Attachment-related psychodynamics. *Attachment and Human Development* **4**, 133–61.

Simpson, J. A. and Rholes, W. S. (1998). *Attachment Theory and Close Relationships.* New York: Guilford Press.

Slade, A. (2000) The development and organisation of attachment: Implications for psychoanalysis. *The Journal of the American Psychoanalytic Association* **48**, 1147–74.

Steele, H. (2002). State of the art: Attachment. *The Psychologist* **15**, 518–22.

Wallin, D. (2007) *Attachment in Psychotherapy.* New York: Guilford Press.

Waters, E., Merrick, S., Treboux, D., Crowell, J. and Albersheim, L. (2000). Attachment security in infancy and early adulthood: A twenty-year longitudinal study. *Child Development* **71**, 684–9.

Weinfield, N. S., Sroufe, L.A. and Egeland, B. (2000). Attachment from infancy to early adulthood in a high-risk sample: continuity, discontinuity, and their correlates. *Child Development* **71**, 695–702.

Weinfield, N. S., Sroufe, L. A., Egeland, B. and Carlson, E. (1999). The nature of individual differences in infant–caregiver attachment. In J. Cassidy and P. Shaver (eds), *Handbook of Attachment: theory, research, and clinical application*, pp. 68–88. New York: Guilford Press.

Chapter 2

Attachment theory in therapeutic practice

Jeremy Holmes

Evidence suggests that what happens in consulting rooms is at best tenuously related to the avowed theoretical perspective of the practitioner. A good example of this is to be found in the well-known study by Castonguay, Goldfried, Wiser, Raue and Hayes (1996) of processes of change in Cognitive Behavioural Therapy (CBT). They found that two key factors in predicting good outcomes were the quality of the therapeutic alliance and the extent to which the client was able to experience previously warded-off emotions in the course of therapy, and that strict adherence to CBT protocol actually led to worse outcomes than where the therapist applied techniques flexibly. Thus 'psychodynamic' features seem to play an important part in a 'CBT' therapy. This suggests that we need to distinguish between the procedural/semantic aspects of psychotherapeutic work and the declared or 'episodic' aspects of a particular theoretical position. My contention in this chapter is that while there are relatively few overtly attachment-based psychotherapies, attachment theory has much to say about the procedural aspects of all therapies, and that it is these that lead to psychic change (Holmes 2001; Slade 2008). Thus attachment ideas and research constitute a meta-position from which to view psychotherapy practice (Holmes 2009). I argue that effective practitioners are intuitively attachment-minded and guided, irrespective of their therapeutic allegiance. I shall base the discussion around therapy's three principal components (Castonguay and Beutler 2006): the therapeutic relationship, meaning-making and change promotion.

The therapeutic relationship

Attachment styles and therapeutic engagement

According to attachment theory, intimate relationships have specific interactional dynamics, prototypically between children and parents and between spouses; sometimes amongst siblings and military or sporting 'buddies'. Threat or illness triggers attachment behaviours. Once activated, these override all other motivations – exploratory, playful, sexual, gustatory, etc. Attachment behaviour involves seeking proximity to a figure able to assuage distress; in the case of children, one who is older and wiser. Once soothed and safe, and only then, is the sufferer able to explore his or her world, inner or outer, in the context of 'companionable interaction' (Heard and Lake 1997) with a co-participant. This model can usefully be applied to the therapist–client relationship.

An important feature of the basic attachment dynamic is that threat-triggered attachment behaviour and exploration are mutually exclusive. In infants and young children this is manifest in observable behaviours – pulling 'in' to the secure base figure when threatened, and turning 'out' into the world of play and exploration when secure. Inhibitions and compromises of this pattern are to be found in insecurely attached children. In adults these shifts are usually more subtle, although most will have had the experience of 'holding onto pain', whether physical or emotional, while in the public arena until the secure presence of a loved one makes 'letting go' possible, usually with physical accompaniments such as holding, hugging and tearfulness.

Thus, the basic interpersonal architecture of therapy is: (a) a person in distress seeking a safe haven, in search of a secure base; (b) a care-giver with the capacity to offer security, soothing and exploratory companionship; and (c) the resulting relationship, with its own unique qualities. This process applies to the initiation of therapy itself, to the start of ongoing sessions, and to moments of emotional arousal as they occur within a session. Since a central therapeutic aim is eliciting and identifying buried feelings (Malan and Della Selva 2006), there will, in the course of a session, be an iteration between affect arousal, activation of attachment behaviours, and their assuagement; companionable exploration of the triggering feelings; further affective arousal and so on.

This process is inevitably coloured by past experience, especially expectations about how a care-giver will respond to expressed distress. This can be construed as 'transference' in that the client brings to the relationship largely unconscious schemata, or internal working models, based on, but not identical with, previous experiences of care-seeking.

Classifying attachment styles in adults, Shaver and Mikulincer (2008) see insecure attachment as a spectrum ranging from deactivation of attachment needs (corresponding to avoidance in children) at one pole, to hyperactivation (corresponding to ambivalent attachment) at the other. This hyperactivation/ deactivation dichotomy captures the relational expectations clients typically bring into the consulting room. Some seem 'switched-off', describing their difficulties in clichéd, minimalist ways, resistant to therapists' probes for feelings. Others overwhelm the therapist and themselves with emotion, seemingly confusing present and past, leaving little space for the therapist to stem the tide of emotion or assuage distress so that difficulties can be reflectively considered. This can be conceptualised as the unassuaged activation of the attachment dynamic.

Real-life therapists are far from passive observers, neutral elicitors of 'material', or objective commentators on their clients' difficulties. A proportion of them will themselves have insecure attachment styles, commonly towards the hyper-activating pole (Diamond et al. 2003). Therapist and patient actively engage in an attachment/exploration cycle, in which the actuality of what the therapist offers, and the client seeks, is counterpoised with deeply ingrained expectations potentially threatening that very process of productive engagement.

Mallinckrodt and his co-workers (Mallinckrodt, Porter and Kivlighan 2005) illustrate how skilful therapists accommodate to, and gradually modify, the presenting stance of the client vis-à-vis attachment. They suggest that successful therapy requires initial 'concordance' (cf. Racker 1968) on the part of the therapist. This means partial acceptance by the therapist of the role allocated by the patient's unconscious expectations and procedures. This might entail allowing for a degree of intellectualising with deactivating clients, waiting patiently for the client to begin to allow feelings to surface, for example in relation to breaks – 'I used to take gaps in my stride, just telling myself that you were a hard-working professional and were entitled to holidays; now I really resent your going away, and wonder who you are going away with'. Conversely, with hyperactivating clients, a degree of boundary flexibility and gratification might be allowable, accepting inter-session letters and text-messages and occasionally offering extra sessions. Later the therapist will move to a 'complementary' (as opposed to 'concordant', Racker 1968), more challenging role, thereby disconfirming maladaptive client expectations and opening the way for psychological reorganisation.

From an attachment perspective, the therapeutic relationship can be seen as the result of two opposing sets of forces. On the one hand the analyst attempts within the limited framework of therapy to provide a secure attachment experience – to identify and assuage attachment needs and to facilitate exploration; on the other, the patient approaches the relationship with prior expectations of sub-optimal care-giving, unconsciously assumes an unloving and/or untrustworthy, or narcissistically self-gratifying care-giver and aims mainly for a measure of security. The attachment viewpoint suggests that the therapeutic relationship is shaped both by the dynamic of its actuality and the distorting effects of transference. Secure therapists redress their clients' attachment insecurities, while insecure ones are more likely to reinforce them. As therapy proceeds, the soothing presence of the analyst enables the client to expose themselves to, tolerate, and learn from increasing levels of anxiety.

Susan, 46, a single parent who had had recurrent major depressive episodes, sought therapy when she developed depression following the break-up of a five-year relationship with a married man. She herself had been brought up by her lone parent mother, a narcissistic woman who had numerous affairs throughout Susan's childhood. In the initial interview Susan described how she longed for closeness, but at the same time felt intruded on whenever she did get close to a man, and how she felt this had contributed to the breakdown of her relationship. She had mentioned at the outset that her funds were limited and that she could only afford infrequent sessions. The therapist suggested that she had learned as a child to keep her distance from her attachment figure, thereby achieving a modicum of security, albeit by protecting herself from her mother's narcissistic intrusions by sacrificing the need for intimacy and understanding. It was likely that she had then reproduced this pattern in her relationships, and that her declaration that she could only manage infrequent sessions suggested that she was setting herself up for a similar experience in therapy. The therapist stated that once a week would normally be a minimum, but that he would be prepared to see her fortnightly but not less often than that, as that would then perpetuate her difficulties rather than helping to overcome them.

Emotional connectedness

What makes a potential secure base 'secure'? How does an infant 'know' to whom to turn when attachment behaviours are activated? How does an attachment hierarchy, normally with mother at the apex, followed by other kin such as aunts, older siblings, father, grandparents and non-kin 'alloparents' (Hrdy 1999) such as child-minders, become established? For adults, at what point does friendship and companionship become 'love', and what is the relationship between this and the establishment of a secure base? (Attempting to tap into this vector, I routinely ask clients at assessment 'Who would you contact first if there were an emergency or crisis in your life?'). When does a therapist move from being a helpful professional to the role of an indispensable attachment figure? Attachment research suggests at least partial answers to some of these questions.

Ongoing intimate proximity, availability, together with the 'knowing' – the holding in mind through absence and interruption that is integral to parental (and spousal) love – are some of the essential ingredients of a secure base. The mother–infant literature suggests that, among other characteristics, a secure base parent also provides responsiveness and 'mastery' (Slade 2005); reliability and consistency; 'mind-mindedness' (Meins 1999); and the ability to repair disruptions of parent–infant emotional connectedness (Tronick 1998). All of these are threads that also run through the fabric of successful therapeutic relationships.

Overall, care-seeker/care-giver emotional connectedness is the key feature of a secure base (Farber and Metzger 2008). The restriction, exaggeration, or uncoupling of such connectedness is what leads to the three varieties of insecure attachment. No less than in secure relationships, in insecure attachments the attachment figure is present in the mind of the care-seeker as a sought target for attachment behaviours, but there is a discrepancy between what is desired and what is available. In analytic psychotherapy, transference analysis attempts to place the minutiae of this disjunction under the therapeutic microscope. Thus in Susan's case the therapist offered the client a chance to look at her insecure attachment pattern within the safety of the therapeutic relationship.

Contingency and marking

There are analogues of therapeutic intimacy in developmental studies of parent–child interaction. Gergely and Watson's landmark paper (Gergely and Watson 1996; see Gergely 2007) focuses on affective sequencing between parents and infants. They identify 'contingency' and 'marking', in the context of intense mutual gaze, as the basis of mirroring sequences in which, to use Winnicott's (1971: 51) phrase, the 'mother's face is the mirror in which the child first begins to find himself'.

'Contingency' describes the way in which the care-giver waits (her response is 'contingent upon') for the infant to initiate affective expression. Her response is then 'marked' by an exaggerated simulacrum of the infant's facial and verbal affective expression. For example, the child might be slightly down-at-mouth; the mother might then, while maintaining intense eye contact with her child, twist her face into a caricature of abject misery, saying, in high-pitched 'motherese', 'Oh, we are feeling miserable today, aren't we…'. She thereby offers the child a visual/auditory representation of his own internal affective state. This sets in motion the child's capacity to 'see' and 'own' his feelings.

Contingency gives the child the message that s/he is an actor, a person who can initiate and make a difference to the interpersonal world in which he or she finds himself, and introduces him to the dialogic nature of human meanings. Marking links representation (initially in the mother's face, then re-represented in his own mind) to the child's own actions and internal feelings, while 'tagging' that these are his/her feelings, not the mother's. This proto-linguistic envelope has a soothing, affect-regulating quality.

When mothers mirror their infant's feelings, 'marking', which is a form of exaggeration or elaboration, means that the image that the infant sees is never an exact match of his or her facial expression. It is partial, not complete, contingency, a rhyme, not a replica. Fonagy and colleagues (2002) placed infants in high chairs in front of two reflective video-screens. One acted like a conventional mirror, the other was able to copy the child's movements but with a time lag so that there was a discrepancy between what the child could see and his or her actions. Up to 3 months, infants selectively chose total contingency when offered a choice of visual feedback (Fonagy et al. 2002). At this stage the child is still mapping the body representation, where total contingency, e.g. between hand movements and the movement of an image across the visual field, is the rule. But over the age of 3 months, when offered a choice between watching a conventional ('total contingency') mirror, or one that subjects their movements to a time lag, infants tend to select the latter (Fonagy et al. 2002), presumably because it represents novelty and interest.

In a comparable auditory mirroring study of 4 month olds (Koulomzin et al. 2002), Beebe and her colleagues showed that both high and low contingency were more likely to lead to insecure attachment classification at 1 year than mid-range or partial contingency. Mothers, who could play comfortably with their children's vocalisations in jazz-like improvisation around them, were more security-producing than those that mirrored them exactly or, at the other end of the spectrum, were incapable of getting on their child's wavelength. Similarly, psychotherapy, however empathic, that merely reflects back what the patient brings without challenge or alteration, may fail to precipitate change, which depends on the continuous interplay of sameness and difference (Holmes 2009).

Gergely and Watson's interactive sequences (see Gergely 2007) thus involve: (a) affect expression by the child; (b) empathic resonance on the part of the mother, able to put herself into the shoes of the child; (c) affect regulation in that the parent tends to up-regulate or down-regulate depending on what emotion is communicated (stimulating a bored child, soothing a distressed one); resultant (d) mutual pleasure and playfulness or, to use Stern's (1985) phrase, the evocation of 'vitality affects', enlivenment, leading to (e) exploratory play/companionable interaction (Heard and Lake 1997).

Similar sequences characterise in-session therapist–client interactions. McCluskey (2005) has shown that initial attunement – a mirroring affect-identifying response on the part of the therapist – in itself is insufficient to make up a satisfactory therapeutic interaction. Further steps are needed in order to release exploration and companionable interaction. Step two is affect-regulatory, as the therapist 'takes' the communicated feeling and, through facial expression, tone of voice and emphasis, modifies or 'regulates' it: softly expressed sad feelings are amplified, perhaps with a more aggressive edge added; manic excitement soothed; vagueness of tone sharpened. Mirroring here becomes dialogic.

In Susan's case she became very tearful and her face distorted with expressed suffering and misery. Without saying much or indeed consciously being aware of any more than adopting a 'witnessing' stance, the therapist mirrored this distress with his physical posture, facial expression and non-verbal murmurings of sympathy. Susan responded to this by, as it were, 'seeing' her own affects through the therapist's eyes and ears – and therefore to an extent objectifying them – by saying with a wry smile, 'By the way, I don't think I'm depressed – just distressed'. One can hypothesise that it is precisely this kind of responsiveness that her self-preoccupied mother would have found very difficult to achieve.

More typically, the therapist makes comments comparable to the 'marking' of the Gergely and Watson schema (see Gergely 2007). The therapist might say: 'You did what?!'; 'That sounds painful'; 'Ouch!!'; 'It sounds as though you might be feeling pretty sad right now'; 'I wonder if there isn't a lot of rage underneath all this'. The therapist communicates to the patient that he has heard and felt her feelings, regulates their intensity, and implicitly or explicitly adds something, e.g. the sadness that underlies mania, the anger that can be an unacknowledged feature of depression. The security associated with being understood leads to enlivenment on the part of the patient. This in turn opens the way for companionable exploration of the content or meaning of the topic under discussion. McCluskey (2005) dubs this sequence Goal Corrected Empathic Attunement (GCEA), in which there is a continuous process of mutual adjustment or 'goal-correction' between client and therapist as they attempt, emotionally and thematically, to entrain the client's affective states and imagine the contexts which engender them. Mentalising (Holmes 2009), see below, can be thought of as an umbrella term covering all aspects of this process.

Triangulation

At the Gergely stage, looking/mirroring is dyadic. 'Marking' signals to the child the message 'mirror', rather than 'reality' – i.e. 'It's a reflection of your feelings you are looking at, not mine'. The mother's face is a reflective surface for the child, but not, under normal circumstances, vice versa. But as development proceeds, visual referencing and elaboration of meaning come to encompass the outer as well as the inner world. Mother and child look together at what is 'over there'. Initially this may take the form of pointing – the child points, perhaps randomly, the mother says, 'Yes, that's ... Daddy, doggie, flower, tree' etc. Thus the mother gradually brings order and meaning, 'thirdness' and the beginnings of simple narrative, to the child's 'buzzing booming' world of sensation.

Cavell (2006), a philosopher and psychoanalyst, theorises this process using the concept of 'triangulation'. From a Kantian perspective, 'reality' is ineffable; it can never be directly apprehended but is always filtered through the mind. Nevertheless, as development proceeds, the child acquires a sense of quiddity – 'thing-ness' – via 'triangulated referencing'. The child reaches out to a cup. The mother says encouragingly, 'Yes, cup'. She lets the child hold and feel and smell it. She 'references' it – they are both looking at the 'same' cup – albeit not quite the same since they both have their unique point of view. The child looks at the mother looking at her looking at the cup. A triangle is formed: mother–child–cup. The child 'triangulates' the reality of the cup, fixed via language, and the overlap of her own experience with that offered by the mother's imaginative identification. The security-inducing care-giver gives the message to the child that he or she has a mind, different from, but similar to, hers, and that despite differing perspectives, the cup exists 'out there'. In psychotherapy, the 'cup' analogue are the patient's feelings and the connections between them and his life-experience. The triangle now is patient, therapist, and the patient's story. Patient and therapist together look at fragments of experience and mentalise them: 'What did you make of that?' 'Looking back, how does that seem to you today?' etc.

This metaphorical mutual gaze helps validate and bring the patient's experience to life. Most therapists (and patients) have an inherent sense of what it feels like to have a 'good session', however painful it may seem at the time. One aspect of this is the strengthened sense of consensual reality that comes from triangulation: 'Yes, that's just how it was', 'That really hits the nail on the head' etc.

Rupture and repair

Like parents and spouses, and indeed anyone whose goal is intimate understanding of another person, therapists regularly 'get it wrong'. Tuckett and his co-authors' category of therapist actions (Tuckett *et al.* 2008: 29), which they define as 'sudden and glaring reactions not easy to relate to the analyst's normal method', can be seen as ruptures comparable to the normal and expectable ruptures in parent–infant connectedness, which in well-functioning parent–infant couples are 'repaired' as the parent responds to the child's signals of distress.

The GCEA framework tells us that being understood reduces anxiety, liberates vitality affects and initiates exploration. Conversely, being misunderstood is anxiety-augmenting and aversive, triggering withdrawal and avoidance and/or defensiveness and anger. But just as security-providing mothers are able to repair lapses in attunement with their infants, so the capacity to repair therapeutic 'ruptures', a concept developed by Safran and Muran (2000), is associated with good outcomes in therapy.

Using the 'still face' paradigm, attachment researchers have looked at attachment styles in relation to the capacity of mother–infant dyads to resume affective contact following a brief one-minute affective withdrawal on the part of the mother in which she is asked to 'freeze' her expression (Crandell, Patrick and Hopson 2003; Tronick 1998). Securely attached children are least disrupted by this procedure. Children with organised insecurity resort to temporary self-soothing via looking at their own faces in the mirror when the link with mother is broken, but can generally resume contact once the break is terminated. Disorganised children are least likely to get back on track with their mothers on resumption, and likely to resort to more entrenched self-soothing, failing to link up again with the security of the mother's gaze even when it becomes once more available.

Extrapolating from these findings to adult psychotherapy, therapists need to be highly sensitive to client reactions to 'freezing' or discontinuities of contact both within sessions and in relation to the normal interruptions of holidays and illness. Even though psychoanalytic psychotherapists are trained to focus on manifestations of 'negative transference', the evidence suggests that clients hold back negative feelings from their analysts no less than in other modalities of therapy (Safran and Muran 2000). An attachment perspective suggests that: (a) in any intimate relationship quotidian misunderstandings are the norm; (b) the implications of these depend in part on prior expectations and attachment styles of both participants; and (c) the therapeutic issue is not so much to eliminate misunderstandings as to focus on the feelings associated with them and find ways to talk about them. Therapist 'enactments' (e.g. starting a session late, drowsiness, inattention or intrusiveness, etc.) need to be non-defensively acknowledged. Reflexive thinking about them by therapist and client together strengthens the therapeutic bond and is itself a change-promoting manoeuvre, enhancing the client's capacity for self-awareness and negotiating skills in intimate relationships.

'Paternal' aspects of the attachment/therapeutic relationship

A key early finding in attachment research was that attachment classification in the Strange Situation was a relational not a temperamental feature, since at 1 year old children could be secure with mother and insecure with father or vice versa, although by 30 months the maternal pattern tends to dominate (Ainsworth *et al.* 1978). Nevertheless, the role of fathers in attachment has been relatively neglected, disorganised attachment because, sadly, most of the children studied, as in Susan's case, come from mother-only families (Lyons-Ruth and Jacobvitz 1999). The Grossman's longitudinal studies (Grossman, Grossman and Waters 2005) are an exception, showing that paternal contributions in childhood to eventual security in early adulthood are as important as those of the mother, and that their combined parental impact is greater than the sum of each alone.

The Grossmans delineate the 'paternal' role as somewhat different from the 'maternal'. (The sexist implications of this dichotomy are acknowledged, perhaps better reframed as 'security-providing' and 'empowering' parental functions.) When asked to perform a brick-building or sporting task (e.g. teaching a child to swim), security-providing fathers offer their offspring a 'You can do it' message, creating a zone of protection within which sensory-motor development can proceed. In the Strange Situation, as compared with mothers, fathers tend to use short bursts of intense distraction and activity as comforting manoeuvres, in contrast to the more gentle crescendo and diminuendo of hugging and soothing that characterises female care-givers.

Comparing parent–child relationships in disorganised and secure children, measures of maternal sensitivity are insufficient to capture security-providing functions. A dimension of 'mastery' also contributes to the variance, communicating not just intimate protectiveness but also the presence of a competent adult in charge of the play-space (Slade 2005). The importance of space – physical and metaphorical – links with the Vygotskian notion of the 'zone of proximal development' where the child is directed to tasks that are neither too easy nor too hard (Leiman 1995), and the 'defensible space' surrounding the child whose security it is the parent's responsibility to guarantee. Similarly, therapists provide for their clients therapeutic space, which is also a 'space of time'.

Effective psychotherapy is both soothing and empowering. In the Western world, 'naming' is construed as a 'paternal'/masculine function. The famous Lacanian pun – 'le no(m) de père' (the name of the father; the no of the father) – encapsulates the 'negative' paternal prohibition that severs the infant's fantasy of merging with the mother, but also the 'positive' liberating, linguistic function that enables one to stand outside, think about and manipulate experience and, ultimately, to understand oneself (expressed in the patronymic). In order to alleviate client anxiety, the therapist needs not just to be empathic, but also to communicate 'mastery' (with its 'paternal' resonance) – a sense that she knows what she is doing, is in control of the therapy and its boundaries (without being controlling), and is relaxed enough to mentalise her own feelings. Mastery and empathy are not mutually exclusive, but denote a good 'primal marriage' of sensitivity and power from which the client can begin to tackle his difficulties.

Meaning

Meaning-making is intrinsic to all therapies. An explanatory framework brings order to the intrinsically inchoate experience of illness, whether physical or mental (Holmes and Bateman 2002). A 'formulation' is both anxiety-reducing in itself and provides a scaffolding for the mutual exploration that follows once attachment anxiety has been assuaged. A symptom or troublesome experience is 'reframed' via an explanatory system that helps make sense of the sufferer's mental (or physical) pain. The use of the word 'sense' here acknowledges that meaning transcends mere cognition and ultimately derives from bodily experiences.

Language

New meanings emerge in the cut and thrust of psychoanalytic work in part through the analyst's close attention to language. Freud saw the inherent ambiguity of language as an entrée to the unconscious, viewing words as 'switches' or junction points between conscious and unconscious thoughts, or, to use a contemporary metaphor, nodal points in neural networks.

In the attempt of Tuckett *et al.* (2008) to categorise psychoanalytic interventions, one group of comments is described as 'polysemic', i.e. having 'many meanings'. As the literary critic Eagleton (2007: 22) puts it: 'language is always what there is more of'. Therapist and patient co-create a space from which to look at feelings, behaviours and speech-acts from all possible perspectives and angles – concrete, metaphorical, sexual, adult, child-like, coercive, intimidated, anxiety-influenced and so on.

> Susan came into therapy with the idea that there was something 'wrong' with her that drove people away – her intolerance of closeness, 'bad temper', etc. The therapist offered a new set of meanings: her fear of intimacy linked with her mother's neglectfulness (better to be self-sufficient than get close to another and then be abandoned); her choice of partner as a continuation of this pattern; her angry outbursts representing the protest of the abandoned child; the underlying fear that if she gave up her fragile self-sufficiency all would fall apart.

In the consulting room, sensitivity to the ebb and flow of attachment and exploration is the hallmark of the skilful therapist. As discussed, GCEA entails 'secure base' responses to client distress. This is in part a matter of timing and tone of voice, but accurate verbal identification of feelings – i.e. the emergence of shared meanings – is in itself soothing. As in any intimate relationship – spousal, parent–child, sibling, close friendship – highly specific meanings derived from the minutiae of a person's life are co-created by therapist and client. Elaborating this personal vernacular or 'ideolect' (Lear 1993; 2009) is a crucial aspect of psycho-therapeutic work. In Bollas' (2007) terminology, the 'receptive unconscious' of the analyst is tuned into the 'expressive unconscious' of the client; the task of the analyst's conscious ego, like that of the good-enough mother in Winnicott's (1971) model of the child playing 'alone in the presence of the mother', is to guard the therapeutic space in a non-intrusive way.

The meaning-making function of therapy picks out significance from this unending flux and free play of the imagination, or stream of consciousness. Once verbally 'fixed', meanings can be considered, by therapist and patient together from all possible angles: tested, refined, held onto, modified, or discarded as appropriate.

Main is credited with attachment theory's decisive 'move to the level of representation' (Main 1999) – i.e. the instantiation in the mind of attachment relationships. Clearly 'representation' is not exclusively nor necessarily verbal. 'Teleological' thinking, characteristic of pre-verbal, 'pre-mentalising' toddlers (Holmes 2009) is both representational and meaningful in the sense that the infant begins to develop a mental map of the interpersonal world based on 'if this, then that' logic. However, the capacity to represent the Self and Others and their relationship verbally is a vital developmental step, enabling children to negotiate the interpersonal world that will be a matrix of all future existence once the physical 'matrix' (i.e. mother) is relinquished. Language underpins a 'self' that becomes both a centre of experience and an object in the world that can be described and discussed and 'worked on' through the vicissitudes of everyday life and, when necessary, in psychotherapy.

Narrative styles and the meaning of meaning

The Adult Attachment Interview suggests that *how* we talk about ourselves and our lives, as much as *what* we talk about, reveals the architecture of the inner world. Like the 'fluid attentional gaze' (Main 1995) of the secure infant who seamlessly negotiates transitions between secure base-seeking, social referencing and exploratory play, Main characterises secure narratives as 'fluid autonomous' – neither over- nor under-elaborated and able to balance affect and cognition in ways appropriate to the topic discussed.

In the context of therapy, secure narrative styles are 'meaningful' in the sense that they facilitate an open-ended 'language game' (Wittgenstein 1958) between therapist and client. 'Meaning' is inherent in the interactive mutuality of a language game. Clearly it is possible to have a private language, as for example in psychosis, but it is only when it can be shared that it becomes meaningful in the sense used here. Therapy can be seen as continuously helping the client to move from private to shared meanings. Insecure attachment styles lead to therapeutic conversations that are under- or over-saturated with meaning (dismissive or enmeshed respectively), or with breaks in meaning (incoherent), depending whether they represent deactivating, hyperactivating or unresolved attachments.

A key part of therapeutic work is moving the client towards the exploration of mutual meanings, based on a more secure narrative style. 'Can you elaborate on that?'; 'What exactly did you mean then?'; 'I can't quite visualise what you are talking about here; can you help?'; 'What did that feel like to you?'; 'I'm getting a bit confused here, can you slow down a bit?'; 'There seems to be something missing in what you're saying; I wonder if there is some part of the story we haven't quite heard about?'. In this kind of dialogue the therapist is probing for specificity, visual imagery and metaphor that enable her to conjure up, in her mind's eye and ear, aspects of the patient's experience. This then becomes a shared object or 'third' (Benjamin 2004; Ogden 1987) that can be 'companionably explored' (Heard and Lake 1997), often a metaphor to be played with and extended.

There is evidence to support the idea that successful therapy is associated with the replacement of insecure by more secure narrative styles (Avdi and Georgaca 2007), towards the acquisition of what I have called 'autobiographical competence' (Holmes 2001). Main's schema describes the fluidity of secure styles, always subject to further 'vision and revision' (Eliot 1986), in contrast to the fixed, overwhelming, or inchoate narratives of insecure attachment.

Finding the right meaning

As therapists we are continuously struggling to find the 'real', 'right', or 'true' meaning of our client's communications, verbal and non-verbal. The client will in turn respond by telling us whether a particular comment on the part of the analyst, or idea they have generated themselves, 'feels right'. In his neurophysiological critique of Cartesian dualism, Damasio (1994) suggests that mind and body work in tandem to let us know when our cognitive and intellectual faculties are on track. Implicit in Cavell's (2006) notion of 'triangulation' is the idea that a child cross-checks the veracity and validity of their perceptions of the outside world with those of the care-giver, and so begins to build up a picture of the real world distinct from his or her perception of it. The Winnicottian ideas of mirroring, contingency/marking and empathic attunement suggest that we learn about our inner world in a comparable way, using the care-giver's understanding to develop our own self-knowledge. In psychotherapy sessions the analyst makes guesses or suggestions about how clients may be feeling; clients then compare this proffered empathic understanding with what their introspection tells them. Exploring whether there is a near-match or a misalignment, therapy helps the client to gradually know him or herself better.

Attachment and empathy, apparently abstract concepts, are ultimately psycho-physical phenomena. Proximity is sought – tactile (hugging, sitting on a lap), auditory (via a telephone) or visual (a picture, which may be in the 'mind's eye'). This lowers arousal – slowed heart rate, less sweating – and releases oxytocin (Zeki 2009). A mentalising conversation (e.g. a therapy session) may also be seen in those terms. The physical posture and tone of voice of the client reveals his or her emotional state. The therapist imaginatively or even actually (via contingently marking and so altering their own physical posture) mirrors this state, which in turn, via 'mirror neurones', triggers a version of the client's emotional state in the therapist's receptive apparatus (Hobson 2002). This can then be introspected, identified, verbalised. In doing so, change is set in train.

Attachment theory's contribution to meaning-making underpins a meta-theoretical perspective in which it is not so much specific interpretations that count, as the restoration or fostering of the capacity to find/make shared meanings, irrespective of their content. Therapist and client come together in a meaningful, shared 'present moment' (Stern 2004). Meaning in itself is not mutative; it is the mutuality of meaning-making that matters. This brings us to the third leg of the psychotherapy tripod – promoting change.

Promoting change

Exposure

An integrative approach to psychotherapeutic work sees a crucial component in psychic change as the exposure to previously avoided/warded off mental pain and trauma. In the safety of the consulting room, past pain is revived and relived. Focusing on this in safety enables sufferers to experience, process, name and gain perspective on the unexpressed feelings that bedevil their relationship to themselves and their intimates. In that it is based on trauma, avoidance and exposure, psychoanalytic approaches here are consistent with cognitive/ behavioural theory, even if the methods – spontaneous free association and transference interpretation as opposed to pen-and-paper self-observation and directed homework exposure tasks – are radically different.

In a series of attachment-influenced studies, Mikulincer and colleagues (reviewed Mikulincer and Shaver 2008; Mikulincer *et al*. 2008) show how the experience of security, even if subliminal, enables insecurely attached people to confront rather than defensively deactivate or hyperactivate mental pain. In one study, participants who had completed a questionnaire tapping into attachment styles were asked to write a description of an incident in which a close partner had hurt their feelings. They were then exposed to security-enhancing subliminal 'primes' (words like 'love', 'secure', 'affection') or neutral ones ('lamp', 'building' etc). Next they were asked to reconsider the hurtful event and to describe how they would feel if it were to occur again. In the neutral priming condition, deactivators reported less, and hyperactivators more, pain than in the initial task. This would be expected if, with the passage of time, pre-existing defences were reinforced. However, in those exposed to the positive prime, both anxiety and avoidance were greatly reduced and the insecurely attached subjects' responses were indistinguishable from those of the securely attached. As Mikulincer and his colleagues (Mikulincer *et al*. 2008: 318) put it:

protective armour can at least temporarily [be] softened by an infusion of felt security ... even a small security boost can allow an avoidant person to be more open to inner pain ... which can then be addressed clinically.

Transposing this into the consulting room, the benign presence of the therapist offers a validating, encouraging environment, helping clients to face, bear, process, live with, master, transcend and incorporate pain and trauma. Positive priming, via the implicit validating presence of the analyst, is a precondition for meaningful exposure to negative emotions. Conversely, support without challenge can be collusive rather than mutative.

Mentalising

According to Gustafson (1986; drawing on Bateson 1972), who based his ideas on Bertrand Russell's 'theory of logical types', psychic change invariably entails taking a perspective at a meta-level, or 'higher logical type', from the problematic behaviours or experience that had led the sufferer to seek help. Attachment research established more than 20 years ago (Fonagy 2008) that the 'Reflective Function' subscale of the Adult Attachment Interview predicted sensitive parenting, irrespective of the trauma history of the individual. Reflective Functioning has now mutated into the concept of mentalising, both as a general mark of psychological social maturity and as a treatment objective in people suffering from Borderline Personality Disorder (Fonagy 2008; Holmes 2009). 'Mentalising', which can be defined as the capacity to see oneself and others as sentient beings with desires, hopes and aims, or 'mind-mindedness' (Meins 1999), clearly fulfils the Gustafson criterion in that it is a species of 'meta-thinking'. Moving from action and impulse to reflecting on one's own and others' mental states is crucial to therapeutic action in psychoanalytic psychotherapy, and perhaps the psychotherapies generally (Allen 2003).

Bleiberg (2006) suggests that mentalising is an essential social skill for group living. Being able to mentalise or to read the intentions of the 'Other' became a vital 'friend-or-foe' appraisal as small groups of hominids learned to collaborate and to cope with competition. However, once the 'Other' is identified as unthreatening, mentalising is inhibited. With the appraiser's guard down, psychic energy is available for other uses. Extreme instances of this are seen in intimate relationships between infants and their mothers, and the mothers and their romantic partners. Brain patterns in both are similar, with inhibition of the neuroanatomical pathways subsuming mentalisation (Zeki 2009). This releases psychic energy from the appraisal task, and perhaps explains the necessary idealisation inherent in such relationships ('my baby/lover/mum is the best baby/lover/mum in the whole world'), in which negative features are ignored or discounted.

A similar sequence may apply in psychotherapy, as the client begins to imbue the therapist and therapeutic situation with secure base properties and to relax into a comfortable state of held intimacy. However, while encouraging the development of trust, the therapist will simultaneously insist that clients examine their feelings about the therapist and the therapeutic relationship – aiming to help clients acquire, activate and extend mentalising skills. A psychotherapy session is recursive in the sense that it loops back on itself in ways that normal relationships tend not to, except perhaps when repair (which can be thought of as an everyday form of 'therapy') is needed. To take a commonplace example, there is often a tussle between therapist and client – especially if a deactivating one – about reactions to breaks. The client may insist that it is perfectly all right for the therapist to have a holiday ('everyone needs time off, especially in your sort of work'), while the therapist relentlessly probes for signs of disappointment, rejection and anger, sometimes much to the client's irritation. The client is encouraged to mentalise the avoided negative affect in the service of therapeutic change. Therapy thus puts the client in a paradoxical 'change/no change', 'inhibit mentalising/mentalise' bind, forcing the emergence of new structures and extending clients' range of interpersonal skills and resources. Clients have no choice but to think about their feelings and identity in ways that would normally be dealt with by repression, avoidance, acting out or projection.

Conclusions

The main argument of this chapter is that psychotherapy process may best be understood by theoretical perspectives – in this case Attachment Theory – orthogonal to those espoused by its practitioners. Attending to the pull and push of the attachment dynamic and freeing oneself from dogma (including dogmatic views on Attachment!) may lead to better therapy, productive research questions and a focus on the mutative ingredients of psychotherapeutic process.

References

Ainsworth, M., Blehar, M., Waters, E. and Wall, S. (1978). *Patterns of Attachment: a psychological study of the strange situation*. Hillsdale, New Jersey: Erlbaum.

Allen, J. G. (2003). Mentalizing. *Bulletin of the Menninger Clinic* **67**, 87–108.

Avdi, E. and Georgaca, E. (2007). Narrative research in psychotherapy: a critical review. *Psychology and Psychotherapy: Research and Practice* **78**, 1–14.

Bateson, G. (1972). *Steps Towards an Ecology of Mind*. New York: Ballentine.

Benjamin, J. (2004). Beyond doer and done to: An intersubjective view of thirdness. *Psychoanalytic Quarterly* **73**, 5–46.

Bleiberg, E. (2006). Treating professionals in crisis: A mentalisation-based specialized inpatient program. In J. Allen and P. Fonagy (eds), *Handbook of Mentalisation-based Treatment*, pp. 233–47. Chichester: Wiley.

Bollas, C. (2007). *The Freudian Moment*. London: Karnac.

Castonguay, L. G. and Beutler, L. (2006). *Principles of Therapeutic Change that Work*. Oxford: Oxford University Press.

Castonguay, L. G., Goldfried, M. R., Wiser, S. L., Raue, P. J. and Hayes, A. M. (1996). Predicting the effect of cognitive therapy for depression: a study of unique and common factors. *Journal of Consulting and Clinical Psychology* **64**, 497–504.

Cavell, M. (2006). *Becoming a Subject*. Oxford: Oxford University Press.

Crandell, L., Patrick, M. and Hobson, P. (2003). 'Still face' interactions between mothers with borderline personality disorder and their 2-month infants. *British Journal of Psychiatry* **183**, 239–49.

Damasio, A. (1994). *Descartes' Error*. New York: Jason Aronson.

Diamond, D., Stovall-McClough, C., Clarkin, J. and Levy, K. (2003). Patient–therapist attachment in the treatment of borderline personality disorder. *Bulletin of the Menninger Clinic* **67**, 227–59.

Eagleton, T. (2007). *How to Read a Poem*. London: Blackwell.

Eliot, T. S. (1986). *Collected Poems*. London: Faber.

Farber, B. and Metzger, J. (2008). The therapist as secure base. In J. Obegi and E. Berant (eds), *Clinical Applications of Adult Psychotherapy and Research*, pp. 46–70. New York: Guilford Press.

Fonagy, P. (2008). The mentalisation-focused approach to social development. In F. N. Busch (ed.), *Mentalisation: theoretical considerations, research findings, and clinical implications*, pp. 3–56. Hove: The Analytic Press.

Fonagy, P., Gergely, G., Jurist, E. L. and Target, M. (2002). *Affect Regulation, Mentalisation and the Development of the Self*. New York: Other Press.

Gergely, G. (2007). The social construction of the subjective self. In L. Mayes, P. Fonagy and M. Target (eds), *Developmental Science and Psychoanalysis*, pp. 39–63. London: Karnac.

Gergely, G. and Watson, J. S. (1996). The social biofeedback theory of parental affect-mirroring: The development of emotional self awareness and self-control in infancy. *International Journal of Psycho-analysis* **77**, 1181–1212.

Grossman, K., Grossman, K. and Waters, E. (2005). *Attachment from Infancy to Adulthood: the major longitudinal studies*. New York: Guilford Press.

Gustafson, J. (1986). *The Complex Secret of Brief Psychotherapy*. New York: Norton.

Heard, D. and Lake, B. (1997). *The Challenge of Attachment for Care-Giving*. London: Routledge.

Hobson, P. (2002). *The Cradle of Thought*. London: Macmillan.

Holmes, J. (2001). *The Search for the Secure Base*. London: Routledge.

——(2009). *Exploring in Security: towards an attachment-informed psychoanalytic psychotherapy*. London: Routledge.

Holmes, J. and Bateman, A. (2002). *Integration in Psychotherapy: models and methods*. Oxford: Oxford University Press.

Hrdy, S. (1999). *Mother Nature*. London: Penguin.

Koulomzin, M., Beebe, B., Anderson, S., Joseph, J., Feldstein, S. and Cown, C. (2002). Infant gaze, head, face and self-touch at 4 months differentiate secure vs. avoidant attachment at 1 year: A microanalytic approach. *Attachment and Human Development* **4**, 3–24.

Lear, J. (1993). An interpretation of transference. *International Journal of Psychoanalysis* **74**, 739–55.

——(2009). Technique and final cause in psychoanalysis: four ways of looking at one moment. *International Journal of Psychoanalysis* **90**, 1299–1317.

Leiman, M. (1995). Early development. In A. Ryle (ed.), *Cognitive Analytic Therapy: developments in theory and practice*, pp. 103–20. Chichester: Wiley.

Lyons-Ruth, K. and Jacobvitz, D. (1999). Attachment disorganisation: unresolved loss, relational violence, and lapses in behavioural and attentional strategies. In J. Cassidy, and P. Shaver (eds). *Handbook of Attachment*, pp. 666–97. New York: Guilford Press.

Main, M. (1995). Recent studies in attachment: overview with selected implications for clinical work. In S. Goldberg, R. Muir and J. Kerr (eds), *Attachment Theory: social, developmental and clinical perspectives*, pp. 276–89. Hillsdale, New Jersey: Analytic Press.

——(1999). Epilogue. In J. Cassidy and P. Shaver (eds), *Handbook of Attachment*, pp. 832–69. New York: Guilford Press.

Malan, D. and Della Selva, P. C. (2006). *Lives Transformed: a revolutionary method of dynamic psychotherapy*. London: Karnac.

Mallinckrodt, B., Porter, M. J. and Kivlighan, D. M. J. (2005). Client attachment to therapist, depth of in-session exploration, and object relations in brief psychotherapy. *Psychotherapy: Theory, Research, Practice, Training* **42**, 85–100.

McCluskey, U. (2005). *To be Met as a Person*. London: Karnac.

Meins, E. (1999). Sensitivity, security and internal working models: bridging the transmission gap. *Attachment and Human Development* **3**, 325–42.

Mikulincer, M. and Shaver, P. (2008). Adult attachment and affect regulation. In J. Cassidy and P. Shaver (eds), *Handbook of Attachment* (2nd edn), pp. 503–31. New York: Guilford Press.

Mikulincer, M., Shaver, P., Cassidy, J. and Berant, E. (2008). Attachment-related defensive processes. In J. Obegi and E. Berant (eds), *Attachment Theory and Research in Clinical Work with Adults*, pp. 293–327. New York: Guilford Press.

Ogden, T. (1987). *The Matrix of the Mind*. Northvale, New Jersey: Aronson.

Racker, H. (1968). *Transference and Counter-transference*. London: Hogarth/Karnac.

Safran, J. and Muran, J. (2000). *Negotiating the Therapeutic Alliance: a relational treatment guide*. New York: Guilford Press.

Shaver, P., and Mikulincer, M. (2008). An overview of attachment theory. In J. Obegi and E. Berant (eds), *Clinical Applications of Adult Psychotherapy and Research*, pp. 17–45. New York: Guilford Press.

Slade, A. (2005). Parental reflective functioning: an introduction. *Attachment and Human Development* **7**, 269–82.

——(2008). The implications of attachment theory and research for adult psychotherapy: research and clinical perspectives. In J. Cassidy and P. Shaver (eds), *Handbook of Attachment* (2nd edn), pp. 672–782. New York: Guilford Press.

Stern, D. (1985). *The Interpersonal World of the Infant: a view from psychoanalysis and developmental psychology*. New York: Basic Books.

——(2004). *The Present Moment in Psychotherapy and Everyday Life*. New York: Norton.

Tronick, E. (1998). Dyadically expanded states of consciousness and the process of therapeutic change. *Infant Mental Health Journal* **19**, 290–9.

Tuckett, D., Basile, R., Birkstead-Breen, D., Bohm, T., Denis, P., Ferro, A., Hinz, H., Jemstedt, A., Mariotti, P. and Schubert, J. (2008). *Psychoanalysis Comparable and Incomparable*. London: Routledge.

Winnicott, D. (1971). *Playing and Reality*. London: Penguin.

Wittgenstein, L. (1958). *Philosophical Investigations*. Oxford: Oxford University Press.

Zeki, S. (2009). *The Splendours and Mysteries of the Brain*. Chichester: Wiley-Blackwell.

Section 2

Clinical problems and presentations

Chapter 3

Attachment theory and compassion focused therapy for depression

Paul Gilbert

Compassion focused therapy (CFT) emerged from a number of major but disparate influences, including clinical observation, evolution theory, attachment theory and Buddhist practices (Gilbert 2000a, 2009a, 2012). Firstly, when working with Cognitive Behaviour Therapy (CBT) for chronic depression in the 1980s, it became clear that some people could generate impressive alternative thoughts to their depressive ones but still said: 'I can see the logic but I don't feel any better' or 'I know logically I am not a failure but I still feel a failure'. This is now well recognised as a difficulty in CBT (Stott 2007). Exploring the emotional textures by which people experienced their alternative thoughts revealed that they were often somewhat harsh and aggressive, rather than kind, understanding and supportive. Attachment theory gave important insights into how we generate such 'kind' emotional textures (Cozolino 2007) and that shame is one of the biggest blocks to feeling affiliative emotions for the self (Gilbert 2010).

The attachment model focuses on the emotional and behavioural mechanisms that enable parent and child to stay in close proximity to each other and that regulate the child's physiological systems, especially emotions. The evolution of attachment is the basis for the experience of early warmth, affiliation and emotional soothing. Attachment loss impacts on these emotion systems, giving rise to anxiety and depression (Bowlby 1969, 1973, 1980; Harlow and Mears 1979; Mikulincer and Shaver 2007). The evolved defensive strategies to disruptions in attachment and affiliation are protest (anger, anxiety and crying) and despair (retardation, loss of positive emotions and hiding). Separated and thus uncared for, mammalian juveniles do not generally survive. The first defensive response to separation, called protest-distress, is therefore to lose interest in any other considerations and attend fully to distress – seeking and calling to the parent. However, if this continues without resolution then the infant attracts predators and is at risk of becoming exhausted and lost. At some point the protest-distress strategy becomes a liability and needs to be 'turned off' and a totally different strategy of conserving resources and minimising signalling is required. The despair defences reduce explorative and distress calling and down-regulate positive affect, inhibiting explorative and resource seeking behaviour (Gilbert 1992, 2007b). There is some evidence for genetic differences in the susceptibility to the intensity of protest and despair responses (Suomi 1997, 1999) that give rise to phenotypic differences arising from variations in affiliative or hostile early environments (Belsky and Pluess 2009).

As Bowlby was articulating the link between attachment and mood, Price (1972) was developing a model that suggested that a down-regulation of positive emotion was defensive when confronted with a more powerful, hostile other. There were many descriptions in the literature of animals who had lost status or were subject to constant down rank aggression, who then went into submissive states of high social avoidance, reduced explorative behaviour, became passive with low drive and took on the appearance of depression (Gilbert 2000b; Price and Sloman 1987).

Rank, attachment and affiliation have very complex interactions (Liotti 2000; Sloman, Gilbert and Hasey 2003). For example, perceptions of low social rank (feeling inferior, shame, being fearful of assertiveness, and vulnerability to social rejection) seem a route into adult depression and other forms of psychopathology (Gilbert 1992, 2000b; Sturman 2011), but those routes are sensitised in early life, particularly by the lack of appropriate attachment relationships. Moreover, shame (the sense of being undesirable to others, bad, unworthy, or inadequate) often underpins depression (Gilbert, 2013). Not only does shame carry a sense of inferiority, but it is one of the biggest blocks to the experience of affiliative emotion. Healing shame requires some experience of connectedness with others, such as kindness, understanding, support, and validation (Gilbert 2007a, 2011). Indeed, even in monkeys who have been rendered subordinate or defeated, their abilities to engage in supportive relationships with other primates has a huge impact on their recovery, including cardiovascular and cortisol indicators of stress (Abbott *et al.* 2003).

From attachment to affiliation and shame

Bowlby (see also Harlow and Mears 1979) argued that the experience of attachment acted as a template by which individuals come to choreograph their perceptions and feelings about other relationships and themselves. Recent researchers have pointed out that attachment influences capacities for empathising, mentalising (Allen and Fonagy 2007; Liotti and Gilbert 2011), and compassion (Gillath, Shaver and Mikulincer 2005). Thus our early experiences of another human being (as loving, available and trustworthy) come to influence (though not determine) our ways of engaging in different types of relationships as we grow up, such as co-operation, friendship formation, sexual and social rank (Cozolino 2007). Belonging to, and taking identity from, groups can also be influenced by attachment history (Baumeister and Leary 1995). Indeed the neurophysiology would indicate that the attachment system is linked to wider systems for the development of affiliative relationships in general, and not just attachment ones (Dunbar 2010; Gilbert 1989; Porges 2007). For example, although the neurohormone oxytocin is known to be important in the evolution and onset of attachment behaviour (Carter 1998), it also plays a role in a range of social and affiliative behaviours including trust, conspecific recognition, empathy and mind reading, and the ability to be soothed by a trusted friend in the face of threat (Carter 1998; MacDonald and MacDonald 2010). So while attachment is key to our beginning of feeling safe or threatened in relationships, we need to think about the wider contexts of social relationships in terms of the affiliative qualities that can be shared between friends and groups in general (Cacioppo and Patrick 2008), which is the basis of social neuroscience (Cacioppo et al. 2000).

Gilbert (1989) suggested that as infants move through childhood and into adulthood, the attachment system links with more complex forms of relating. This is because different social (archetypal) tasks await the child on their maturational journey, such as forming alliances, identifying with groups, working in teams, developing sexual interest and relating, becoming a parent and developing authority (and adapting/accommodating to higher authority) within a group. Many of these tasks and goal orientations will focus the growing child-to-adult on their social reputation and how they (think they) exist in the minds of others; on the competitive dynamics of life but also caring and supporting others; the processes of 'getting along' and 'getting on'. Key for humans is that social competition and social rank have evolved to become increasingly less focused on aggression and more focused on winning approval or being liked by others. This aspect became known as our social attention holding potential, SAHP (Gilbert 1989, 1997). There is, for example, evidence that people ground their self-esteem by believing they have traits that others will value (Santor and Walker 1999). The dimension of being valued is a different dimension to being cared for. Some people (especially in the older populations) can get depressed not because they feel uncared for but because they feel they have nothing to contribute; no-one needs or wants them. It is the feeling that one cannot contribute that can therefore be a major issue for some depressed people (Gilbert 1984).

SAHP can be positive and negative – when it is negative, individuals have issues of shame and stigma. When SAHP is first experienced positively in the loving gaze and embrace of an affectionate parent, we have the emotional experience of existing positively in the mind of another. The positive emotion in the face of the mother leads to positive emotion in the infant (Schore 1994, 2010; Trevarthen and Aitken 2001). In fact, the evolution of being interested in and monitoring our attractiveness in the minds of others is linked to humans being sensitive to multiple caregivers (aunts and grandmothers) and carries on throughout life (Hrdy 2009). Indeed, even our competitive behaviour now is orientated around attractiveness and wanting 'to be chosen' (Barkow 1989; Gilbert 1992). Shame is an experience of feeling undesired and unattractive to others, vulnerable to criticism, rejection or even persecution (Gilbert 1998). It is useful, therefore, for therapists to understand the evolutionary roots of dynamics of shame and how shame can be one of the most important disruptors of affiliative capacities in therapy, increasing risk of concealments, dropout and acting out (Dearing and Tangney 2011; Gilbert 2007a, 2011). Shame and affiliation therefore share complex, dynamic and reciprocal relationships. Shame can arise from disruptions in affiliation and affiliation can heal shame.

Neurophysiology of attachment and affiliation

It is now understood that basic motivational systems such as finding food, sexual partners, seeking status, and the various human derivatives, are linked to actions by emotion. Take any motive, and if we are successful we get a buzz of positive emotion, but when it is blocked, thwarted or we fail, we experience negative emotion. In this respect, emotions are motive trackers. There is evidence that depressed people are motivated (they *want* to achieve certain things) but they lack feeling/emotion in being able to do it or anticipate a negative emotion in trying (Dalgleish *et al.* 2011). Lack of interest may come from repeated efforts of failing to experience positive emotion in the context of trying or as a result of high levels of threat (White, Laithwait and Gilbert, in press). Key to understanding the link between motivational systems like attachment and affiliation, then, is how different types of emotion are regulated by them.

To answer this we first need to recognise that we are now able to identify three types of affect regulation systems, all of which play fundamental roles in attachment and affiliative psychology (Depue and Morrone-Strupinsky 2005). These are the:

- *Threat and self-protection focused system*, which enables detecting, attending, processing and responding to threats. There is a menu of threat-based emotions such as anger, anxiety and disgust, and a menu of defensive behaviours, such as fight, flight, submission and freeze.
- *Drive, seeking and acquisition focused system*, which enables the paying of attention to advantageous resources and, with some degree of 'activation', an experience of pleasure in pursuing and securing them.
- *Contentment, soothing and affiliative focused system*, which enables a state of peacefulness and openness when individuals are no longer threat focused or seeking resources, but are satisfied and experience positive well-being. Over evolutionary time, this system of calming has been adapted for many functions of attachment and affiliative behaviour. The system is linked to the endorphin-oxytocin systems which function to promote trust and affiliative behaviour. Recipients of affiliation experience calming of the threat system (MacDonald and Macdonald 2010).

These three systems are depicted in Figure 3.1.

One of the most important developments in the last 10 years has been the understanding that positive emotion is of (at least) two fundamental types. The first is linked to drives and is associated with feelings of excitement, social dominance, pleasure and anticipation of reward. The second is a positive affect system that is associated with soothing/affiliative affects, neither seeking positives nor responding to the threat, which creates feelings of calming, soothing and well-being. These emotions are especially linked to the endorphins and to some degree oxytocin (Dunbar 2010). This type of positive affect, linked with well-being, is associated with parasympathetic arousal, calm mind and ease of sleeping.

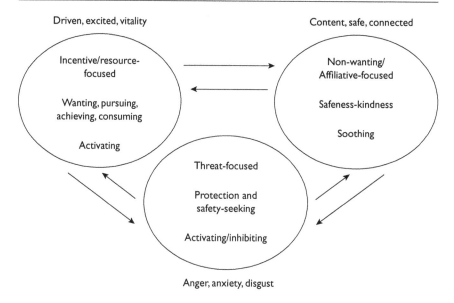

Driven, excited, vitality   Content, safe, connected

Incentive/resource-focused   Non-wanting/Affiliative-focused

Wanting, pursuing, achieving, consuming   Safeness-kindness

Activating   Soothing

Threat-focused

Protection and safety-seeking

Activating/inhibiting

Anger, anxiety, disgust

Figure 3.1 Three types of affect regulation system
From Gilbert, The Compassionate Mind *(2009b), reprinted with permission from Constable and Robinson Ltd.*

Therefore, attachment and affiliative relationships down-regulate the threat system (e.g. Guerra *et al.* 2012) and provides sufficient safeness for people to be able to engage in explorative behaviour (Gilbert 1989), mentalise, reflect and change (Allen and Fonagy 2007; Liotti and Gilbert 2011; Wallin 2007).

The point is that, without recognition of the distinction between these two very different types of positive emotion, it can be difficult to think about which type of positive emotion (or both) has gone off-line in depression and what needs to be done to bring it on-line. There are many theories that focus on drive emotions, and indeed the neuropharmacology of depression tends to focus on the monoamines and drive and threat systems. While the focus on drive emotions, achievement and doing can be helpful (Dimidjian *et al.* 2006), as can unconscious threat emotions such as anger (Wachtel 2011), we should also focus on the importance of the attachment, affiliation, endorphin and oxytocin systems, which are about slowing, calming and creating a sense of safeness from which exploration can occur. It is this safeness (or what Bowlby called a 'secure base') that provides a platform to go out, seek and have the confidence to try things. In addition the concept of 'safe haven' refers to how the child can return to a secure base, for calming and reassurance, if they become threatened or distressed. So there are both encouraging and soothing qualities to attachment. Indeed, self-report measures that distinguish drive emotions (feeling energised, active) from soothing affect (warm, secure) suggest that it is the latter which are particularly (negatively) linked to depression and anxiety (Gilbert *et al.* 2008). Kelly, Zuroff, Leybman and Gilbert (2012) found that a measure of general social safeness and capacities for feeling connected to others were a better predictor of vulnerability psychopathology than negative affect, positive affect or needs for social support. So it is possible that the general day-to-day tone of the affiliative (endorphin-oxytocin) system plays a role in resilience.

Disruptions of this affect system are associated with feelings of separation, disconnection and aloneness. Indeed, for many people who have psychopathology, including depression, the experience of aloneness, especially when they are feeling at their worst, is very common (Cacioppo and Patrick 2008). The experience of aloneness and disconnectedness or 'shut off-ness', as part of the emotional complex a person is feeling is actually a focus for compassion focused therapy (Gilbert 2010).

So, using the three circle model, we can see that depression involves disruption in all three systems – and should not be seen as only a disturbance of positive affect (Gilbert 2007a, b, in press). This can be depicted in diagram form in Figure 3.2.

Attachment and affiliative disruption

Many problems in psychopathology, and especially depression, are linked to the difficulties of attachment and soothing/affiliation systems to regulate the drive and threat system (Gilbert 1993, 2009). One reason this occurs is because the parent could have been a source both of comfort and also of fear, producing approach avoidance conflicts (Liotti and Gumley 2008). So, for example, if parents have frightened the child, the child can hardly turn to them for comfort, or if they do, he or she must behave in a highly submissive way (Gilbert 1992, 2007). This is commonly seen as creating in the child a state of 'fright without resolution' in that there is no-one to act as a soothing caring other (Liotti 2009).

Shame can also create 'fright without resolution or solution' because the very thing that will heal shame is the affiliative validating experience, or even a forgiving experience from another. Shame is, however, the fear that one will lose whatever affiliation and care there is if one reveals 'the shameful'. It is a Catch-22 situation. In this sense, shame creates avoidance or sometimes aggressive counter-defences – all of which completely disrupt the capacity for connective, affiliative relationships. The management of shame within therapy therefore becomes central (Dearing and Tangney 2011).

Logically it might seem that the best thing for shame-prone individuals to do is to engage in more affiliation – which is true up to a point. However, this is problematic. Some years ago I saw a recorded lecture by John Bowlby in which he noted that the kindness and support of the therapist can activate the attachment system. When this happens the 'system' will open up whatever memories have been encoded there. Sometimes the emotional memories coded in the attachment system are ones of neglect, abuse, yearning, aloneness and shame and reactivating those could be traumatic. This can also be understood in conditioning terms (Gilbert 1992). For example, normally one's own sexual arousal, or imagining a holiday, is pleasant. However, if one has been raped on holiday then having memories of holidays or sexual feelings triggered will be not pleasant but deeply traumatic. This is just one of a number of ways in which stimulating the attachment and affiliative system can at first be aversive. The therapist needs to work through this, of course, because not to do so leaves the patient without a major affect regulating system. They can again get stuck in a kind of 'threat without resolution'.

People can have a fear of affiliative feelings for many reasons (Gilbert *et al.* 2011). Whatever the reasons, one of the consequences is that the movement towards affiliation actually produces intense approach–avoidance conflicts (Liotti 2000, 2009). When shame is involved as a block to affiliative feelings, the most common problem is the person's ability to deal with overwhelming sadness and grief (Gilbert and Irons 2005), which not uncommonly they block. There are many therapies that recognise the fear of affiliative emotion but do not necessarily make that the focus of therapy – nor do they suggest that practising affiliative motives and emotions should be central to therapy itself. Sometimes they rely on the therapeutic relationship being the key focus for compassion development.

Compassion focused therapy

Compassion focused therapy (CFT) suggests that one of the key difficulties for many people with depression and other emotion regulation difficulties is that for various reasons the three affect regulation systems are out of balance, this type of pattern of change in affect systems is shown in Figure 3.2. Given the enormous importance of the soothing affiliative system in affect regulation, this is a central (but not the only) focus of CFT.

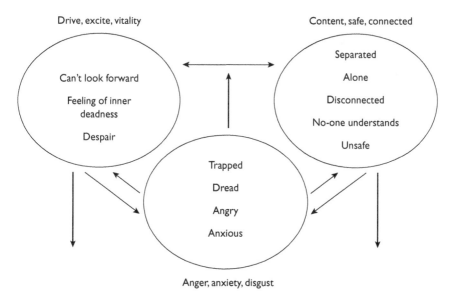

Figure 3.2 Experiences associated with three major affect regulation systems in depression

In addition to using standard therapeutic interventions, such as building an appropriate safe and validating therapeutic relationship, Socratic questioning, teaching people how to monitor their thoughts and feelings, using inference chains and behavioural experiments, a good deal of the work for depression in CFT focuses on building compassionate capacity (Gilbert 2007b, 2010; Gilbert and Choden 2013). In CFT it is like basic muscles: unless some degree of compassion (strength, a kind of inner secure base and safe haven) is available to the patient, it can be difficult to engage with threat-based experiences.

The model of compassion is also quite specific in CFT (Gilbert 2005, 2009). We make a distinction between the ability to compassionately approach and engage suffering and the compassionate capacity for alleviation, holding and softening suffering. This is often represented as two interacting 'psychologies' of attributes (engagement abilities) and skills (alleviation) (Gilbert 2010, 2012).

The engagement aspect of compassion involves motivation to engage and learning how to be attentionally sensitive to suffering (including what is happening in one's body and emotions). It also involves the ability to be emotionally moved by what one attends to or experiences 'sympathy for' (for example, if you attend to another person in distress, are you left cold by it or do you attune into it and feel connected, emotionally moved); and distress tolerance (sometimes when people become distressed they engage in avoidance, dissociation and denial). It further involves empathy, which links with mentalising, the ability to think about and reflect on what is happening and the potential sources of suffering (clearly one cannot do that if one is not motivated or able to tolerate distress); and non-judgement (which means we do not criticise or fight with what comes up in us as we explore the nature of our own or other people's suffering).

These two psychologies of 'engagement and alleviation' can guide the therapist almost like walking – first one foot/aspect, then the next – and show him or her how to explore where key problems lie. For example, some patients with depression can engage with their suffering but do not know how to do anything about it, or do so in very critical, hostile ways. In contrast, some individuals are very reluctant to engage with the source of their suffering, such as early trauma or the implications of the need to change lifestyle. Some individuals struggle with mentalising and empathy competencies and these can compromise motivation. So CFT does not engage too much with suffering (e.g. trauma memories) until there is sufficient capacity for compassionate holding, alleviation and soothing – one foot should not get too far ahead of the other.

CFT therefore seeks to build motivation and these abilities, skills and competencies to address suffering and the causes of suffering in compassionate, containing ways. The concepts of a secure base and safe haven is very important, because this is the point to return to if the threat system gets too highly activated (Holmes 2001). While CFT can proceed in very standard ways through guided discovery, validation, encouragement and creating a secure base and safe haven in the therapeutic relationship, CFT suggests that we need to go beyond this and teach patients how to actually cultivate and practise generating patterns of compassionate activity inside themselves (Dalai Lama 1995, 2001); so that they can create their own inner secure base and safe haven. Hence compassionate mind training becomes a part of the overall structure of the therapy. There are therefore a number of unique aspects to CFT which have some overlap with Buddhist concepts of compassion cultivation (Gilbert 2009a; Gilbert and Choden 2013). These involve sharing the evolutionary model, helping people to understand the nature of depression as an evolved potential and the importance of social shaping of our identities and sense of self (e.g. if I had been adopted as a baby into a violent drug gang then this version of Paul Gilbert would not exist, but rather one who is more violent and even murderous). These are key to de-shaming processes. In addition we build compassionate capacity by focusing on the generating experience of practising compassionate behaviours, being open to compassion from others, and developing self compassion. The therapist uses a mixture of building the therapeutic relationship and a range of imagery and sensory body-focused exercises (Gilbert and Choden 2013). In addition, we focus on developing compassionate attention, compassionate thinking, compassionate behaviour and compassionate feeling. All these are designed to help balance the three affect regulation systems and to develop a particular kind of self-identity.

There is good evidence that imagery can work better than verbal interventions (Stopa 2009), and that guided positive imagery can be helpful for depression (Holmes, Lang and Shah 2009). CFT uses a series of imagery tasks, some of which are adaptations from Buddhist imagery practices (Leighton 2003), whereas others were developed with patients themselves (Gilbert 2009; Gilbert and Choden 2013). There is evidence that practising imagining one's 'best possible self' is related to increased optimism (Meevissen, Peters and Alberts 2011), and practising positive self-imagery by recalling a time when one felt relaxed and positive is related to higher levels of self-esteem and reduced anxiety in response to anxiety-provoking vignettes (Stopa, Brown and Hirsch 2012). There is also growing evidence, based on an increasing number of outcome studies, that compassion focused practices have a major role to play in the treatment of psychopathology (Gilbert 2011; Hofmann, Grossman and Hinton 2011).

CFT for depression, and other conditions, builds on many other therapies but its central focus is that the attachment and affiliative systems often require more attention and cultivation. CFT suggests that in the context of a supportive relationship we can literally teach people with depression to cultivate compassionate ways of thinking and being in the world that will have major impacts on their attention, thinking, behaviour and feeling and the very essence of the sense of self these will then re-orientate motivations and balance emotion regulation systems.

Conclusion

Evolutionary insights have illuminated some of the reasons we and other animals are vulnerable to reduced positive affect and increased negative affect which is the basis of depression (Gilbert 2013). It also reveals how attachment became the major regulator of threat, with huge impacts on a range of physiological processes. However, it was not just attachment between child and parent that was vital in human evolution, but the evolution of general affiliative relationships that supported pair bonding and alliance formation (Dunbar 2010). Within these contexts we live not only in the physical world but in the world of the minds of others when we seek to be valued and respected and wanted. Shame is the experience of living negatively in the minds of others and this has an impact on blocking us from affiliative connections and affiliative emotions, processes that are so vital for emotion regulation and well-being. In addition, shame is commonly linked to self-criticism, which blocks the capacity for self kindness support and encouragement. Compassion focused therapy explicitly addresses these issues. If our internal self-with-self relationship is hostile then there is no source for joy, love and soothing – and the world turns dark and empty.

References

Abbott, D.H., Keverne, E.B., Bercovitch, F.B., Shively, C.A., Mendoza, S.P. and Saltzman, W. (2003). Are subordinates always stressed? A comparative analysis of rank differences in cortisol levels among primates. *Hormones and Behavior* **43**, 67–82.

Allen, J.G. and Fonagy, P. (2007). *Handbook of Mentalisation-Based Treatment.* Chichester: Wiley.

Barkow, J.H. (1989). *Darwin, Sex and Status: biological approaches to mind and culture.* Toronto: University of Toronto Press.

Baumeister, R.F. and Leary, M.R. (1995). The need to belong: desire for interpersonal attachments as a fundamental human motivation. *Psychological Bulletin* **117**, 497–529.

Belsky, J. and Pluess, M. (2009). Beyond diathesis stress: differential susceptibility to environmental influences. *Psychological Bulletin* **135**, 885–908.

Bowlby, J. (1969). *Attachment and Loss, Volume 1: Attachment.* London: Hogarth Press.

——(1973). *Attachment and Loss, Volume 2: Separation: anxiety and anger.* London: Hogarth Press.

——(1980). *Attachment and Loss, Volume 3: Loss: sadness and depression.* London: Hogarth Press.

Cacioppo, J.T. and Patrick, B. (2008). *Loneliness: human nature and the need for social connection.* New York: W.W. Norton and Company.

Cacioppo, J.T., Berston, G.G., Sheridan, J.F. and McClintock, M.K. (2000). Multilevel integrative analysis of human behavior: social neuroscience and the complementing nature of social and biological approaches. *Psychological Bulletin* **126**, 829–43.

Carter, C.S. (1998). Neuroendocrine perspectives on social attachment and love. *Psychoneuroendorinlogy* **23**, 779–818.

Cozolino, L. (2007). *The Neuroscience of Human Relationships: attachment and the developing brain.* New York: W. W. Norton.

Dalai Lama (1995). *The Power of Compassion.* India: HarperCollins.

——(2001). *An Open Heart: practising compassion in everyday life.* London: Hodder and Stoughton.

Dalgleish, T., Hill, E., Morant, N. and Golden, A.M.J. (2011). The structure of past and future lives in depression. *Journal of Abnormal Psychology* **120**, 1–15.

Dearing, R.L. and Tangney J.P. (eds) (2011). *Shame in the Therapy Hour*. Washington: American Psychological Society.

Depue, R.A. and Morrone-Strupinsky, J.V. (2005). A neurobehavioral model of affiliative bonding. *Behavioral and Brain Sciences* **28**, 313–95.

Dimidjian S., Hollon, S.D., Dobson, K.S., Schmaling, K.B., Kohlenberg, R.J., Gallop, R.J., Rizvi, S.L., Gollam, J.K., Dunner, D.L. and Jacobson, N.S. (2006). Randomized trial of behavioral activation, cognitive therapy, and anti-depressant medication in the acute treatment of adults with major depression. *Journal of Consulting and Clinical Psychology* **74**, 658–70.

Dunbar, R.I.M. (2010). The social role of touch in humans and primates: behavioural function and neurobiological mechanisms. *Neuroscience and Biobehavioral Reviews* **34**, 260–8.

Gilbert, P. (1984). *Depression: from psychology to brain state*. London: Lawrence Erlbaum Associates Ltd.

——(1989). *Human Nature and Suffering*. Hove: Lawrence Erlbaum Associates Ltd.

——(1992). *Depression: the evolution of powerlessness*. Hove: Lawrence Erlbaum Associates Ltd.

——(1993). Defence and safety: their function in social behaviour and psychopathology. *British Journal of Clinical Psychology* **32**, 131–53.

——(1997). The evolution of social attractiveness and its role in shame, humiliation, guilt and therapy. *British Journal of Medical Psychology* **70**, 113–47.

——(1998). What is shame? Some core issues and controversies. In P. Gilbert and B. Andrews (eds), *Shame: interpersonal behavior, psychopathology and culture*, pp. 3–38. New York: Oxford University Press.

——(2000a). Social mentalities: internal 'social' conflicts and the role of inner warmth and compassion in cognitive therapy. In P. Gilbert and K.G. Bailey (eds), *Genes on the Couch: explorations in evolutionary psychotherapy*, pp.118–50. Hove: Psychology Press.

——(2000b). Varieties of submissive behaviour: their evolution and role in depression. In L. Sloman and P. Gilbert (eds), *Subordination and Defeat: an evolutionary approach to mood disorders*, pp. 3–46. Hillsdale, New Jersey: Lawrence Erlbaum.

——(2005). Compassion and cruelty: a biopsychosocial approach. In P. Gilbert (ed.), *Compassion: conceptualisations, research and use in psychotherapy*, pp. 3–74. London: Routledge.

——(2007a). *Psychotherapy and Counselling for Depression*, 3rd edn. London: Sage.

——(2007b). The evolution of shame as a marker for relationship security. In J.L. Tracy, R.W. Robins and J.P Tangney (eds), *The Self-conscious Emotions: theory and research*, pp. 283–309. New York: Guilford Press.

——(2009a). Evolved minds and compassion focused imagery in depression. In L. Stopa (ed.), *Imagery and the Threatened Self: perspectives on mental imagery and the self in cognitive therapy*, pp. 206–31. London: Routledge.

——(2009b). *The Compassionate Mind*. London: Constable-Robinson; Oaklands, CA: New Harbinger.

——(2010). *Compassion Focused Therapy: distinctive features* (The CBT Distinctive Features Series). London: Routledge.

——(2011). Shame in psychotherapy and the role of compassion focused therapy. In R.L. Dearing and J.P. Tangney (eds), *Shame in the Therapy Hour*, pp. 325–54. Washington: American Psychological Society.

——(2012). Compassion focused therapy. In W. Dryden (ed.), *Cognitive Behaviour Therapies*, pp. 140–65. London: Sage.

——(2013). Depression: the challenges of an integrative, biopsychosocial evolutionary approach. In M. Power (ed.), *Mood Disorders: a handbook of science and practice*, 2nd edn. pp. 229–88. Chichester: J. Wiley.

Gilbert, P. and Choden (2013). *Mindful Compassion*. London: Constable-Robinson.

Gilbert, P. and Irons, C. (2005). Focused therapies and compassionate mind training for shame and self-attacking. In P. Gilbert (ed.), *Compassion: conceptualisations, research and use in psychotherapy*, pp. 263–325. London: Routledge.

Gilbert, P., McEwan, K., Mitra, R., Franks, L., Richter, A. and Rockliff, H. (2008). Feeling safe and content: a specific affect regulation system? Relationship to depression, anxiety, stress and self-criticism. *Journal of Positive Psychology* **3**, 182–91.

Gilbert, P., McEwan, K., Gibbons, L., Chotai, S., Duarte, J. and Matos, M. (2011). Fears of compassion and happiness in relation to alexithymia, mindfulness and self-criticism. *Psychology and Psychotherapy* **84**, 239–55.

Gillath, O., Shaver, P.R. and Mikulincer, M. (2005). An attachment-theoretical approach to compassion and altruism. In P. Gilbert (ed.), *Compassion: conceptualisations, research and use in psychotherapy*, pp. 121–47. London: Routledge.

Guerra P., Sánchez-Adam A., Anllo-Vento L., Ramírez I. and Vila J. (2012). Viewing loved faces inhibits defense reactions: a health-promotion mechanism? PLoS ONE 7(7): e41631. doi:10.1371/journal.pone.0041631.

Harlow, H.F. and Mears, C. (1979). *The Human Model: primate perspectives*. New York: Winston and Sons.

Hofmann, S.G., Grossman, P. and Hinton, D.E. (2011). Loving-kindness and compassion meditation: potential for psychological interventions. *Clinical Psychology Review* **31**, 1126–32.

Holmes, J. (2001). *The Search for the Secure Base: attachment theory and psychotherapy*. Hove: Brunner-Routledge.

Holmes, E.A., Lang, T.J. and Shah, D.M. (2009). Developing interpretation bias modification as a 'Cognitive Vaccine' for depressed mood: imagining positive events makes you feel better than thinking about them verbally. *Journal of Abnormal Psychology* **118**, 76–88.

Hrdy, S.B. (2009). *Mothers and Others: the evolutionary origins of mutual understanding*. Harvard: Harvard University Press.

Kelly, A.C., Zuroff, D.C., Leybman, M.J. and Gilbert, P. (2012). Social safeness, received social support, and maladjustment: testing a tripartite model of affect regulation. *Cognitive Therapy and Research* (published online) DOI 10.1007/s10608-011-9432-5.

Leighton, T.D. (2003). *Faces of Compassion: classic bodhisattva archetypes and their modern expression*. Boston: Wisdom Publications.

Liotti, G. (2000). Disorganised attachment, models of borderline states and evolutionary psychotherapy. In P. Gilbert and B. Bailey (eds). *Genes on the Couch: explorations in evolutionary psychotherapy*, pp. 232–56. Hove: Brunner-Routledge.

——(2009). Attachment and dissociation. In P. Dell and J.A. O'Neil (eds), *Dissociation and the Dissociative Disorders: DSM-V and beyond*, pp. 53–66. New York: Routledge.

Liotti, G. and Gilbert, P. (2011). Mentalizing, motivations and social mentalities: theoretical considerations and implications for psychotherapy. *Psychology and Psychotherapy* **84**, 9–25.

Liotti, G. and Gumley, A. (2008). An attachment perspective on schizophrenia: the role of disorganized attachment, dissociation, and mentalization. In A. Moskowitz, I. Schafer and M. J. Dorahy (eds), *Psychosis, Trauma, and Dissociation: emerging perspectives on severe psychopathology*, pp. 117–34. Oxford: John Wiley & Sons.

MacDonald, K. and MacDonald, T.M. (2010). The peptide that binds: a systematic review of oxytocin and its prosocial effects in humans. *Harvard Review of Psychiatry* **18**, 1–21.

Meevissen, Y.M.C., Peters, M.L. and Alberts, H.J.E.M. (2011). Become more optimistic by imagining a best possible self: effects of a two week intervention. *Journal of Behavior Therapy and Experimental Psychiatry* **42**, 371–8.

Mikulincer, M. and Shaver, P.R. (2007). *Attachment in Adulthood: structure, dynamics, and change*. New York: Guilford Press.

Porges, S.W. (2007). The polyvagal perspective. *Biological Psychology* **74**, 116–43.

Price, J.S. (1972). Genetic and phylogenetic aspects of mood variations. *International Journal of Mental Health* **1**, 124–44.

Price, J.S. and Sloman, L. (1987). Depression as yielding behaviour: an animal model based on Schjelderup-Ebbe's pecking order. *Ethology and Sociobiology* **8** (Suppl.), 85–98.

Santor, D. and Walker, J. (1999). Garnering the interests of others: mediating the effects among physical attractiveness, self-worth and dominance. *British Journal of Social Psychology* **38**, 461–77.

Schore, A.N. (1994). *Affect Regulation and the Origin of the Self: the neurobiology of emotional development*. Hillsdale, New Jersey: Lawrence Erlbaum.

——(2010). Attachment trauma and the developing right brain: origins of pathological dissociation. In. P.F. Dell and J.A. O'Neil (eds), *Dissociation and the Dissociative Disorders: DSM-V and beyond*, pp. 107–41. London: Routledge

Sloman, L., Gilbert, P. and Hasey, G. (2003). Evolved mechanisms in depression: The role and interaction of attachment and social rank in depression. *Journal of Affective Disorders* **74**, 107–21.

Stopa, L. (ed.) (2009). *Imagery and the Threatened Self: perspectives on mental imagery and the self in cognitive therapy*. London: Routledge

Stopa, L., Brown, M.A. and Hirsch, C.R. (2012). The effects of repeated imagery practice on self-concept, anxiety and performance in socially anxious participants. *Journal of Experimental Psychopathology* **3**, 223–42.

Stott, R. (2007). When the head and heart do not agree: a theoretical and clinical analysis of rational-emotional dissociation (RED) in cognitive therapy. *Journal of Cognitive Psychotherapy: An International Quarterly* **21**, 37–50.

Sturman, E. (2011). Involuntary subordination and its relation to personality, mood, and submissive behavior. *Psychological Assessment* **23**, 262–76.

Suomi, S.J. (1997). Early determinants of behavior: evidence from primate studies. *British Medical Bulletin* **53**, 170–84.

——(1999). Attachment in rhesus monkeys. In J. Cassidy and P.R. Shaver (eds), *Handbook of Attachment: theory, research and clinical applications*, pp. 181–97. New York: Guilford Press.

Trevarthen, C. and Aitken, K. (2001). Infant intersubjectivity: research, theory and clinical applications. *Journal of Child Psychology and Psychiatry* **42**, 3–48.

Wachtel, P.L. (2011). *Therapeutic Communication: knowing what to say when*. New York: Guilford Press.

Wallin, D.J. (2007). *Attachment in Psychotherapy*. New York: Guilford Press.

White, R., Laithwait, H. and Gilbert, P. (in press). Negative symptoms in schizophrenia: the role of social defeat. In A. Gumley, A. Gillham, K. Taylor and M. Schwannauer (eds), *Psychosis and Emotion: the role of emotions in understanding psychosis, therapy and recovery*. London: Routledge.

Chapter 4

Responding to threat

Using attachment-related interventions in cognitive behavioural therapy of anxiety disorders

Gail Myhr

Introduction

The natural goal of the attachment system is to increase a person's sense of security in the world (Bowlby 1982). Early attachment relationships affect not only the perceived level of threat and safety in the person's world (Liotti 2007), but also the strategies the person uses to attenuate that sense of threat (Main 2000). The conceptualisation of attachment security as an important determinant of human thinking, emotional processing and behaviour, both in times of distress and in novel situations, dovetails with the cognitive behavioural model of anxiety disorders.

Central to the cognitive behavioural model of anxiety is the notion of perceived personal vulnerability to threat (Beck, Emery and Greenberg 1985). Individuals with anxiety disorders exaggerate threats from both external and internal sources, and underestimate their capacity to cope with these threats. They respond to their fears with behavioural avoidance and the employment of 'safety behaviours' or strategies to reduce anxiety in threatening situations (Abramowitz, Deacon and Whiteside 2011). Not surprisingly, insecure attachment has been associated with anxiety in both clinical and non-clinical populations (Bifulco *et al.* 2006; Mikulincer and Shaver 2007). Greater attachment insecurity, compared to controls, has been measured in individuals with specific phobia (Mikulincer and Shaver 2007), social anxiety disorder (Eng *et al.* 2001), obsessive compulsive disorder (Myhr, Sookman and Pinard 2004), generalised anxiety disorder (Cassidy *et al.* 2009), and post traumatic stress disorder (Kanninen, Punamaki and Qouta 2003). Furthermore, the extent of attachment insecurity is directly related to symptom severity (Bifulco *et al.* 2006).

While the pattern of attachment behaviour (or attachment 'style') and extent of attachment security are considered to be relatively stable across the lifespan (Fraley *et al.* 2011; Waters *et al.* 2000), psychotherapy has been found to alter both in the direction of greater attachment security (Levy *et al.* 2006; Travis *et al.* 2001). In the cognitive behavioural therapy (CBT) literature, Guidano and Liotti (1983) were the first to advance the notion that attachment-related beliefs, feelings and behaviour, activated within the therapeutic relationship, could be examined using a CBT approach, leading to healthy changes in patients' internal working models (IWMs) of attachment (Guidano and Liotti 1983; Liotti 2007). IWMs refer to those internalised representations, derived from early experiences with caregivers, that affect one's view of oneself as competent and worthy of attention, and one's expectations of others as responsive and available in times of need (Bowlby 1982).

This chapter draws on Guidano and Liotti's early work and specifies how the knowledge of patients' attachment styles and IWMs can inform not only the management of the therapeutic relationship, but also the specific targets and interventions in CBT for anxiety disorders.

Insecure attachment and the cognitive model of anxiety

The cognitive behavioural model of emotional distress posits that, in any given situation, a person's thoughts, feelings, and behaviour are inter-related. Consequently, insecure attachment can impact a person's thoughts and behaviours in such a way as to increase anxiety.

Thinking

In the cognitive model, anxious individuals suffer from a heightened sense of personal vulnerability to threat, fuelled by their thought content as well as by characteristic thinking patterns, known as cognitive biases (Beck, Emery and Greenberg 1985). Important cognitive biases in anxiety include attentional biases (Bar-Haim *et al.* 2007) – the tendency to scan the environment for threats – and interpretative biases such as overestimating the probability of a negative event and exaggerating the dire consequences should it happen (catastrophisation) (Allen, McHugh and Barlow 2008).

These thought processes are fuelled by the content of underlying beliefs. Themes important in anxiety includes assumptions related to control ('If I don't prepare for the worst, bad things will happen'), perfectionism ('Mistakes lead to disaster'), inflated responsibility ('If something bad happens, it will be my fault so I must do what I can to prevent it'), intolerance of uncertainty ('I can't take a chance…') and personal vulnerability ('If something goes wrong, I won't be able to handle it') (Casey *et al.* 2004; Taylor *et al.* 2010).

Many of these content areas directly relate to IWMs (Bowlby 1982), i.e. beliefs about one's capacity to cope with adversity and whether attachment figures will be available or helpful in times of stress (Doron and Kyrios 2005). Derived from early interactions with caregivers, these attachment-related expectations of the self and others are crucial determinants of anxiety in exploring novel situations and in dealing with stress.

If early attachment figures are reliable and consistent sources of soothing and help, the child learns that their attachment-related emotions are legitimate and that the attachment figure can be called upon for comfort and soothing, even when the attachment figure is not present during the distressing episode (Liotti 2007). This is a feature of secure attachment (Main 2000).The securely attached child explores his environment more readily, safe in the knowledge that he can rely on his attachment figure in the case of difficulty (Main 2000).

If, however, the attachment figures of childhood respond intermittently to the child's distress, at times proving helpful and at other times proving intrusive or inept, the child learns to increase the intensity of requests for emotional soothing. This is a feature of insecure attachment characterised by 'hyperactivating' attachment strategies and overly dependent behaviour. Through this organised strategy, the child's 'clinginess' within the attachment relationship ensures that he does not miss any sporadic soothing which might come his way (Main 2000).

On the other hand, if early attachment figures respond with impatience or ridicule or neglect to the young child's requests for comfort and help, the child learns to suppress their attachment-related emotions and to become more self-reliant. This is a feature of an avoidant insecure attachment style, with the use of 'deactivating attachment strategies' and compulsive self-reliance. Through this strategy, the avoidant child manages his attachment relationships to minimise the likelihood of rejection and abandonment (Bartholomew 1990; Main 2000).

IWMs and attachment strategies, originating in childhood, are thought to underlie adult attachment representations, with research indicating stability in these over time (Fraley et al. 2011; Waters et al. 2000). Prototypes of adult attachment typically measure two dimensions: attachment anxiety and attachment avoidance (Fraley and Waller 1998). The attachment anxiety dimension refers to an increased sensitivity to abandonment and has been associated with 'hyperactivating' attachment strategies characterised by heightened vigilance to threats, increased expressiveness of fears and needs, worry about attachment figures' availability and excessively dependent, clingy behaviour. Individuals scoring high on this dimension can be called 'preoccupied' or 'anxiously attached' individuals.

By contrast, the attachment avoidance dimension refers to avoidance of emotional closeness with attachment figures and has been associated with 'deactivating attachment strategies' such as dismissal of emotional threats, denial of personal needs, exaggerated self-reliance and downplaying needs of support from attachment figures. Individuals scoring highly on this dimension can be considered to have an 'avoidant' attachment style.

'Secure' individuals are conceptualised as having low attachment anxiety and low avoidance. They are independent, but also comfortable with intimacy and depending on others in times of stress (Fraley and Waller 1998).

Bowlby's IWM (1982) – representing beliefs, emotions and behavioural tendencies of self and other within attachment relationships – resemble the CBT construct of 'schemas' (Beck 1979). Schemas refer to underlying organising structures consisting of a person's core beliefs about themselves, others and the world around them, with emotional and behavioural components. Schemas guide a person's attention towards certain aspects of the world around him and mould data to fit with the schema-related beliefs (confirmation bias). While schema can encompass many themes (e.g. competence, entitlement, alienation), schema related to expectations about attachment figures, attachment-related emotions and behavioural strategies to maintain attachment relationships can be seen as equivalent to IWMs (McBride and Atkinson 2009) and worked on in an explicit fashion in therapy.

These patterns of attachment reflect not only beliefs about the self and others, but also influence cognitive domains relevant to anxiety. People with avoidant attachment styles, who believe that they are alone to solve their problems and must do all they can to prevent things from going awry, may have related beliefs about perfectionism, responsibility and control. Preoccupied patients, who believe that they can't cope alone and must guarantee the availability of others, may have related beliefs about the subjugation of one's personal needs to those of others, the dangerousness of anger and the catastrophisation of emotional distress.

Behaviour

Two behaviours which serve as key maintaining factors in anxiety are avoidance and safety behaviours (Salkovskis 1991). Avoidance can range from the obvious, such as an OCD patient who crosses the street to avoid a potentially contaminated garbage can, to the more subtle, such as a panic disorder patient who avoids arguments with his spouse to prevent increasing his heart rate and bringing on a panic attack. Safety signals/behaviours are those behaviours that allow the anxious person to endure a difficult situation with a sense of safety. These may include a wide variety of actions such as carrying medication in case of a panic attack, attending social situations only if accompanied, or seeking excessive reassurance about medical issues from the internet. Avoidance and safety behaviours prevent the person from learning that what they fear may not happen or that, whatever does happen, they can cope.

Secure individuals, with internalised attuned and responsive attachment figures, will display skilful 'secure base' behaviour in order to explore the world and elicit comfort in times of stress (Waters and Cummings 2000). They will be comfortable taking risks and facing challenging new situations, and will seek comfort or instrumental help from attachment figures when the going gets rough. Conversely, insecurely attached individuals use the 'secure base' less skilfully, perceiving attachment figures as unresponsive, unavailable or unhelpful. The deactivating or hyperactivating attachment strategies used by insecure individuals, while originally effective in optimising early inadequate attachment relationships, now lead to greater anxiety, greater avoidance and efforts to minimise risk of all kinds.

Attachment and case conceptualisation in CBT

CBT of anxiety involves facing what is feared (exposure), eliminating safety behaviours, changing anxiogenic thinking and increasing emotional awareness and self-regulation. Therapy begins with case conceptualisation, integrating information about habitual ways of thinking and behaving in anxiety-provoking situations, with empirically supported models of the anxiety disorder in question.

Attachment-informed CBT incorporates information about attachment styles and related schemas into case conceptualisation (Liotti 2007; McBride and Atkinson 2009; Tasca *et al.* 2004). This requires assessment of thoughts, emotions and behaviours within attachment relationships – past and present. Typical questions include:

- When you were young, to whom did you go for help when you had a problem or were upset?
- After you went to X, what would be the usual result of this?
- If the answer was 'no one, I had to solve my own problems': Why was this so?
- Suppose you had expressed your distress to your parents, what might have happened?
- How were disagreements dealt with?
- How did they deal with emotions in general?
- How do these past experiences influence you today?
- Who do you go to if you have a problem in your life now? What is the usual result?
- If you are comfortable asking help from others, does this ever pose a problem for you? Is it hard for you to do things independently?
- If you tend to solve things on your own, what keeps you from asking for help?
- Are you satisfied with the level of intimacy with X?
- How do you and X deal with disagreements?

From these questions can be derived underlying assumptions about the self, expectations about attachment figures and typical behaviour within attachment relationships used to attenuate stress and regulate emotion. Pertinent assumptions have stems like: 'If I am upset, then…', 'If I get close to X, then…', 'If I ask for help, then X will…' etc. Self-report questionnaires, such as the Experiences in Close Relationships scale (Brennan, Clark and Shaver 1998), can aid clinicians in identifying their patients' attachment styles.

The CBT therapist as a 'secure base'

Patients enter CBT for anxiety disorders because something is inordinately threatening for them and they have not been able to manage it using their habitual strategies. These conditions activate the attachment system; inviting therapists to serve as 'secure bases' from which help can be sought (Bowlby 1988; Waters and Cummings 2000). CBT's 'collaborative empiricism' highlights one secure base function: the exploration of patients' internal and external worlds. The 'felt safety' of an engaged and responsive therapist allows patients to articulate hypotheses about what is feared and facilitates the testing of these hypotheses, through the joint process of guided discovery. Changes in thinking and behaviour, whether through exposure exercises, acting more assertively at work, or examining painful beliefs in session, engender increased anxiety in the short-term, requiring therapists to fulfil the second secure base function, that of 'safe haven' providing soothing and comfort in times of threat (Bowlby 1988). Asking patients to face what they fear most requires therapists to convey something like: 'I know this is hard, but I have confidence in you and in this therapy. You are not alone in this – I am beside you'.

Recognising attachment system activation in the therapeutic alliance

CBT begins with patients and therapists interacting on equal ground, working towards shared therapeutic goals in what can be called the 'joint, goal-oriented mode' (Liotti 2007). Over time, a deepening emotional bond in the alliance reflects the activation of the attachment system and the use of the therapist as secure base. This signals a shift from the 'joint goal-oriented mode' to an 'attachment-caregiving' mode. Liotti has suggested that there are three signs that this has happened (Liotti 2007). First, patients become increasingly emotionally vulnerable in session and express, explicitly or implicitly, the wish for soothing by their therapists. Second, therapists become aware of an increased sense of protectiveness towards their patients. Moments occur in therapy where therapists have an acute sense that 'something else is required of me' that is not necessarily geared towards the stated goals of therapy. Third, patients' attachment-related schemas may become apparent in their dialogue, especially with the notion that the therapist is a kind of rescuer from suffering.

A 46 year-old businessman began CBT for panic disorder and agoraphobia. Mr. A was an independent man who functioned well at home and at work, but was unable to drive on the highway or take a plane for fear of having a panic attack. Family vacation plans suffered and there were business trips he could not attend because of his fears. When his oldest daughter planned her wedding on a Caribbean island, he consulted in a desperate bid to be able to attend.

After several sessions of exploring avoided situations, safety behaviours and pertinent beliefs, a plan was made to begin exposure. When asked to choose a starting point, he looked at his list of avoided situations for a moment, then burst into tears. The therapist became aware of an acute sense of tenderness towards him, and inquired gently whether he could explain what was going on inside of him. He blew his nose and said 'No, I'm ok, let's go on'. When she commented that this was not easy work they were doing together and that she could see it was upsetting to him, he answered tearfully: 'You must think I'm so pathetic. A grown man, afraid of driving his wife to the shopping mall! This is hopeless'.

> The therapist remarked: 'You have been struggling with these fears alone for many years and it might be uncomfortable for you to share them with me. Are you interested in what I am *really* thinking?' When he looked up at her, she went on to say: 'I am just getting to know you, but I know you well enough to recognise the courage and determination it took for you to come and discuss your fears with me. I am so glad you did. I, for one, am extremely hopeful that with your courage and determination, and my help, you will achieve your goals'. He was silent in response to this. When she pressed him for a response, he said that if she felt that way, he could allow himself to hope things would get better too.

In the above vignette, the therapist recognised the three signs of attachment system activation. First, she saw in his emotional vulnerability activation of the attachment system and an implicit request for comfort in a usually avoidant individual. Second, she noticed her own feeling of tenderness in response to his distress, which led her to respond to him in a highly personal, attachment-related way. Rather than giving information about the likelihood of improvement with CBT, she reassured him that she would be his 'secure base' – that he was not alone, that she was interested in his emotional state, that she was committed to helping him, and that she was not critical of him but rather appreciative of his qualities. Third, having recognised his avoidant attachment style in the initial assessment, and having assessed his expectation of attachment figures as being 'critical' or unhelpful, she deliberately disclosed her own true feelings and welcomed his need for her, so he could begin the process of changing attachment-related schema.

Therapists' recognition of attachment system activation, validation of attachment-related emotions and establishing oneself as a helpful, consistent and non-critical 'secure base' leads to a reduction of anxiety in their patients and a resumption of the joint therapy venture, once again focused on the tasks of therapy (Liotti 2007). Effective CBT is characterised by fluid shifts between the joint goal-oriented mode and the intensely personal attachment-caregiving mode at times of stress or dismay. In the process, patients' expectations of attachment figures may undergo transformation, ideally leading to greater attachment security.

Therapeutic stance with respect to attachment-related schema

Emotionally charged moments in session are golden opportunities to elicit pertinent thoughts, underlying assumptions, emotions and behavioural responses in an attachment-related situation. How these situations are dealt with by therapists may, over time, modify attachment-related expectations and behaviours.

For example, patients whose childhood caregivers were experienced as incessantly critical may view benign comments by their therapists as criticisms and withdraw in silent protest. The task-oriented approach and the use of homework in CBT provide many potential situations where patients may feel their performance is being evaluated. Therapists should elicit their patients' thoughts and feelings during such moments and explore the observed behavioural responses (e.g. withdrawal). By welcoming their patients' articulation of the true feelings underlying the withdrawal, acknowledging their own contribution to the therapeutic 'strain', and perhaps by disclosing their actual non-critical feelings towards their patients (Safran and Muran 2000), therapists can help their patients consider new attachment-related schema in which attachment figures are interested in their true feelings, appreciative of their efforts and genuinely welcoming self-expression.

Closely related to patients' expectations of attachment figures are the strategies patients employ to get their attachment needs met – whether secure, deactivating or hyperactivating. Secure patients flexibly move between dependence on the therapist (attachment-caregiving mode) and work on the problem at hand (joint goal-oriented mode). Avoidant patients, having learned to ignore or minimise emotions, overvalue cognition and devalue the importance of connection and dependence on others, will be more comfortable in the joint goal-oriented mode and may resist discussion of attachment related issues (Dozier *et al.* 2001). Conversely, preoccupied patients, utilising hyperactivating attachment strategies, pull for more time to be spent in the attachment-caregiving mode with their therapists and less time in moving towards non-attachment related therapy goals (Liotti 2007).

According to Bowlby, therapists must challenge the usual strategies patients use to process emotion in the context of attachment relationships by acting in ways opposite to the patient's expectations (Bowlby 1982). These 'non-complementary' actions on the part of the therapist vary by attachment style (Dozier and Tyrrell 1998).

The avoidant patient

With avoidant patients, therapists should recognise emotional avoidance, validate unarticulated feelings, draw attention to the attachment-related needs, and underline the importance of the therapeutic and other attachment relationships. The therapist must non-defensively normalise dependency and deepen intimacy, even in the face of sarcasm or dismissal.

Mr. B was in treatment for Obsessive Compulsive Disorder (OCD) featuring pathological doubt. His attachment style was avoidant, with extensive use of deactivating strategies. His condition reduced his efficacy at work and made everyday actions fraught with anxiety over doing the wrong thing.

During therapy, Mr. B's father entered the hospital in the terminal stages of cancer. While visiting him, Mr. B attempted to express thanks to his father for having provided him with many good opportunities in life. Mr. B's father responded in a gruff dismissive way and changed the subject. A nurse, overhearing this, intervened, saying to Mr. B's father that what his son was saying was important and that he should hear him out. But Mr. B's father turned his head and appeared not to hear.

As Mr. B recounted this poignant scene is his dry, matter-of-fact way, his therapist found herself becoming tearful. She recognised the effort it must have taken Mr. B to overcome his usual emotional avoidance to communicate with his dying father, and how ultimately disappointing this interaction must have been. This prompted her to ask what he was feeling as he was telling her this story. He replied with apparent irritation that he felt nothing: 'I said what I had to say to my father, and one can't expect more than that'. While it would have been easier to simply agree with this rationalisation and move on, the therapist persisted: 'Well, I am proud of what you did to express yourself to your father, and I find myself feeling sad that he didn't respond to you differently'.

Mr. B quickly replied: 'The problem with you psychologists is that you have no lives of your own and you rely on other people's feelings to have a life'. The therapist replied gently: 'Well, any way you want to look at it, it must have been a tough night for you.' Mr. B looked at her for a long moment, then he appeared uncertain. 'I'm confused. What are we talking about here?' She repeated her earlier comments and he grew pensive for several long minutes. Then he began to speak again of this episode with greater emotional depth.

In this vignette, the therapist, knowing Mr. B's avoidant attachment style, recognised the courage it took to attempt an emotional connection with his father, and was privy to the kind of rebuff that had probably played itself out many times in Mr. B's childhood. She responded in a 'non-complementary' way by bringing her own emotional reaction into the story, and empathising with what she imagines he might have felt. She ignored Mr. B's attempt to derail the conversation with a personal attack by sticking to her goal of validating his attachment-related emotions and trying to foster a sense of connection in the therapeutic relationship.

The anxiously attached patient

Non-complementary interventions for anxiously attached patients include resisting patient requests for excessive reassurance and stressing the therapist's confidence that other ways exist to reduce the patient's suffering. Here the message is that 'I am here for you', but also, 'I have confidence that there are things you can do on your own to reduce your suffering'. Skilful use of cognitive behavioural techniques can give patients concrete tools to reduce their anxiety and model attachment figures who are consistent and helpful (Liotti 2007).

Ms C suffered from hypochondriasis. She had attachment anxiety and had employed hyperactive attachment strategies with her husband and previous therapists over the years. Recently she had become convinced that she had symptoms of multiple sclerosis. She had consulted many medical doctors and had been finally sent for CBT by her exasperated GP. Despite her therapist's attempts to structure her sessions and methodically tackle her tendency to catastrophise minor physical sensations, she would frequently derail the agenda by describing her symptoms in detail, crying intensely and asking her therapist whether he thought she had a serious illness. While she attended sessions faithfully, she didn't do her homework, which consisted of simple monitoring of her symptoms, triggers and underlying thoughts and behavioural responses.

Finally, the therapist said to her: 'I get the feeling that you and I are working at cross purposes; that we're almost not on the same team! I know there are practical ways of dealing with these kinds of worries that are very effective, and I am eager to show you. I am confident that you could learn them. But as long as you continue to seek my reassurance about your symptoms, we don't have the time to try them. So why don't we do an experiment? How many hours of pure reassurance do you think it will take to make you feel better? I will book them in, and we can try that and see what effect that has on how you feel. We can write down right now what you predict will happen to your anxiety with this plan, and what alternate predictions could be'.

Ms C was delighted with the idea of being able to ask for as much reassurance as she wanted. After four sessions of straight reassurance, her anxiety was worse than ever. She noticed that she experienced temporary relief during the session, but that shortly after she found herself worrying about details of the reassuring comments. At the beginning of the fifth session, she asked her therapist about those other treatment options. The experiment had brought home to her how reassurance was making her anxiety worse.

In this vignette, the therapist demonstrated to Ms C his confidence that he could help her, not by being a source of reassurance, but by specific techniques that she could eventually do on her own. Aware of his role as an attachment figure, he was careful to act quietly confident and unexasperated by her clinginess. 'Concrete, consistent help' was offered (Liotti 2007) and was eventually requested by the patient through the process of guided discovery. In this way, the patient started taking charge of her own life and moved towards a more secure relationship with her therapist.

Using attachment-related schema to inform behavioural interventions: 'external exploration'

Cognitive behavioural therapy of anxiety involves confronting what is feared, either through an exposure exercise or a behavioural experiment to test a relevant belief. Both the anticipation and execution of these interventions will augment anxiety and activate the attachment system. An individual's predominant attachment style may play a role in such technical parameters as the choice of therapist-assisted versus independently conducted exposure. Avoidant patients, in their efforts to minimise felt distress, may not pay attention to the full exposure experience. Subsequent lack of progress may lead to self-recrimination for being unable to do this independently. Anticipating this, therapists should avoid joining in the minimisation of these tasks and encourage attention to the emotional aspects of the exposure ('This exercise would be tough for anyone. How can you and I make it easier for you? Shall we do it together first?'). The choice of therapy-assisted exposure (with the advantage of detecting subtle safety behaviours and efforts at neutralisation) may result in learning not only about the confronted danger, but also the helpfulness of others in dealing with threat and the relief that comes with emotional connection.

For anxiously attached patients, therapist-assisted exposure may be less desirable: the tendency to be more mindful of the therapist's presence than the confronted fear may diminish the results of exposure. Thus the preference may be for independent exposure, with early exercises easy enough to accomplish alone. Patients will learn that not only is what they fear not as dangerous as they thought, but also that they can actually cope with the threat alone.

'External exploration' may include testing other kinds of behaviour in the world. Insecure individuals with anxiety disorders have managed their attachment relationships in characteristic ways to minimise their anxiety. Anxiously attached individuals, who feel they cannot cope alone, may find it difficult to disagree with significant others for fear of being abandoned. Conversely, avoidant individuals, who expect no soothing or help from family members, may cause conflict by having to have things 'just so' in their efforts to stave off catastrophic outcomes for which they will feel solely responsible. Thus behavioural targets in attachment-informed treatment of anxiety disorders may include conflict resolution, self-assertion and emotionally authentic interpersonal communication.

Using attachment-related schema to inform cognitive interventions: 'internal exploration'

Cognitive strategies involve the exploration of patients' internal worlds – their deepest beliefs, their expectations of others and of themselves. Cognitive strategies emphasise the articulation and re-evaluation of these beliefs through the exploration of automatic thoughts in problematic situations, or as they emerge in behavioural experiments. Targeting cognitions that maintain anxiety will often simultaneously target attachment-related cognitions, especially in the insecurely attached individual.

> Ms D, with an anxious attachment style, was in treatment for social anxiety. She was clingy with her husband and unable to attend social situations or do grocery shopping without him. As therapy progressed and she became more confident in dealing with strangers alone, she subtly expressed dissatisfaction with this man on whom she had so heavily relied. While he was generally good to her, she felt hurt at the way he referred to her, when irritated, as 'a mental case'. When her therapist asked if she had ever protested such treatment, she replied: 'Oh I couldn't'. When the therapist gently persisted, wondering what would happen if she did express herself to him, she said: 'I'm sure he would be furious'. 'And if he were furious?' 'Well, probably nothing, but I would feel bad, as if I had done something wrong. And I hate feeling that way.' This example permitted her therapist to explore pertinent underlying beliefs related to anger ('anger is to be avoided at all costs'), and her own perceived fragility in the face of negative affect ('I can't handle feeling bad'). In the context of the therapeutic relationship, the patient considered an alternate belief about anger as a valuable source of information and re-evaluated her inability to tolerate short-term emotional discomfort, in the interest of attaining greater emotional authenticity with her partner.

Implicit versus explicit attachment-related interventions

Many attachment-related interventions are implicit, such as decisions to self-disclose in order to offer a contrast to expectations of attachment figures. At the same time, CBT is highly collaborative, with case conceptualisations and targets of therapy elaborated jointly. Habitual beliefs and behaviours – including attachment-related ones – are described in patients' own words, and are explicitly referred to throughout therapy as they are modified. Attachment-related interventions can be made explicit through drawing attention to particular in-session interactions of emotional salience. Patients can be asked what they expected their therapists to say or do, to articulate what actually happened and how that made them feel. Through careful examination of felt experience, patients can consider new attachment-related schema and how to test these with current attachment figures.

Summary

Attachment-related schema influence the sense of personal vulnerability to threat and behavioural avoidance characterising individuals with anxiety disorders, as well as their use of attachment relationships in the attenuation of this threat. Attachment-informed CBT involves the use of interventions to augment felt security in the service of facing what is feared. This involves recognisng the activation of the attachment system, managing the therapeutic alliance to counter attachment-related schemas, and choosing cognitive and behavioural targets that may underlie both the anxiety disorder and attachment security.

References

Abramowitz, J.S., Deacon, B.J. and Whiteside, S.P.H. (2011). *Exposure Therapy for Anxiety: principles and practice.* New York: Guilford Press.

Allen, L.B., McHugh, R.K. and Barlow, D.H. (2008). Emotional disorders: a unified protocol. In D.H. Barlow (ed.), *Clinical Handbook of Psychological Disorders: a step-by-step treatment manual,* 4th edn, pp. 216–49. New York: Guilford Press.

Bar-Haim, Y., Lamy, D., Pergamin, L., Bakermans-Kranenburg, M.J. and van IJzendoorn, M.H. (2007). Threat-related attentional bias in anxious and nonanxious individuals: a meta-analytic study. *Psychological Bulletin* **133**, 1–24.

Bartholomew, K. (1990). Avoidance of intimacy: An attachment perspective. *Journal of Social and Personal Relationships* **7**, 147–78.

Beck, A.T., Emery, G. and Greenberg, R. (1985). *Anxiety Disorders and Phobias: a cognitive perspective.* New York: Basic Books.

Beck, A.T., Rush, A.J., Shaw, B. and Emery, G. (1979). *Cognitive Therapy of Depression.* New York: Guilford Press.

Bifulco, A., Kwon, J., Jacobs, C., Moran, P.M., Bunn, A. and Beer, N. (2006). Adult attachment style as mediator between childhood neglect/abuse and adult depression and anxiety. *Social Psychiatry and Psychiatric Epidemiology* **41**, 796–805.

Bowlby, J. (1982). *Attachment and Loss, Volume 1: Attachment.* New York: Basic Books.

——(1988). *A Secure Base.* New York: Basic Books.

Brennan, K.A., Clark, C.L. and Shaver, P.R. (1998). Self report measurement of adult attachment: An integrative overview. In J.A. Simpson and W.S. Rholes (eds), *Attachment Theory and Close Relationships,* pp. 46–76. New York: Guilford Press.

Casey, L.M., Oei, T.P.S., Newcombe, P.A. and Kenardy, J. (2004). The role of catastrophic misinterpretation of bodily sensations and panic self-efficacy in predicting panic severity. *Journal of Anxiety Disorders* **18**, 325–40.

Cassidy, J., Lichtenstein-Phelps, J., Sibrava, N.J., Thomas, C.L. Jr. and Borkovec, T.D. (2009). Generalized anxiety disorder: connections with self-reported attachment. *Behavior Therapy,* **40**, 23–38.

Doron, G. and Kyrios, M. (2005). Obsessive compulsive disorder: A review of possible specific internal representations within a broader cognitive theory. *Clinical Psychology Review* **25**, 415–32.

Dozier, M. and Tyrrell, C. (1998). The role of attachment in therapeutic relationships. In J.A. Simpson and W.S. Rholes (eds), *Attachment Theory and Close Relationships,* pp. 221–48. New York: Guilford Press.

Dozier, M., Lomax, L., Tyrell, C.L. and Lee, S.W. (2001). The challenge of treatment for clients with dismissing states of mind. *Attachment and Human Development* **3**, 62–76.

Eng, W., Heimberg, R.G., Hart, T.A., Schneier, F.R. and Liebowitz, M.R. (2001). Attachment in individuals with social anxiety disorder: the relationship among adult attachment styles, social anxiety, and depression. *Emotion* **1**, 365–80.

Fraley, R.C. and Waller, N.G. (1998). Adult attachment patterns: a test of the typological model. In J.A. Simpson and W.S. Rholes (eds), *Attachment Theory and Close Relationships*, pp. 77–114. New York: Guilford Press.

Fraley, R.C., Vicary, A.M., Brumbaugh, C.C. and Roisman, G.I. (2011). Patterns of stability in adult attachment: An empirical test of two models of continuity and change. *Journal of Personality and Social Psychology* **5**, 974–92.

Guidano, V.F. and Liotti, G. (1983). *Cognitive Processes in Emotional Disorders: a structural approach to psychotherapy*. New York: Guilford Press.

Kanninen, K., Punamaki, R.L. and Qouta, S. (2003). Personality and trauma: adult attachment and posttraumatic distress among former political prisoners. *Peace and Conflict: Journal of Peace Psychology* **9**, 97–126.

Levy, K.N., Meehan, K.B., Kelly, K.M., Reynso, J.S., Weber, M., Clarkin, J.F. and Otto, F. (2006). Change in attachment patterns and reflective function in a randomized control trial of transference-focused psychotherapy for borderline personality disorder. *Journal of Consulting and Clinical Psychology* **74**, 1027–40.

Liotti, G. (2007). Internal working models of attachment in the therapeutic relationship. In P. Gilbert and R.L. Leahy (eds), *The Therapeutic Relationship in the Cognitive Behavioral Therapies*, pp. 143–61. New York: Routledge.

Main, M. (2000). The organized categories of infant, child, and adult attachment: Flexible vs. inflexible attention under attachment-related stress. *Journal of the American Psychoanalytic Association* **48**, 1055–96.

McBride, C. and Atkinson, L. (2009). Attachment theory and cognitive behavioral therapy. In J.H. Obegi and E. Berant (eds), *Attachment Theory and Research in Clinical Work with Adults*, pp. 434–58. New York: Guilford Press.

Mikulincer, M. and Shaver, P.R. (2007). Attachment bases of psychopathology. In M. Mikulincer, and P.R. Shaver (eds), *Attachment in Adulthood: structure, dynamics and change*, pp. 369–404. New York: Guilford Press.

Myhr, G., Sookman, D. and Pinard, G. (2004). Attachment security and parental bonding in adults with obsessive-compulsive disorder: a comparison with depressed out-patients and healthy controls. *Acta Psychiatrica Scandinavica* **109**, 447–56.

Safran, J.D. and Muran, J.C. (2000). *Negotiating the Therapeutic Alliance: a relational treatment guide.* New York: John Wiley and Sons.

Salkovskis, P.M. (1991). The importance of behavior in the maintenance of anxiety and panic: a cognitive account. *Behavioural Psychotherapy* **19**, 6–19.

Tasca, G.A., Taylor, D., Ritchie, K. and Balfour, L. (2004). Attachment predicts treatment completion in an eating disorders partial hospital program among women with anorexia nervosa. *Journal of Personality Assessment* **83**, 201–12.

Taylor, S., Coles, M.E., Abramowitz, J.S., Wu, K.D., Olatunji, B.O., Timpano, K.R., McKay, D., Kim, S.K., Carmin, C. and Tolin, D.F. (2010). How are dysfunctional beliefs related to obsessive-compulsive symptoms? *Journal of Cognitive Psychotherapy* **24**, 165–76.

Travis, L.A., Bliwise, N.G., Binder, J.L. and Horne-Moyer, H.L. (2001). Changes in clients' attachment styles over the course of time-limited dynamic psychotherapy. *Psychotherapy: Theory, Research, Practice, Training* **2**, 149–59.

Waters, E. and Cummings, E.M. (2000). A secure base from which to explore close relationships. *Child Development* **71**, 164–72.

Waters, E., Merrick, S., Treboux, D., Crowell, J. and Albersheim, L. (2000). Attachment security in infancy and early adulthood: A twenty-year longitudinal study. *Child Development* **71**, 684–9.

Chapter 5

Attachment theory and psychosis

Matthias Schwannauer and Andrew Gumley

Introduction

Psychosis is characterised by severe and distressing changes in self experience. The individual experiences a pervasive sense of interpersonal threat combined with a sense of vulnerability that undermines basic assumptions of safety, security, intimacy and attachment. Psychosis signifies stigmatising negative life trajectories generating feelings of hopelessness or triggering defensive denial and sealing over. Emotional recovery from psychosis is governed by an integration of affective experience, interpersonal adaptation and constructive help-seeking in the face of crisis. A central theory that has been developed to explain the link between emotional distress, adaptation and help-seeking is attachment theory. Attachment theory has been one of the most influential concepts in psychology, informing developmental models of human behaviour and interaction as well as approaches to psychopathology and psychotherapy. We argue that attachment theory also has the potential to aid our understanding of key processes in the development and maintenance of psychosis (Liotti and Gumley 2009). Following a brief description of attachment classification in infancy and adulthood, this chapter will describe the way in which attachment theory can inform our understanding of psychosis. This will be followed by a description of how concepts and ideas from attachment theory can be used to help facilitate recovery.

Attachment classification and psychopathology

Insecure attachment strategies are adaptive and develop throughout childhood in order to help the individual cope with a sub-ideal attachment context (Bowlby 1988). From an attachment perspective, there are two key interpersonal strategies available to help the infant in such an environment to regulate affect and distress: deactivating affect (dismissive strategies) or hyperactivating affect (preoccupied strategies). Disorganised (or unresolved) attachment status is not an attachment pattern as such. It refers to the absence or the collapse of organised attachment strategies due to exposure to trauma and/or loss. The description refers to infants most often parented by carers who are either frightening, frightened or both. In this context, the infant's source of security is also a source of fear. The infant's conflict between approach (safeness) and avoidance (fear) strategies is temporarily resolved by dissociative responding.

Bowlby (1973) proposed that the experience of interactions with attachment figures in childhood becomes internalised and carried forward into adulthood as mental models that he termed 'Internal Working Models' (IWMs). These implicit structures embedded in procedural memory systems regulate cognitive, affective and behavioural responses during subsequent interpersonal interactions. Through IWMs, therefore, early attachment relationships form the prototype for interpersonal relationships throughout life, and indeed serve to shape the nature and functioning of individuals' interpersonal networks. It is generally well established that early adverse experiences such as early loss and trauma are strongly linked to emotional and psychological problems in adulthood (Brown *et al*. 1986; Hofstra, van der Ende and Verhulst, 2002; Rutter 2000) and psychosis in particular (Read *et al*. 2005). However, this association between early loss and/or trauma and later adult psychopathology is no longer understood as arising from a direct relationship between early adverse events and later psychopathology. A significant number of those who experience adverse events in childhood do not develop problems in adulthood. The association between earlier life experiences and later psychopathology is seen as being influenced by a range of different factors, including how experiences are processed and incorporated into autobiographical narratives: a core function of the attachment system.

There have been numerous studies describing the impact of early attachment experiences on individuals' interpersonal functioning and emotional regulation (summarised in Fonagy 1998; Fonagy *et al*. 2002). Theories describing causal mechanisms linking attachment experiences with later interpersonal functioning and emotional regulation highlight the centrality of concepts of mentalisation and reflective function (Fonagy 1998; Fonagy *et al*. 2002). Mentalisation refers to 'mind mindedness', which is the ability or willingness to identify and understand thoughts and feelings, including the thoughts and feelings of others. Reflective function describes the process by which 'mind mindedness' is acquired. For example, in infancy this function is provided by the caregiver's appropriate attunement to, and reflecting (or mirroring) of, the infant's intentional and emotional expressions. This social biofeedback assists the infant in developing a second order symbolic representational system for organising their affective and mental states and thus the ability to regulate negative and unwanted emotions. The mirrored expression and response of the caregiver moderates affect in such a way that it is different and separate from the primary experience. The infant starts to associate positive changes in their emotions with the control they have over this process, leading to an understanding of having the ability to self-regulate. In adults reflective functioning is evidenced by an awareness of the nature of mental states and how they underpin the behaviour of the self and others (Fonagy 1998).

An influential framework for understanding attachment states of mind in adulthood has been provided by Mary Main's work (Main, Kaplan and Cassidy 1985; Main 1990, 1999). This conceptualisation of adult states of mind with regard to attachment provides analogous categories to infant attachment behaviour. Secure attachment in infancy is mirrored by a 'freely autonomous' adult attachment state of mind. Secure adults are able to behave with flexibility and openness in relationships. They are able to reflect openly on, and communicate information about, their own state of mind without excessive distortions or censorship. They are also more able to reflect on and attune to the mental states of others. Autonomous adults communicate an autobiographical narrative that is free-flowing, fresh, reflective, sensitive to context and collaborative with another person. They respond to painful experiences in self and others with expressions of compassion, forgiveness and warmth.

Avoidant infant attachment associates with an adult stance that is 'dismissing' of attachment. 'Dismissing' adults minimise and avoid attachment-related experiences and therefore autobiographical memories related to attachment experiences tend to be under elaborated. The 'dismissing' adult's ability to reflect on his or her own affective experience, and attune to the minds, intentions and mental states of others, is diminished. Anxious/ambivalent infant attachment is paralleled by 'preoccupied/ enmeshed' adult attachment. In a preoccupied state of mind with respect to attachment, adults are valuing of attachment but are insecure, ruminative and distressed. Often adults with preoccupied states of mind are concerned with themes of abandonment and rejection. Finally, disorganised infant attachment behaviour predicates an unresolved subcategory in adulthood, reflecting trauma with regard to loss and abuse. Adults with disorganised and unresolved attachments will characteristically show disorganisation of affect regulation and behaviour and problems in monitoring the coherence of discourse. This is characteristic of the approach–avoidance conflict that we often see in adults seeking help for past trauma and abuse. It is, however, important to note that, to a greater or lesser degree, we all have unresolved attachment-related issues and therefore elements of dysregulation. It is just that some people's interpersonal experience – as a result of extensive childhood trauma – is dominated by these issues (Wallin 2007).

Attachment and psychosis

A growing number of studies have investigated attachment theory and its relevance for psychological models of psychosis (Berry, Barrowclough and Wearden 2007; Read and Gumley 2008). Generally, samples of individuals with psychosis tend to have higher levels of insecure attachment than control groups (Couture, Lecomte and Leclerc 2007; Dozier 1990; Ponizovsky, Nechamkin and Rosca 2007) and there is some evidence to suggest that insecure attachment may be associated with an earlier onset of psychosis and longer periods of hospitalisation (Ponizovsky, Nechamkin and Rosca 2007). Studies have also found higher levels of insecure-dismissing attachment in people with a diagnosis of psychosis (Dozier et al.1991; Mickelson, Kessler and Shaver 1997; MacBeth et al. 2011). High levels of insecure attachment, and insecure-dismissing attachment in particular, have been replicated using different methods of assessing attachment and in first episode and multiple episode samples.

A number of studies have examined individual symptoms of psychosis and their association with attachment. In line with findings of high levels of dismissing attachment in psychosis, there is consistent evidence of associations between attachment avoidance, assessed using self-report measures of attachment and positive symptoms of psychosis (Berry, Barrowclough and Wearden 2007; Kvrgic et al. 2012; Ponizovsky, Nechamkin and Rosca 2007). Ponizovsky, Nechamkin and Rosca (2007) also found associations between attachment anxiety, which is similar to preoccupied attachment, and positive symptoms, but this was not replicated by the two later studies, suggesting that associations between preoccupied attachment and psychosis might not be as robust. Individuals with dismissive attachment styles may employ minimising and dismissive affect regulation strategies to cope and adapt to the dysregulated affect that accompanies psychosis. Externalising strategies, such as paranoid delusions or positive psychotic symptoms, may also be conceptualised as an attempt to externalise emotional arousal whilst minimising its impact. Furthermore, this pattern of attachment avoidance and down regulation of interpersonal and emotional distress may contribute to our understanding of the development of negative symptoms in psychosis. Studies using self-report measures of attachment have also found evidence of associations between attachment avoidance and negative symptoms (Berry, Barrowclough and Wearden 2007; Ponizovsky, Nechamkin and Rosca 2007).

The growing body of research into attachment theory and psychosis has not only investigated relationships between attachment and symptoms, but has also investigated associations between insecure attachments and factors that are likely to facilitate or impede recovery. The quality of the individual's social relationships is a key factor in influencing the course of psychosis (Penn et al. 2004) and there is evidence of associations between insecure attachment and difficulties in forming relationships with others in this group (Couture, Lecomte and Leclerc 2007; Berry, Barrowclough and Wearden 2007). The majority of studies investigating attachment and interpersonal relationships in psychosis have studied the impact of insecure attachment on therapeutic relationships, possibly because attachment theory is in part a theory of help-seeking behaviour and also because of the well established effect of the quality of therapeutic relationships on outcomes (Horvath and Symonds 1991). Studies have used different methods to assess therapeutic relationships, including engagement with services, adherence to treatment, therapeutic interactions, therapeutic alliance and attachment to services (Berry et al. 2008; Blackburn, Berry and Cohen 2010; Dozier 1990; Dozier et al. 2001; Kvrgic et al. 2011; MacBeth et al. 2011). Across all these studies, there is evidence that insecure attachments are associated with more difficulties in therapeutic relationships and, in line with associations between dismissing attachment and more severe symptoms, some studies have found that dismissing attachment may have a particularly negative influence on engagement and therapeutic alliance (Dozier 1990; Dozier et al. 2001; Berry, Barrowclough and Wearden 2007; Kvrgic et al. 2011; MacBeth et al. 2011). If individuals with a dismissing pattern of attachment do not seek help in the context of the onset or relapse of psychosis, this narrows the opportunity for early detection and intervention. The impact of this avoidance on families and mental health teams can lead to more coercive strategies of intervention, such as involuntary hospital admissions. These coercive strategies are likely to reinforce avoidance of help-seeking and impede emotional recovery (Gumley *et al.* 2010).

It may be easier to form therapeutic relationships with individuals with preoccupied attachment compared to individuals with dismissing attachment and there is evidence of more symptom reporting and treatment adherence in this group (Dozier 1990; Kvrgic *et al.* 2011). Nonetheless, as preoccupied attachment is typified by sensitivity to rejection, it might be associated with more ruptures in alliance or over-dependence in therapeutic relationships (Daniel 2006). There is also evidence to suggest that it is important to consider interactions between therapists and clients' attachment patterns. For example, one study of case managers and patients with severe and enduring mental health problems found that dyads of case managers and patients who differed in terms of their attachment strategies reported better therapeutic alliance and outcomes than dyads with similar attachment strategies (Tyrell *et al.*1999).

Bowlby's (1980) theory of loss and grief has also been used as a framework to understand emotional adjustment to psychosis. Responses to bereavement that are atypical fall into two distinct areas, on a continuum ranging from chronic mourning to prolonged absence of mourning (Middleton *et al.* 1993). In attachment terms, the chronically mourning individual mirrors the preoccupied/anxious individual who makes persistent attempts to retain proximity or attention of any attachment figure as part of a pervasive and enduring interpersonal schema. This attenuates the feelings of anxiety, distress and disorganisation associated with any loss or separation. In contrast, the absence of grief mirrors the dismissing/avoidant individual. Bowlby (1980) saw this as indicative of 'defensive exclusion', an internal mechanism of downplaying the emotional impact to minimise distress to the self. This strategy was hypothesised to leave fragmented shards of 'raw' memories and feelings about the loved one. Individuals who attempt to block off, minimise and deny the occurrence of psychosis have been described as having a 'sealing over' recovery style.

McGlashan (1987) argues that in recovering from psychosis, individuals adopt either a 'sealing over' or an 'integrative' recovery coping style. The former is characterised by a difficulty in recognising and understanding psychotic experiences and the latter is characterised by recognising the links between previous psychotic and present experiences. Individuals with a diagnosis of psychosis tend to use avoidant coping strategies like 'sealing over' more often than 'integrative' styles, although integrative styles have been related to less frequent relapse and better social functioning (McGlashan 1987). Individuals who 'seal over' their experiences of psychosis isolate these experiences from other domains of their life and thus may not experience explicit memories of previous episodes. In this case the associations may be more implicit. Therefore internal events reminiscent of relapse may cue feelings of fear and dread (Gumley and MacBeth 2006; Gumley, White and Power 1999). Similar to findings in the trauma literature (Ehlers and Clark 2000; Schacter, Israel and Racine 1999), individuals are likely to struggle to source the origins of these feelings ('affect without recollection') and therefore they may become vigilant for other forms of threat, for example scanning for interpersonal danger.

Birchwood (2003) argues that individuals need an internal secure base to integrate and explore experiences of psychosis. Earlier difficulties in attachment relationships can adversely affect the development of this internal secure base and thus result in a 'sealing over' recovery style. In support of this theory, studies have found evidence of associations between insecure attachment and/or reports of difficulties in earlier relationships with parents and a 'sealing over' recovery style in response to psychosis (Drayton, Birchwood and Trower 1998; Tait et al. 2004; Mulligan and Lavender 2009). This sealing over recovery style has also been associated with less engagement with services (Tait et al. 2004).

As outlined above, attachment patterns and psychosis have largely been linked on a theoretical level in an attempt to enhance and develop current conceptualisations of symptoms, social relationships, engagement with services and recovery style. By contrast, the impact of mentalisation and reflective function on the experience of, adaptation to, and recovery from psychosis is largely unexplored. Deficits in the related concept of 'Theory of Mind' have, however, been implicated in schizophrenia (Frith 1992). There is now robust evidence to show that 'Theory of Mind' is impaired among persons with a diagnosis of schizophrenia compared to non-clinical controls and that this impairment exists in patients in remission, indicating that it is not merely a consequence of acute symptoms and may reflect a more stable vulnerability factor (Sprong et al. 2007). Indeed, 'Theory of Mind' deficits have been found in persons at high genetic risk of developing schizophrenia (Schiffman et al. 2004; Marjoram et al. 2006) and among those with schizotypy (Pickup 2006). Conceptualisations of the 'Theory of Mind' as a form of cognitive capacity tend to be exclusively focused on cognitive and rational aspects, understanding and insight, whereas related concepts of reflective function and mentalisation include a strong emphasis on affective and relational components of behaviours and social interactions and have been less well researched. Reflective function and mentalisation stem from the interaction of affect mirroring, the reflection of the individual's own mental and emotional state in that of others. Well developed reflective function is associated with the ability to form and revise thoughts about beliefs and feelings and the ability to understand the perspective of others. This capacity allows individuals to successfully adapt to significant life events and changing contexts. It is important to note that the discussed concepts of 'theory of mind', reflective function, metacognition and mentalisation describe overlapping and related areas of cognitive, emotional and relational ability and awareness, and place differentiating emphasis on cognitive, interpersonal and affective aspects, but are at times used interchangeably. There is a strong need for further research to clarify how these concepts relate to each other and their associated mechanisms.

The only study that has directly investigated attachment states of mind and mentalisation in psychosis to date is a study by MacBeth, Gumley, Schwannauer and Fisher (2011). In a small sample of 34 first episode psychosis patients, the authors established a clear association between AAI-based attachment states of mind and reflective function. Participants with an insecure dismissive classification had lower mentalisation skills than the secure and preoccupied classification groups. The study also found that reflective function was associated with social functioning. This study did not find a direct association between reflective function and psychotic symptoms, which may indicate that although individuals experience difficulties in mentalisation, this difficulty is not reducible to a single cognitive deficit or symptom. Rather, difficulties in understanding one's own thoughts and feelings and those of others may influence the affective experience of psychosis and social functioning. We argue that processes of mentalisation are therefore important targets in therapeutic work.

Implications for psychological treatment

Early developmental experiences characterised by attachment disruptions and/or traumatic experience lead to the evolution of IWMs that may be impoverished, overly rigid or disorganised. This results in difficulties in self-reflection, affect regulation and understanding the mental states of self and others. Psychological therapy provides the opportunity for a corrective attachment-related experience that has the potential to re-orientate attachment-related behaviours, enhance emotional containment and consequentially update IWMs. The therapist's orientation throughout therapy is the collaborative development of a coherent client narrative that optimises the evolution of self-reflectiveness, the crafting of alternative helpful beliefs and appraisals, and the development of adaptive coping and interpersonal behaviours. Underpinning this process, the therapist carefully nurtures the therapeutic alliance and provides the client with a safe haven and secure base from which to explore difficult issues. For this reason there is a strong emphasis on interpersonal functioning as it unfolds in the patient's external context and internal representations, and their unfolding in the context of the therapeutic relationship. Siegel (1999) proposes five basic elements of how caregivers can foster a secure attachment in the children under their care. These elements are: collaboration, reflective dialogue, repair, coherent narratives, and emotional communication. We argue that these elements are also key in therapeutic work with people with a diagnosis of psychosis.

Collaboration

Secure relationships are based on collaborative and carefully attuned communication. The therapeutic relationship is central to therapy in people with psychosis. The collaborative working alliance becomes an important scaffold to facilitate the development of clients' understandings of their own experience and their understanding of the beliefs and intentions of others. In terms of fostering collaboration, a number of authors, including Jeremy Holmes (2003), Harris

(2004) and Robert Leahy (2008), have emphasised the importance of tailoring therapy style to attachment style in the first few months of therapy. Our clinical experiences have led us to feel that such an approach is extremely helpful in supporting recovery from psychosis. In this context, there are two central therapeutic processes: these involve the development of 'safe haven' to enable the experience of safeness, the expression of distress and help-seeking in context of crisis; and the promotion of 'secure base', involving the promotion of autonomy, choice, freedom, curiosity, courage and compassion. Collaboration relies on balancing these fundamental components of attachment security. For example, during the initial stages formulation is used to strengthen therapeutic bonding, whereas later, formulation and reformulation of problem understanding and shared goals might be used to highlight important therapeutic tasks or to identify the relationship between historical events and current problems, which is also evident in the therapeutic relationship itself. In formulating the client's difficulties it is important to attend to the quality of the client's narrative and to notice their ability to openly reflect and consider past experiences as important in the current context.

Susan, a 19-year-old service user following her second episode of psychosis, found it difficult to make best use of vocational opportunities offered through the service and to engage in peer-based groups and activities. Following an episode of inpatient stay she lost contact with her old friends and people she knew at her college. When she was talking about her experience of psychosis she was also reluctant to explore how this had affected her and to consider the impact on her as a young person. Given Susan's initial reluctance to explore experiences, the initial engagement focused on development of the therapeutic frame as a safe haven to express problems in relation to valued goals, and the use of formulation as a means of mapping problem areas to goals and specifying the activities of therapy. Using a timeline which provided a map linking key life events, their impact and her use of social supports enabled Susan to consider the advantages and disadvantages of withdrawal from others and minimisation of their influence on her. The unintended consequence of this 'safe haven' strategy was to block access to feelings of support and social connectedness and thus ultimately to undermine safeness and security by increasing loneliness and isolation. Therefore, Susan was able to formulate the 'secure base' treatment goal to consider new social situations as different from past events, to attend to interactions as they unfolded; a linked goal was to use these new opportunities of interactions with peers to share some of her experiences and to be open about her reluctance to talk about herself. She found that others on the whole responded positively to her, giving her the experience and understanding that her own appraisal of herself and her experience was not necessarily that of others.

Reflective dialogue

'Secure base' relationships are characterised by attuned communication; openness to both positive and negative aspects of experience; an acceptance of pain and suffering in relation to experiences of loss, separation, threat and abuse; a valuing of relationships as influential; and a curiosity about the nature of relationships and their influence on mental states and behaviour. Reflective discourse provides a framework within which individuals are able to consider the influence of their experiences and construct new or altered meanings. There is a focus on the person's internal experience, where the therapist attempts to make sense of client narratives and then communicate their understanding in a way that helps the client create new meanings and perspectives on their emotions, perceptions, thoughts, intentions, memories and beliefs. An example in relation to the use of the client's narrative as a means to understand their internal experiences and their capacity to reflect is to draw attention to the emotional context and to other, comparable emotional experiences, in order to facilitate a re- or co-construction of the experience from another perspective, including their current feelings when thinking about the event. Questions like 'Can you think of other situations in which you felt similar?', 'Looking back how do you think X felt when you...', or 'What do you think may have happened if you...' can be used to elicit thoughts and emotions in relation to past experiences that are reflective of current feelings about the events, and to consider the importance of their emotional experience now in responding to similarly challenging or distressing situations. Reflective dialogue can only take place in the context of safe haven and thus moving to a more reflective mode of discourse is permitted by the necessary establishment of collaboration.

Repair

When attuned communication is disrupted there is a focus on collaborative repair, allowing the client to reflect upon misunderstandings and disconnections in their interpersonal experiences. Disrupted communication threatens safe haven, and the focus on repair enables a refocusing on problems, goals and change strategies. Within the structure of safe haven, interpersonal problems and ruptures can be detected and explored that might not otherwise be volunteered or raised by the client. This is important when considering that the client may be highly avoidant and unaware of possible problems. Process factors within therapy, such as those expressed in concepts derived from psychodynamic therapies (e.g. transference and counter-transference), can be utilised within therapy as a means to enable the therapist's reflective functioning, particularly with respect to how their own responses within therapy may facilitate or interfere with recovery. The establishment of a containing and reflective therapeutic relationship will enable therapeutic change to take place within an interpersonal context that can in itself provide an essential and corrective emotional experience. In this context it can be helpful to think about possible ruptures and 'stuckness' in therapy in attachment terms. For example, a client with a disorganised or unresolved attachment state of mind may draw the therapist into very strong but fragmented and contradictory narratives about past experiences. They may also have a ready tendency to identify the therapist with other important people in their past lives and assume that the therapist will feel similarly about them as people in the past did. It is vitally important in these instances to be able to take a mentalising stance and maintain an 'observing distance' by identifying and verbalising what is currently happening between client and therapist, including the identification of feelings of both. In the context of an unresolved attachment state of mind, the therapist may notice herself being tempted to provide solutions or to act by reformulating the client's narrative prematurely, rather than noticing her urge to resolve the client's distress through action and thus mirror the client's inability to tolerate distress in the moment. By verbalising the affect felt at the time and highlighting its importance for their shared ability to think about the impact of the experience, the therapist is more likely to progress the session than by focusing on the detail or content of the narrative.

Coherent narratives

The connection of past, present and future is central to the development of a person's autobiographical self-awareness. The development of coherent narratives within therapy aims to help foster the flexible capacity to integrate both internal and external experiences over time. This can be achieved by focusing on the specific details of autobiographical memory in a client's description of a particular event, resisting the tendency to abstract or generalise from the experience, and by carefully separating feelings at the time from the feelings triggered by the remembering and verbalising of these memories. Coherence in the co-construction of the narrative can further be achieved by focusing on the client's perspective at the time, so, for example, aligning the guilt felt now in relation to interpersonal trauma with the possibilities of having been able to understand what was happening at the time they were much younger. The therapeutic narrative gives an indication of the levels of processing and understanding achieved by the client and can be used to focus therapeutic discourse. For example, when discussing trauma, it is not unusual for narrative to become fragmented, difficult to follow and impoverished. This acts as a signal to the therapist of the presence of problematic or unresolved experiences. Trauma and loss can disrupt the development of a coherent narrative and care should be taken in accessing strong negative affect. The therapist needs to work with the client and carefully consider the client's ability to regulate strong negative affect in the context of the therapeutic relationship.

Emotional communication

The therapist maintains close awareness not only of the cognitive contents of narrative but also of clients' emotional communications. In focusing on negative or painful emotions within sessions, the therapist appropriately communicates and encourages self-reflection, understanding, acceptance and soothing. In their process experiential approach to psychotherapy, Greenberg and colleagues (1993) have emphasised therapeutic tasks that facilitate experiential rather than conceptual processing of events. The routes to therapeutic change are via the empathic exploration of the therapeutic narrative, the recognition of affect that is expressed directly or indirectly in the narrative, and the therapist's ability to reflect on the process of meaning-making and interpretation of affect that is contained in the client's report. Within this care-giving framework provided by the therapist, key aspects of attachment security are characterised by empathy, forgiveness, compassion and the capacity to make appearance reality distinctions. Therefore there is an explicit attempt to help the person to develop an internal compassionate and self-soothing stance towards their prior experiences and themselves. The therapist works collaboratively with the client to develop and strengthen these underdeveloped self-nurturing strategies. As part of this process, the development of these skills in relating to the self and others is meshed with changes in the clients' beliefs about themselves and others. For example, where it becomes apparent that a client tends to become very self-critical and derogating towards her own behaviours and reactions when talking about particular experiences, it is helpful to openly notice this within the session and to draw attention to these shifts in emotions and self-appraisal. Characteristics of safe haven and secure base are actively utilised to promote the development of therapeutic strategies. Cultivating a secure base orientation involves the development of characteristics of courage, openness, curiosity and exploration, whilst safe haven involves the development of attunement, acceptance, caring, empathy, warmth, compassion, forgiveness. The crucial therapeutic task is finding a balance between these two domains that optimises supporting the service user in responding to painful thoughts, feelings and memories with these characteristics of secure attachment. This can unfold in a variety of techniques focused on developing cognitive, emotional, attentional and behavioural skills (Gumley *et al.* 2010; Gumley and Clark 2012).

Implications for mental health services

Attachment theory is invaluable in incorporating a formulation of insecure and threat based recovery strategies within the context of therapist and client relationships. However, working with people with a diagnosis of psychosis also requires a co-ordinated multi-disciplinary response to clients' needs. It seems unreasonable to work with a client to encourage and develop their help-seeking behaviours if the help that they receive is not the help that they were seeking in the first instance. Goodwin and colleagues (2003) proposed that a key function of multi-disciplinary teams is to facilitate a 'secure base' through providing continuity and consistency of care, providing sensitive and appropriate responses to affective distress, and providing emotional containment during times of crisis. A crucial challenge for services is developing capacity to provide a safe haven for service users to seek help in the context of feelings of distress and threat. This involves developing service capacities to tolerate listening to painful and distressing stories whilst responding in an attuned and responsive way. In addition, services need to balance safe haven with secure base by supporting service users in developing autonomy, choice, curiosity and exploration. Achieving this balance within services can present special challenges to the development of collaboration and the enabling of service user choice and positive risk-taking. Attachment theory provides a coherent framework within which to understand these recovery based challenges.

Conclusions

We have argued that attachment theory provides a key framework within which to understand processes involved in recovery from psychosis. Although further research is required to maximise the potential of attachment theory in this area, it is encouraging that there is a growth in empirical studies demonstrating associations between insecure attachment and symptoms of psychosis, as well as key factors associated with blocked recovery such as the therapeutic relationship, a 'sealing over' recovery style and poorer mentalisation skills. We have argued that the therapeutic relationship is a key vehicle to facilitate recovery from psychosis. The therapeutic relationship provides a context in which to establish security and trust to enable the development of a coherent narrative and the reinforcement of productive coping. The psychotherapeutic framework for this may involve both a sensitisation and tolerance of affect that allows for increased mentalising capacity. This process is not without its challenges. Constructing a safe haven/secure base can, for some, create feelings of vulnerability and threat that produce apparently contradictory or unexpected emotional or coping responses that in themselves can elicit confused or unhelpful reactions from services. This can produce an unintended confirmation of negative expectations of others. Therefore these apparently contradictory responses need to be understood and explored in the person's life context. This is the work of applying attachment theory to recovery in terms of overcoming the basic blocks and fears related to affiliation. The development of a secure base for recovery provides a bridge for help-seeking, distress tolerance and distress reduction in the future. This has profound implications not just for individual therapists but also for how services reflect on their own helpful (and unhelpful) responses to individuals and their families.

References

Berry, K., Barrowclough, C. and Wearden, A. (2007). A review of the role of adult attachment style in psychosis: unexplored issues and questions for further research. *Clinical Psychology Review* **27**(4), 458.

Birchwood, M. (2003). Pathways to emotional dysfunction in first-episode psychosis. *British Journal of Psychiatry* **182**, 373–5.

Blackburn, C., Berry, K. and Cohen, K. (2010). Factors correlated with client attachment to mental health services. *The Journal of Nervous and Mental Disease* **198**(8), 572–5.

Bowlby, J. (1973). *Attachment and Loss, Volume 2: Separation: anxiety and anger.* London: The Hogarth Press.

——(1980). *Attachment and Loss, Volume 3: Loss: sadness and depression.* London: The Hogarth Press.

——(1988). *A Secure Base: clinical applications of attachment theory.* London: Brunner-Routledge.

Brown, G.W., Andrews, B., Harris, T.O., Adler, Z. and Bridge, L. (1986). Social support, self-esteem and depression. *Psychological Medicine* **16**, 813–31.

Couture, S., Lecomte, T. and Leclerc, C. (2007). Personality characteristics and attachment in first episode psychosis: impact on social functioning. *Journal of Nervous and Mental Disease* **195**, 631–9.

Daniel, S.I. (2006). Adult attachment patterns and individual psychotherapy: A review. *Clinical Psychology Review* **26**(8), 968.

Dozier, M. (1990). Attachment organisation and the treatment use for adults with serious psychopathological disorders. *Development and Psychopathology* **2**, 47–60.

Dozier, M., Lomax, L., Tyrrell, C. L. and Lee, S.W. (2001). The challenge of treatment for clients with dismissing states of mind. *Attachment and Human Development* **3**, 62–76.

Dozier, M., Stevenson, A., Lee, S. and Velligan, D. (1991). Attachment organisation and familial overinvolvement for adults with serious psychopathological disorders. *Development and Psychopathology* **3**, 475–89.

Drayton, M., Birchwood, M. and Trower, P. (1998). Early attachment experience and recovery from psychosis. *British Journal of Clinical Psychology* **37**, 269–84.

Ehlers, A. and Clark, D.M. (2000). A cognitive model of posttraumatic stress disorder. *Behaviour Research and Therapy* **38**(4), 319–45.

Fonagy, P. (1998). Moments of change in psychoanalytic theory: discussion of a new theory of psychic change. *Infant Mental Health Journal* **19**, 163–71.

Fonagy, P., Gergely, G., Jurist, E.L. and Target, M. (2002). *Affect Regulation, Mentalisation and the Development of the Self.* London: Karnac.

Frith, C.D. (1992). *The Cognitive Neuropsychology of Schizophrenia.* Hillside, NJ: Lawrence Erlbaum and Associates Inc.

Goodwin, F.K., Fireman, B., Simon, G.E., Hunkeler, E.M., Lee, J. and Revicki, D. (2003). Suicide risk in bipolar disorder during treatment with lithium and divalproex. *JAMA: The Journal of the American Medical Association* **290**(11), 1467–73.

Greenberg, P.E., Stiglin, L.E., Finkelstein, S.N. and Berndt, E.R. (1993). The economic burden of depression in 1990. *Journal of Clinical Psychiatry* **54**(11), 405–18.

Gumley, A. and Clark, S. (2012). Risk of arrested recovery following first episode psychosis: An integrative approach to psychotherapy. *Journal of Psychotherapy Integration* **22**, 287–97.

Gumley, A.I. and MacBeth, A. (2006). A trauma based model of relapse in psychosis. In W. Larkin and A.T. Morrison (eds), *Trauma and Psychosis*, pp. 283–304. Hoboken, NJ: John Wiley and Sons Ltd.

Gumley, A.I., White, C.A. and Power, K.G. (1999). An interacting cognitive subsystems model of relapse and the course of psychosis. *Clinical Psychology and Psychotherapy* **6**, 261–78.

Gumley, A.I., Braehler, C., Laithwaite, H., MacBeth, A. and Gilbert, P. (2010). A compassion focused model of recovery after psychosis. *International Journal of Cognitive Psychotherapy* **3**, 186–201.

Harris, T. (2004). Discussion of the Special Issue: chef or chemist? Practicing psychotherapy within the attachment paradigm. *Attachment and Human Development* 6(2), 191–207.

Hofstra, M.B., van der Ende, J. and Verhulst, F.C. (2002). Child and adolescent problems predict DSM-IV disorders in adulthood: A 14-year follow-up of a Dutch epidemiological sample. *Journal of the American Academy of Child and Adolescent Psychiatry* 41, 182–9.

Holmes, J. (2001). *The Search for the Secure Base: attachment theory and psychotherapy.* Hove: Brunner-Routledge.

——(2003). Borderline personality disorder and the search for meaning: An attachment perspective. *Australian and New Zealand Journal of Psychiatry* 37(5), 524–31.

Horvath, A.O. and Symonds, B.D. (1991). Relation between working alliance and outcome in psychotherapy: A meta-analysis. *Journal of Counseling Psychology* 38(2), 139.

Kvrgic, S., Beck, E.M., Cavelti, M., Kossowsky, J., Stieglitz, R.D. and Vauth, R. (2012). Focusing on the adult attachment style in schizophrenia in community mental health centres: validation of the Psychosis Attachment Measure (PAM) in a German-speaking sample. *International Journal of Social Psychiatry* 58(4), 362–73.

Leahy, R.L. (2008). The therapeutic relationship in cognitive-behavioral therapy. *Behavioural and Cognitive Psychotherapy* 36(6), 769.

Liotti, G. and Gumley, A.I. (2009). An attachment perspective on schizophrenia: Disorganized attachment, dissociative processes, and compromised mentalisation. In A. Moskowitz, M. Dorahy and I. Schaefer (eds), *Dissociation and Psychosis: converging perspectives on a complex relationship*, pp. 117–33. Hoboken, NJ: John Wiley and Sons Ltd.

MacBeth, A., Gumley, A., Schwannauer, M. and Fisher, R. (2011). Attachment states of mind, mentalisation, and their correlates in a first-episode psychosis sample. *Psychology and Psychotherapy: Theory, Research and Practice*, 84, 1–112.

Main, M., Kaplan, N. and Cassidy, J. (1985). Security in infancy, childhood, and adulthood: A move to the level of representation. In I. Bretherton and E. Waters (eds), *Growing Points of Attachment Theory and Research: Monographs of the Society for Research in Child Development*, Vol. 50, pp. 66–104. Chicago: Chicago University Press.

Marjoram, D., Miller, P., McIntosh, A.M., Cunningham Owens, D.G., Johnstone, E.C. and Lawrie, S. (2006). A neuropsychological investigation into 'Theory of Mind' and enhanced risk of schizophrenia. *Psychiatry Research* 144(1), 29–37.

McGlashan, T.H. (1987). Recovery style from mental illness and long-term outcome. *The Journal of Nervous and Mental Disease* 175(11), 681–5.

Mickelson, K.D., Kessler, R.C. and Shaver, P.R. (1997). Adult attachment in a nationally representative sample. *Journal of Personality and Social Psychology* 73, 1092–1106.

Middleton, W., Moylan, A., Raphael, B., Burnett, P. and Martinek, N. (1993). An international perspective on bereavement related concepts. *Australasian Psychiatry* 27(3), 457–63.

Mulligan, A. and Lavender, T. (2009). An investigation into the relationship between attachment, gender and recovery from psychosis in a stable community-based sample. *Clinical Psychology and Psychotherapy* 17(4), 269–84.

Penn, R.D., Miesel, K.A., Stylos, L., Christopherson, M.A., Nagavarapu, S. and Roline, G.M. (2004). *U.S. Patent No. 6,731,976*. Washington, DC: U.S. Patent and Trademark Office.

Pickup, G. (2006). Theory of mind and its relation to schizotypy. *Cognitive Neuropsychiatry* 11(2), 117–92.

Ponizovsky, A., Nechamkin, Y. and Rosca, P. (2007). Attachment patterns are associated with symptomatology and course of schizophrenia in male inpatients. *American Journal of Orthopsychiatry* **77**, 324–31.

Read, J. and Gumley, A. (2008). Can attachment theory help explain the relationship between childhood adversity and psychosis? *Attachment: New Directions in Psychotherapy and Relational Psychoanalysis* **2**(1), 1–35.

Read, J., van Os, J., Morrison, A.P. and Ross, C.A. (2005). Childhood trauma, psychosis and schizophrenia: a literature review with theoretical and clinical implications. *Acta Psychiatrica Scandinavia* **112**, 330–50.

Rutter, M. (2000). Resilience reconsidered: Conceptual considerations, empirical findings, and policy implications. In J.P. Shonkoff and S.J. Meisels (eds), *Handbook of Early Childhood Intervention*, 2nd edn, pp. 651–82. New York: Cambridge University Press.

Schacter, D.L., Israel, L. and Racine, C. (1999). Suppressing false recognition in younger and older adults: the distinctiveness heuristic. *Journal of Memory and Language* **40**(1), 1–24.

Schiffman, J., Lam, C.W., Jiwatram, T., Ekstrom, M., Sorensen, H. and Mednick, S. (2004). Perspective-taking deficits in people with schizophrenia spectrum disorders: a prospective investigation. *Psychological Medicine* **34**(8), 1581–6.

Siegel, D.J. (1999). *The Developing Mind: toward a neurobiology of interpersonal experience*. New York: Guilford Press.

Sprong, M., Schothorst, P., Vos, E., Hox, J. and van Engeland, H. (2007). Theory of mind in schizophrenia: meta-analysis. *British Journal of Psychiatry* **191**, 5–13.

Tait, L., Birchwood, M. and Trower, P. (2004). Adapting to the challenge of psychosis: personal resilience and the use of sealing-over (avoidant) coping strategies. *The British Journal of Psychiatry,* **185**(5), 410–15.

Tyrrell, C.L., Dozier, M., Teague, G.B. and Fallot, R.D. (1999). Effective treatment relationships for persons with serious psychiatric disorders: The importance of attachment states of mind. *Journal of Consulting and Clinical Psychology* **67**, 725–33.

Wallin, D.J. (2007). *Attachment in Psychotherapy*. New York: Guilford Press.

Chapter 6

Understanding attachment, trauma and dissociation in complex developmental trauma disorders

Kathy Steele and Onno van der Hart

Introduction

The heart of psychotherapy is in understanding and changing the ways in which individuals experience, develop and maintain human relationships. Attachment theory and the field of interpersonal neurobiology have gifted us with a nuanced and powerful understanding of relationships, the mental representations of self and other that shape relationships, and the regulatory and organising functions of attachment. No one is more in need of help with attachment and regulation than those who have been chronically abused and neglected in childhood. These individuals generally suffer from a wide array of symptoms that can be understood as complex developmental trauma disorders, including Complex Posttraumatic Stress Disorder (C-PTSD), trauma-related Borderline Personality Disorder (BPD) and the Dissociative Disorders. Our emphasis in this chapter will be on working with attachment problems in patients who have a dissociative disorder.

Individuals who experienced chronic childhood interpersonal traumatisation have had their development adversely impacted early in life across broad areas of functioning. This leaves them with an unstable foundation for future healthy development and adaptation, putting them at risk for ongoing psychological, physiological and relational problems. These developmental issues distinguish them from those who have classic PTSD related to a single traumatising incident that has not altered the individual's early developmental trajectory (Courtois and Ford 2009).

Although in recent years mental health professionals have developed a much greater understanding of the relationship between childhood abuse and neglect and attachment difficulties across the lifespan, many clinicians have yet to grasp the central role of dissociation in generating and maintaining serious symptoms, including many major attachment difficulties. In fact, dissociation is not only an intrapsychic phenomenon but also an interpersonal one, being highly reactive to what is happening in relationships in the present (Liotti 2009). Thus we will place a special emphasis in this chapter on working with dissociation in the context of attachment.

The chapter begins with a description of how early secure attachment supports regulation and integration of the child, and how abuse, neglect and severe attachment disruptions adversely affect development. These overwhelming experiences create fertile ground for the child to dissociate, as she or he has the impossible task of trying to live normal daily life while under chronic threat. Dissociation in trauma is described, so that clinicians have a solid foundation and rationale for integrative treatment interventions. Specific trauma-related phobias that maintain dissociation and their treatment are discussed.

Treatment of dissociation and related attachment problems will be delineated within a phase-oriented treatment approach that is the current standard of care (Boon, Steele and Van der Hart 2011; Chu 2011; Cloitre, Cohen and Koenen 2006; Courtois and Ford 2009; Davies and Frawley 1994; Howell 2011; ISSTD 2011; Van der Hart, Nijenhuis and Steele 2006). Phase-oriented treatment is based on the premise that early trauma and attachment disruptions limit integrative capacity and impede self and relational regulation skills. Therefore, treatment begins with an initial phase of stabilisation, ego strengthening, and skills building. The second phase focuses on treatment of traumatic memory and the final phase on a more adaptive integration of the individual's functioning across all domains. Within each phase, treatment of trauma-related phobias that maintain dissociation will be addressed. Due to space limitations, treating the phobia of attachment and of attachment loss in the first phase of treatment will be emphasised in this chapter.

Attachment, trauma and dissociation

Children need safe, consistent and predictable relationships for healthy development of self-regulation, maturation and integration (Porges 2011; Schore 2003). These types of relationships can only occur when we feel safe. It is difficult to maintain a sense of relationship when in danger, particularly when it involves severe, or life, threat. Fortunately, evolution has endowed us with the capacity to distinguish between safety and threat so that we can have secure relationships that support our development and integration.

The integrative functions of safe attachment

When we feel safe, an inborn neural organisation or action system called the social engagement system helps us to regulate ourselves and connect well with others (Porges 2011). The social engagement system is the physiological foundation for secure attachment. Via the vagal nerve branches, our physiology is organised to support social behaviour such as movement, hearing and speaking that facilitates bonding and attachment. Specifically, the vagal nerve supplies the muscles that control the social cues of eye gaze, facial expression, head movements and prosody (the rhythm, stress and intonation of our voices). The vagal nerve also helps control heart rate and thus our arousal level. The social engagement system helps us maintain a calm state of being that promotes growth, integration and restoration (Porges 2011).

Secure attachment supports the hard wiring of the child's brain that will determine to a large degree how well he or she is able to regulate and relate to others across the lifespan (Schore 2003). Consistent activation of the social engagement system via secure attachments helps maintain a regulated psychobiological foundation that supports ongoing integration of the child's personality, that is, the consistent and predictable ways of being that define the child. The child learns not only to depend safely upon others to help soothe and reassure but also to self-regulate and to integrate experience and a consistent sense of self across time and situations.

Activation of action systems of daily life

Secure attachment and the social engagement system support activation of other inborn action systems necessary for adaptive functioning in life (Van der Hart, Nijenhuis and Steele 2006). These include exploration (so that we can be curious and learn about our environment), play (supports learning and relating to others), caregiving, socialness (so we can relate within groups), energy management (healthy eating, sleeping and rest patterns) care-taking, and sexuality (so that we can reproduce and maintain our species) (Lichtenberg and Kindler 1994; Panksepp 1998; Van der Hart *et al*. 2006).

Inhibition of defence

Secure attachment not only activates functions that support adaptive living, it also inhibits unnecessary defence. For example, a child might be frightened by dogs, but the parent reassures and supports the child in slowly approaching and petting a friendly dog and gradually teaches the child to read the cues of whether it is safe to approach a particular dog. Secure attachment has deactivated the defensive reaction in the child and supports the child's return to a regulated state where ongoing integration can continue.

Defence against threat

Serious threat automatically activates defence and overrides the action systems of daily life, including the social engagement system. A chronically fearful and insecure person experiences persistent problems in many of the functions that are organised by these action systems, which we can easily see in chronically traumatised individuals. For example, in addition to relational problems, they often have trouble being curious and trying new things (*exploration*), may have anxiety in groups (*socialness*), have sleep and eating difficulties (*energy management*), sexual problems (*sexuality*), tend to over or under care-take others (caretaking), and are unable to enjoy themselves through play (Van der Hart *et al*. 2006).

From an evolutionary standpoint, secure attachment itself is an important first-line defence against threat, as living within a protective group or being in the care of a stronger, more able person is much safer than being out on one's own (Porges

2011). For example, when a young child feels discomfort or distress, or is mildly threatened, the first thing he or she will do is call out for a caregiver. This is a natural defence called the *attachment cry*, and involves panic, frantic searching and crying, and clinging behaviours (Ogden, Minton and Pain 2006; Steele, Van der Hart and Nijenhuis 2001; Van der Hart *et al.*; Van der Kolk 1987). Its purpose is to engage the caregiver for support, help and reassurance, so that the child can return to a calm, comfortable state.

However, when threat becomes too great, the child no longer searches for an attachment figure but instead automatically reacts with evolutionary prepared defences: freeze, flight, or fight, each mediated by the sympathetic nervous system, resulting in extreme hyperarousal. When threat is severe enough to be perceived as life threatening, the child may collapse in a kind of death feint, mediated by the (dorsal vagal) parasympathetic system, resulting in extreme shut down and hypoarousal (Porges 2011; Van der Hart *et al.* 2006). For infants and young children, even non-violent severe attachment disruptions such as neglect or abandonment can be physiologically interpreted as a life-threatening catastrophe, evoking chronic defence (Bowlby 1969/82; Liotti 2009; Schore 2003). These defence reactions are readily observed in chronically traumatised patients, and recognising and treating them is an essential part of treatment.

Dissociation

When the child's caregiver is seriously abusive or neglectful, the natural capacities to distinguish between safety and threat, to become securely attached and engage in all the functions of daily life, to defend oneself when in danger and to integrate experience over time become greatly complicated and confused. The abused child is dysregulated on a chronic basis without sufficient relational support to return to a normal baseline that supports integration. Most importantly, the child is faced with the impossible task of simultaneously approaching the caregiver out of need and an inborn need to attach, and avoiding or defending against the same person. Under these conditions of chronic threat, the child dissociates, unable to make sense of and integrate the highly discrepant needs to attach and defend at the same time. As Liotti (2009) noted, this approach and avoidance 'exceeds the limited capacity of the infant's mind for organising coherent conscious experiences or unitary memory structures' (p. 55).

Dissociative attachment

The child develops a dissociative attachment style called disorganised/disoriented or D-attachment (Liotti 1992, 2009; Main and Hesse 1990; McFadden 2011; Steele *et al.* 2001; Van der Hart *et al.* 2006). D-attachment is strongly related to ongoing and chronic dissociation (Barach 1991; Blisard 2003; Chu 2011; Howell 2011; Liotti 1992, 2009; Lyons-Ruth *et al.* 2006; Ogawa *et al.*1997; Steele *et al.* 2001; Van der Hart *et al.* 2006). D-attachment involves dissociation of the personality, which is a shorthand term for our usual and enduring ways of being. Dissociation occurs between ways of being that involve engagement in daily life and attachment strategies and ways of being in which the individual is rigidly fixed in defences (attachment cry, freeze, flight, fight, and collapse). In the face of perceived threat, the individual may switch in an uncoordinated way between these very different ways of being, resulting in what appear to be disorganised or contradictory actions. In fact, these behaviours indicate an underlying dissociation of his or her personality.

A well-integrated person experiences all ways of being as belonging to him or herself: 'I am *me*, in the past and the present, and in all ways of my being.' But a dissociative person's ways of being are not coordinated, they become activated at the wrong time or in the wrong situations and are even actively in conflict with each other. For example, a person might have a terrified, frozen child sense of self in which he or she is mute and unable to move or think; an angry adolescent sense of self in which he or she is perpetually enraged and avoidant of relationships, and hates the child part; and an adult sense of self in which he or she is primarily interested in work and avoidant of the child and adolescent parts (Van der Hart *et al.* 2006).

Dissociative parts of the personality

These compartmentalised functions (sense of self and related feelings, thoughts, perceptions, predictions, and behaviours) are referred to as dissociative parts of the personality (Van der Hart *et al.* 2006). They are also called self-states, alters, identities and other terms in the literature. By using the term 'parts of the personality' we do not mean that a person has more than one personality, a common misconception of dissociative disorders. Rather, the individual has more than one sense of self within a single personality, each of which is related to particular action systems and generally have rather limited ways of being. Each part has its own unique first-person perspective (that is, a sense of 'me, myself, and I') that is different from another part (Nijenhuis and Van der Hart 2011). These parts are fixed in relatively rigid patterns of thinking, feeling, perceiving and acting. They are not very open to change and learning.

Next, we discuss two basic organisations of dissociative parts, one type organised by the action systems of daily life, including social engagement, and the other organised by the various defences. These distinctions have important treatment implications that will be discussed throughout the chapter.

Apparently Normal part of the Personality (ANP)

Dissociative parts mediated by action systems of daily life (attachment, exploration, care taking, sexuality, etc.) have been called 'apparently normal' parts of the personality (ANP), based on the dissociative individual's need to function normally in daily life to the degree possible, in spite of significant symptoms (Van der Hart *et al.* 2006). ANP involves the ways of being in which the individual deals with daily life in the present as an adult. Typically the patient as ANP is highly avoidant of any reminders of trauma. In many cases, a single ANP is the major 'shareholder' of the personality and is the part of the patient that acts in the world and presents to therapy. In more severe cases, there may be more than one ANP, for example one that goes to work, one that takes care of the children, one that socialises.

In terms of attachment, the patient in ANP mode may have a wide range of capacities and functions. Often he or she is quite avoidant and depressed as ANP, but more functional individuals may be able to engage in at least some relatively healthy relationships. Treatment is geared toward improving function in daily life and helping the patient as ANP accept and respond empathically to other dissociative parts.

Emotional part of the Personality (EP)

Other dissociative parts are fixated in traumatic memories, in which the individual is often relatively unaware of the present, or at least responds to the present as though it were the past. We call this living in trauma-time (Van der Hart, Nijenhuis and Solomon 2010). These parts are typically organised by defences (attachment cry, flight, fight, freeze or collapse) and have been called 'emotional' parts of the personality (EP) because of their chronic and intense hyper- or hypoarousal (Van der Hart *et al.* 2006). Because EPs are fixed in defence, threat is perceived where it does not exist, particularly in relationships. The attention of these parts is narrowed to attend only to threat cues and so they often miss cues that might indicate the present is safe. For example, the patient as EP can become afraid when the therapist frowns in effortful listening, misperceiving the frown as an indication of anger. In this part of the personality, the patient is unable to step back and observe the situation as a whole, putting the frown into the proper context, or at least checking out what it means with the therapist. He or she only reacts with fear.

The therapist helps ANP and EP aspects of the patient become less avoidant and more accepting of each other, eventually leading to more adaptive and integrative functioning for the person as a whole. The individual must learn to accept each part as an aspect of his or her self, though this can take time for those who are extremely avoidant.

Trauma-related phobias: why dissociation becomes chronic

Dissociation is maintained over time first and foremost because the individual whose development has been disrupted may not have the integrative capacity to fully accept and realise what is dissociated. This is why skills building is an essential part of the first phase of treatment, so that the capacity to function and integrate is strengthened as much as possible. Secondly, because integrative capacity has been lacking for so long, the individual has developed major avoidance strategies to prevent confrontation with what has been dissociated. This leads to a series of inner-directed phobias.

Trauma-related phobias typically involve severe conflicts and fear, shame, or disgust of the dissociative individual's experience and of various dissociative parts. These phobias may be triggered strongly in relational contexts. They include:

- the phobia of mental actions, that is, of inner experience;
- the phobia of dissociative parts;
- the phobia of traumatic memory;
- the phobia of attachment and attachment loss;
- the phobia of healthy risk taking and change;
- and the phobia of intimacy.

Each dissociative part is typically isolated from other parts by these phobias that involve painful conflicts, defensive strategies and resistances to therapy. For example, an angry part might feel disgusted by a needy part and punish the patient when needs are expressed, while the needy part feels overwhelmed, criticised and afraid of the angry part.

Overcoming inner-directed phobias is a central task in fostering integration of the individual as a whole. Phobias are addressed in large part in sequence within the three phases of treatment, beginning with the broad phobia of inner experience (thoughts, emotions, sensations, wishes, perceptions, predictions, etc.) and the patient's experience with safety and threat in initial contacts with the therapist (Steele *et al.* 2001, 2005; Van der Hart *et al.* 2006).

Phase-oriented treatment of complex developmental trauma disorders

Phase-oriented treatment involves three overlapping phases of treatment. The initial phase focuses on safety, skills building, stabilisation, symptom reduction and building a co-operative therapeutic alliance in the face of multiple and contradictory transferences. Once a modicum of safety has been established and sufficient skills are in place, the second phase commences, in which traumatic memories and enactments are addressed more thoroughly. In this phase important work on insecure attachment to perpetrators is also accomplished. This phase is followed by a third phase of grieving, solidifying and furthering integrative gains, becoming more accepting of life as ever-changing, and promoting healthy risk-taking to develop more intimate and meaningful relationships. A return to earlier phases is often necessary over the course of treatment, according to the needs of the patient. The foundation for therapy with severely traumatised individuals is a secure therapeutic relationship that has strong boundaries.

Phase I: establishing safety, stabilisation and skills building

In this first phase of treatment, patients must first learn stabilisation skills, including how to establish and maintain safety, arousal and impulse regulation, the ability to reflect on experience (Fonagy 1997), energy management, relational skills, executive functioning, and skills to overcome chronic dissociation, as well as other daily life skills (Boon *et al.* 2011; Chu 2011; Cloitre *et al.* 2006; Courtois and Ford 2009; ISSTD 2011; Steele *et al.* 2005; Van der Hart *et al.* 2006). The therapist should take an initial stance of interest and modulated empathy with the patient as ANP, neither overly warm nor distant in feeling tone and not too probing (Steele *et al.* 2001; Van der Hart *et al.* 2006).

Establishing safety

Much emphasis has been placed on the primacy of the therapeutic relationship. However, what is often missed is the need for the patient to first experience a physical sense of safety that allows for curiosity and co-operation, prior to attachment with the therapist. Dissociative parts that are fixed in fight, flight, freeze, or collapse defences (EPs) are focused on cues of threat, not relationship. Early in therapy, therefore, relational interventions should generally be preceded by those that address safety and collaborative co-operation, following the principle that attachment cannot occur as long as serious threat is perceived. This involves more than just cognitive awareness of safety, because patients often lament, 'I *know* I am safe, but I don't *feel* safe!' The therapist helps the patient identify the physical sensations and postures that accompany being safe in order to have an experiential 'knowing' or felt sense of safety (Ogden *et al.* 2006), sometimes alternating awareness back and forth between a sensation associated with danger and one associated with safety. It is only then that work can proceed on earning secure attachment, with its felt sense of (relational) security.

Working in a window of tolerance

Treatment should be conducted in such a way that it remains within the patient's overall window of affective and integrative tolerance (Boon *et al.* 2011; Ogden *et al.* 2006; Van der Hart *et al.* 2006). The best overall indication of whether therapy is being well paced is how well the patient is functioning in daily life. In general, if functioning over time is status quo or improving, therapy is likely going well. Learning, co-operation and secure attachment cannot exist outside the range of what the patient can tolerate.

All parts of the patient, beginning with the patient as ANP, need to learn to recognise early signals of distress and practise distress tolerance and other regulatory skills (Boon *et al.* 2011). The therapist should track small changes in the patient from moment to moment so that dysregulation can be addressed immediately it begins to occur (Ogden *et al.* 2006). For example, the therapist can notice that the patient's speech has become shaky, her mouth is dry, she is shifting in her seat and looking around the room. Instead of continuing to talk, the therapist can ask the patient to notice what she is experiencing and together they can work toward regulation. The therapist is thus using his or her own capacities for regulation and reflection to help the patient learn self-regulatory skills. This is an essential component of secure attachment that builds safety and co-operation and lays the groundwork for integration.

Orienting parts to the present

Dissociative parts, in particular EPs, are often disoriented to time, place and even person, living in trauma-time in which they perceive danger. This makes it extremely difficult for the individual to have safe relationships, including with the therapist. To this end, 'all parts' are encouraged to focus on present experience in the room with the therapist. Parts are first oriented to place, and then to person, as efforts to develop attachment might be too activating at first. For example, 'Let all parts of you look around the room and see where you are. Can you notice something that can be a reminder to your whole mind of the safe present?' Parts more oriented to the present are encouraged to inwardly remind other parts of the present. Focusing on current reality for all parts of the patient is an important integrative action that supports more accurate perceptions of the present and more capacity to respond appropriately.

Overcoming the phobia of inner experience

The patient must become increasingly aware of, tolerate and understand inner experiences that consist of mental actions. All interventions incorporate implicit and explicit approaches that support overcoming this phobia. The patient, first as ANP, must learn to accept feelings, thoughts, sensations, wishes, needs, fantasies and perceptions without assigning value judgements to them. The patient is routinely encouraged to be aware of and explore his or her present experience (Ogden *et al.* 2006). The therapist should be consistently curious with the patient about inner experience in the moment. For example, the therapist might ask, 'As we are talking about your job, what do you experience right now? Can you notice if parts of you have some thoughts or feelings about it?' In this way the therapist constantly attends to process that accompanies content, and is able to slow down and address the patient's immediate experience.

Overcoming the phobia of attachment and attachment loss

The phobia of attachment in some parts of the personality is paradoxically accompanied by an equally intense phobia of attachment loss (rejection, abandonment, criticism) in other parts. The therapist should recognise that both attachment and attachment loss are feared, and therefore must find a delicate balance between enmeshment and distancing emotions and behaviours (counter transferences), both of which may be extremely intense for the therapist (Dalenberg 2000; Steele *et al*. 2001).

Coping with counter transference

One of the most essential interventions in working with the attachment phobia is for the therapist to understand and work with his or her countertransference reactions, rather than act on them. The therapist is pulled toward extreme emotions with these patients like no others. These may include rage, hatred, shame, guilt, disgust, fear, despair, hopelessness, helplessness, intense love and loneliness (Dalenberg 2000; Davies and Frawley 1994; Steele *et al*. 2001). The therapist can also be seduced by feelings of omnipotence and overwhelming care-taking ('I can save this person'), engendered by the patient's own wishes and the unresolved past of the therapist. Supervision and consultation for these difficult emotions are strongly recommended, even for experienced therapists (Chu 2011; Courtois and Ford 2009; Dalenberg 2000; Steele *et al*. 2001; Van der Hart *et al*. 2006).

Working with the conflict between attachment and attachment loss

The patient's combination of attachment minimising and maximising strategies should be recognised by the therapist (Steele *et al*. 2001; Van der Hart *et al*. 2006). The more need is evoked for the patient in the relationship with the therapist, the more defensive parts (EPs) become fearful and enraged, fearing the therapist's withdrawal or rejection. They are ashamed of dependency and greatly fear vulnerability. They turn shame and anger inward toward needy parts, resulting in dysregulation and often in self-destructive behaviours (drinking, self-harm, etc.). These situations, in turn, create more crises, perpetuating a maladaptive need–shame–rage cycle (Boon *et al*. 2011). The most important interventions are for the therapist (1) to consistently encourage adult aspects of the patient (ANPs) to acknowledge dependency needs and accept responsibility for child parts in collaboration with the therapist; and (2) to help the patient resolve the conflict between these young needy parts and defensive parts that avoid attachment.

The phobia of attachment loss is often mediated by the attachment cry, the early defence of calling out for a caregiver. Many young child-like EPs are fixed in this defence. Behavioural manifestations typically include difficulty ending and leaving sessions, crisis calls in between sessions, panic when the therapist goes away, and frantic expression of need and other attempts at frequent contact with the therapist outside of sessions. These behaviours are unfortunately often labelled as 'manipulative', but actually represent efforts to attain safety via care-taking and attachment, since these parts are dissociated from adult inner resources that could be soothing and helpful.

Treatment does not call for the therapist to meet every need and demand and be constantly available, but rather to be consistent and predictable (Steele *et al.* 2001). In fact, the therapist needs to set appropriate boundaries and limits on contact outside of session. This helps prevent too many dependency behaviours that can upset the equilibrium of the patient, and allows him or her to bring dependency needs into the therapy room where they can be talked about. The following case example illustrates some ways of working with this conflict.

Marge is a 48-year-old woman with a dissociative disorder who was extremely phobic of a child part that cried all the time, calling out for help, and also of an inner critical part that was always telling the child part to 'shut up' internally. This inner conflict was so intense that the patient began calling the therapist frequently between sessions to get help with her anxiety. The therapist first helped the patient verbalise more about her conflict about dependency on the therapist and addressed her concerns. Then she asked for permission to address the critical part and determined that the function of this part was to maintain safety by keeping the 'crybaby' quiet so that the child part would not 'cry too much and get in trouble'. This critical part was living in trauma-time, unaware of the present, and was well-defended by rage against dependency needs. The therapist helped orient the critical part to the present and agreed that she also did not want the child part (or any part of Marge) to be in such a painful state. The therapist then encouraged Marge to understand the function of the critical part, as well as the dependency yearnings of the child part. She gradually became less phobic and more compassionate of these parts of herself and could accept their functions. The therapist supported an alliance between the critical part and the adult self of the patient, which in turn were able to support the child part in being acknowledged and helped in appropriate ways. This significantly calmed the inner conflict.

Overcoming the phobia of dissociative parts

By definition, at least some dissociative parts are avoided because the patient experiences them as feared, shameful or disgusting. As noted above, dissociative individuals tend to wish either that the therapist would 'get rid of' parts, or work with them without the involvement of the patient as ANP. Beginning early in therapy, the therapist should encourage active inner communication and co-operation between the patient as ANP and other parts in a paced manner that fosters integration over the long term. The therapist might say something like, 'I can empathise with your wish for those needy and angry parts of you to disappear. Yet, in all these years, you have not been able to make that happen. That is because these aspects of you are a normal part of being human. I am confident that together, you and I can begin to make sense out of all these ways of being, and help you deal with them so that you feel more safe and comfortable with every part of yourself'.

Treatment is directed first towards helping the patient as ANP understand and become more empathic and engaged with all parts of him or herself, orienting parts to the present, establishing safety and inviting all parts to become involved in a co-operative therapeutic alliance. The therapist may often say something like, 'It is important that you and I invite all parts of you [or every part of your mind, or you in all your ways of being] to listen and give feedback about what we are discussing now'. When the therapist works with parts living in trauma-time (EPs) in the first phase of treatment, it should be to establish safety, orient to the present and develop co-operation in therapy and in daily life with other parts, rather than exploring traumatic material.

Once the patient is stable, functioning in daily life to the degree possible, can engage in regulation, and has some inner awareness and co-operation, the treatment of traumatic memories can take a more prominent place in therapy.

Phase 2: integrating traumatic memories

The major phobia addressed in Phase 2 is that of traumatic memories, many of which involve severe attachment disruptions or trauma. In addition, disorganised attachment to abusive and neglectful family members must also be addressed. In this chapter, we focus on the attachment aspects of Phase 2. Further reading on the treatment of traumatic memories can be found in Chu 2011; Kluft 1996; Van der Hart *et al.* 2006; and Van der Hart, Steele, Boon and Brown 1993.

Treatment of insecure attachment to the perpetrator

The inner conflict between attachment to and defence against caregivers who are perpetrators becomes heightened when traumatic memories are reactivated. Some patients may be enmeshed with their families in the present, unable to set healthy boundaries and limits. Simultaneously, certain dissociative parts of the individual may hold strong feelings of hatred, anger, shame, neediness, or terror toward family perpetrators and others (Steele *et al.* 2001).

The therapist must empathically explore all the patient's conflicted feelings and beliefs related to perpetrators and not blame them, remembering that one part of the patient can have an un-ambivalently positive view of the perpetrator, while another holds a completely negative view. For example, the therapist can say, 'I can empathise that parts of you hate your mother – she hurt you so very much. On the other hand, I can also empathise with feelings of love and yearning that some parts of you experience – she was sometimes kind. I wonder if perhaps all parts of you might join in understanding and accepting how these very different feelings can co-exist. Let's explore how you manage this painful conflict'.

Working with perpetrator-imitating parts

One particular type of part that bears mentioning is those that imitate the perpetrator. They have so strongly identified with the perpetrator that they literally experience themselves as being that person as he or she was in the past. Interventions with these parts should begin early in therapy and are intensified in the second phase of treatment (Blisard 2003; Boon *et al.* 2011; Chu 2011; Howell 2011; Steele *et al.* 2001; Van der Hart *et al.* 2006). Treatment is directed toward time orientation to the present, challenging the fixed belief that the part is the original perpetrator and providing psychoeducation about the original survival value of these parts so that empathy can be developed. The therapist should first focus on safety and co-operation rather than attachment with these parts.

Overcoming phobia of traumatic memory

This is one of the most difficult phobias to overcome, requiring high and sustained integrative capacity. The intensity and duration of exposure, or guided synthesis, must be matched to the patient's overall capacity to integrate these painful experiences (Van der Hart *et al.* 2006). As memories of attachment trauma surface, traumatic transference will heighten. The therapist should be acutely aware of multiple and contradictory transference and countertransference enactments.

It is essential that the therapist help the patient remember rather than relive traumatic experiences. This is accomplished by careful pacing that ensures the patient is grounded in the present, within his or her window of tolerance, and in contact with the therapist during these sessions (Van der Hart *et al.* 2006).

Phase 3: Personality integration and rehabilitation

Phase 3 involves higher levels of integration, such that dissociative parts are accepted and integrated as aspects of a single self and personality. It is also a time for the patient to focus increased energy on creating a more fulfilling and adaptive life. During this period of therapy, the phobia of attachment and attachment loss returns in the form of developing new and healthy relationships and risking intimacy.

Though begun early in Phase 1, ongoing resolution of the phobia of healthy risk taking and change becomes a more targeted focus of Phase 3. As the patient makes efforts to be more involved in present life over the course of this phase, he or she increasingly experiences the conflict between the desire to change and intense fears of doing so. In fact, adaptive change in this phase of treatment requires some of the most difficult integrative work of painful grieving and risk taking.

The patient should be assisted in approaching the phobia of intimacy in a graduated manner; overcoming fear of emotional intimacy prior to physical and sexual intimacy (as opposed to just having sex), as the last two require the first to be in place. Usually there is extreme resistance to the experience of loss, an inevitable risk associated with intimacy. Many individuals say, 'I would rather not have any relationship than run the risk of getting hurt so badly again.' The patient must slowly learn to tolerate the very ordinary conflicts and difficulties that arise within normal intimate relationships. This requires adequate conflict resolution skills, empathy, regulation and reflective functioning skills, and the ability to distinguish between minor and major relationship problems (Boon *et al.* 2011; Courtois and Ford 2009; Steele *et al.* 2001; Van der Hart *et al.* 2006). A case example follows.

> Greg met a nice woman in an evening class he was taking. He had immediate fears that she would not like him, which his therapist challenged and helped him overcome. Then a part of him began having fantasies of getting married to her, without even going on a date. Greg's therapist slowed him down and helped him realise he was retreating into a fantasy to avoid the hard work and risk of building a relationship. The therapist helped him take one small step at a time: making small talk, showing interest in what the woman was talking about, learning about the timing of sharing more vulnerable things. Greg asked the woman to go out for coffee but she was not able to go during the time he asked. He was devastated, and a part of him got angry in defence and wanted nothing to do with her. But gradually he was able to accept the possibility that it was not a rejection. The therapist continued to help Greg work with his fear of getting close and his fear of loss. After a few weeks, he asked again, and the woman accepted his offer.

Finally, it is common for additional traumatic memories and dissociative parts to emerge in Phase 3 in response to a growing capacity to integrate. During such times, Phase 1 and Phase 2 issues need to be revisited. Patients who cannot successfully complete Phase 3 and reach the point where they no longer have dissociation of the personality often continue to have difficulty with normal life, despite significant relief from traumatic intrusions (Kluft 1993).

Integration

All interventions across the course of therapy should promote a higher capacity for integration in the patient. The more the therapist is even-handedly inclusive of all parts in therapy, accepts them as inter-related aspects of one individual rather than separate 'personalities' and encourages the patient as a whole to accept these parts of him or herself, the more consistently integration is likely to occur. Additional techniques to promote integration among dissociative parts are beyond the scope of this chapter, and may be found in Boon *et al.* 2011; Chu 2011; Van der Hart *et al.* 2006; and Kluft 1993, 2006.

Conclusion

Attachment disruptions and attachment trauma are inherent in chronic childhood traumatisation and affect not only the relationships of adult survivors in daily life but also the therapeutic relationship. Early attachment trauma may manifest in therapy in the patient's phobias of attachment and of attachment loss vis-à-vis the therapist, often simultaneously present among different dissociative parts of the personality and known as D-attachment. Phase-oriented treatment, as the standard of care, pertains to all dimensions of therapy, but also, and especially, to helping patients to overcome their attachment-related phobias.

The focus on overcoming attachment-related phobias evolves over the course of these phases, with initial establishment of a felt sense of safety prior to attachment. In Phase 1 work with attachment phobias of ANPs are emphasised, while in Phase 2 conflicts among parts (EPs and ANPs) regarding attachment to the perpetrator is addressed. In Phase 3, the patient as a whole person strives toward greater intimacy (and adaptive risk taking) in relationships.

References

Barach, P.B. (1991). Multiple personality disorder as an attachment disorder. *Dissociation* **4**, 117–23.

Blisard, R. (2003). Disorganized attachment, development of dissociated self states, and a relational approach to treatment. *Journal of Trauma and Dissociation* **4**, 27–50.

Boon, S., Steele, K. and Van der Hart, O. (2011). *Coping with Trauma-related Dissociation: skills training for patients and therapists.* New York/London: W.W. Norton and Co.

Bowlby, J. (1969/1982). *Attachment and Loss, Volume 1: Attachment.* New York: Basic Books.

Chu, J. (2011). *Rebuilding Shattered Lives: the responsible treatment of complex post-traumatic and dissociative disorders,* 2nd edn. New York: Wiley.

Cloitre, M., Cohen, L.R. and Koenen, K.C. (2006). *Treating Survivors of Childhood Abuse: psychotherapy for the interrupted life.* New York: Guilford Press.

Courtois, C. and Ford, J. (2009). *Complex Traumatic Stress Disorders: an evidence-based guide.* New York: Guilford Press.

Dalenberg, C. (2000). *Countertransference and the Treatment of Trauma.* Washington, DC: American Psychological Association Press.

Davies, J. and Frawley, M.G. (1994). *Treating the Adult Survivor of Childhood Sexual Abuse: a psychoanalytic perspective.* New York: Basic Books.

Fonagy, P. (1997). Multiple voices vs. meta-cognition: an attachment theory perspective. *Journal of Psychotherapy Integration* **7**, 181–94.

Howell, E.F. (2011). *Understanding and Treating Dissociative Identity Disorder: a relational approach.* New York: Routledge.

International Society for the Study of Trauma and Dissociation [ISSTD] (2011). Guidelines for treating dissociative identity disorder in adults, third revision. *Journal of Trauma and Dissociation* **12**, 115–87.

Kluft, R.P. (1993). Clinical approaches to the integration of personalities. In R.P. Kluft, and C.G. Fine (eds), *Clinical Perspectives on Multiple Personality Disorder,* pp. 101–33. Washington, DC: American Psychiatric Press.

——(1996). Treating the traumatic memories of patients with dissociative identity disorder. *American Journal of Psychiatry* **153**, 103–10.

——(2006). Dealing with alters: a pragmatic clinical perspective. *Psychiatric Clinics of North America* **29**, 281–304.

Lichtenberg, J.D. and Kindler, A.R. (1994). A motivational systems approach to the clinical experience. *Journal of the American Psychoanalytic Association* **42**, 405–20.

Liotti, G. (1992). Disorganized/disoriented attachment in the etiology of dissociative disorders. *Dissociation* **5**, 196–204.

——(2009). Attachment and dissociation. In P.F. Dell and J.A. O'Neil (eds), *Dissociation and the Dissociative Disorders: DSM-V and beyond*, pp. 53–65. New York: Routledge.

Lyons-Ruth, K., Dutra, L., Schuder, M.R. and Bianchi, I, (2006). From infant attachment disorganisation to adult dissociation: relational adaptations or traumatic experiences. *Psychiatric Clinics of North America* **29**, 63–86.

Main, M. and Hesse, E. (1990). Parents' unresolved traumatic experiences are related to infant disorganized/disoriented attachment status: is frightened and/or frightening behavior the linking mechanism? In M.T. Greenberg, D. Cicchetti and E.M. Cummings (eds), *Attachment in the Preschool Years*, pp. 161–82. Chicago: University of Chicago Press.

McFadden, J. (2011). The role of disorganized attachment and insecure environment in the development of pathological dissociation and multiple identities. *Journal of Analytic Psychology* **56**, 348–53.

Nijenhuis, E.R.S. and Van der Hart, O. (2011). Dissociation in trauma: a new definition and comparison with previous formulations. *Journal of Trauma and Dissociation* **12**, 416–45.

Ogawa, J.R., Sroufe, L.A., Weinfield, N.S., Carlson, E.A. and Egeland, B. (1997). Development and the fragmented self: longitudinal study of dissociative symptomatology in a nonclinical sample. *Development and Psychopathology* **9**, 855–79.

Ogden, P., Minton, K. and Pain, C. (2006). *Trauma and the Body: a sensorimotor approach to psychotherapy*. New York/London: W.W. Norton and Co.

Panksepp, J. (1998). *Affective Neuroscience: the foundations of human and animal emotions*. New York: Oxford University Press.

Porges, S.W. (2011). *The Polyvagal Theory: neurophysiological foundations of emotions, attachment, communication, and self-regulation*. New York/London: W. W. Norton and Co.

Schore, A.N. (2003). *Affect Dysregulation and Disorders of the Self*. New York/London: W. W. Norton and Co.

Steele, K., Van der Hart, O. and Nijenhuis, E.R.S. (2001). Dependency in the treatment of complex PTSD and dissociative disorder patients. *Journal of Trauma and Dissociation* **2**, 79–116.

——(2005). Phase-oriented treatment of structural dissociation in complex traumatisation: overcoming trauma-related phobias. *Journal of Trauma and Dissociation* **6**, 11–53.

Van der Hart, O., Nijenhuis, E.R.S. and Solomon, R. (2010). Dissociation of the personality in complex trauma-related disorders and EMDR: theoretical considerations. *Journal of EMDR Practice and Research* **4**, 76–92.

Van der Hart, O., Nijenhuis, E.R.S. and Steele, K. (2006). *The Haunted Self: structural dissociation of the personality and the treatment of chronic traumatisation*. New York/London: W.W. Norton and Co.

Van der Hart, O., Steele, K., Boon, S. and Brown, P. (1993). The treatment of traumatic memories: synthesis, realisation, and integration. *Dissociation* **6**, 162–80.

Van der Kolk, B.A. (1987). The separation cry and the trauma response: Developmental issues in the psychobiology of attachment and separation. In B.A. van der Kolk (ed.), *Psychological Trauma*, pp. 31–62. Washington, DC: American Psychiatric Press.

Chapter 7

Attachment theory and personality disorders

Kenneth N. Levy, Kevin B. Meehan and Christina M. Temes

Introduction

Bowlby (1977) contended that internal working models of attachment help explain 'the many forms of emotional distress and personality disturbances, including anxiety, anger, depression, and emotional detachment, to which unwilling separations and loss give rise' (p. 201). Bowlby postulated that insecure attachment lies at the centre of disordered personality traits, and he tied the overt expression of felt insecurity to specific characterological disorders. Given that personality disorders are highly prevalent, chronic and debilitating to those who suffer from them, it is imperative to identify etiological factors contributing to the development and maintenance of these disorders. As will be discussed, attachment theory and research provide a comprehensive framework within which personality pathology can be understood. In this chapter we will review the empirical literature on attachment theory, with a focus on assessment and intervention for personality disorders (PDs). Further, we will demonstrate the clinical utility of attachment theory and research for conceptualising personality pathology.

Theory and assessment of attachment

Bowlby (1977) held that childhood attachment underlies the 'later capacity to make affectional bonds as well as a whole range of adult dysfunctions' including 'marital problems and trouble with children, as well as . . . neurotic symptoms and personality disorders' (p. 206). Thus Bowlby (1973, 1982) postulated that early attachment experiences have long-lasting effects that persist across the lifespan, are among the major determinants of personality organisation, and have specific clinical relevance. Longitudinal studies have confirmed the predictability of later functioning and adaptation from infant attachment styles, with considerable, although variable, stability of attachment classification from infancy to adulthood (Hamilton 2000; Waters *et al.* 2000; Weinfield, Sroufe, and Egeland 2000), which is dependent on intervening experiences in relationships (Fraley 2002; Grossmann, Grossmann and Waters 2005; Lewis, Feiring and Rosenthal 2000; Waters *et al.* 2000).

From the seminal work of Bowlby, attachment theory and research have evolved into two traditions (interview and self-report), each with its own methodology for assessing attachment patterns.

Interview

Main and her colleagues developed the Adult Attachment Interview (AAI: George, Kaplan and Main 1985), which evaluates the interviewee's conception of how early attachment relationships have influenced adult personality by probing for specific memories that both corroborate and contradict how the attachment history has been conceptualised. Secure attachment on the AAI is characterised by a well-organised, undefended discourse style in which emotions are freely expressed, and by a high degree of coherence exhibited in the discussion of attachment relationships, regardless of how positively or negatively these experiences are portrayed. These individuals maintain a balanced and realistic-seeming view of early relationships, value attachment relationships, and view attachment-related experiences as influential to their development.

In contrast, dismissive attachment is characterised by a devaluation of the importance of attachment relationships on the AAI, or relationships are portrayed in an idealised fashion with few corroborating examples. These individuals are judged to have low 'coherence of mind' because of the vagueness and sparseness of their descriptions, as well as the inconsistency between the vaguely positive generalisations and 'leaked' evidence to the contrary. Preoccupied attachment is characterised by parental relationships on the AAI described with pervasive anger, passivity and attempts to please parents, even when the relationship is described as positive. These individuals have a tendency towards incoherence in their descriptions, with excessively long, grammatically entangled sentences, reversion to childlike speech, and confusion regarding past and present relationships.

The Unresolved/disorganised classification is assigned when an individual displays lapses in the monitoring of reasoning or discourse when discussing experiences of loss and abuse. These lapses include highly implausible statements regarding the causes and consequences of traumatic attachment-related events, loss of memory for attachment-related traumas, and confusion and silence around discussion of trauma or loss. Cannot Classify is assigned when an individual displays a combination of contradictory or incompatible attachment patterns, or when no single state of mind with respect to attachment is predominant. This occurs when the individual shifts attachment patterns in mid-interview, when the individual demonstrates different attachment patterns with different attachment figures, or when the individual shows a mixture of different attachment patterns within the same transcript or passage.

Self-report

In contrast to Main's focus on relationships with parents, Hazan and Shaver (1987) and colleagues (Shaver, Hazan and Bradshaw 1988), using a social psychological perspective, evaluate romantic love as an attachment process. They translated Ainsworth's descriptions of the three infant attachment types (Ainsworth et al. 1978) into a single-item, vignette-based measure in which individuals characterised themselves as secure, avoidant, or anxious-ambivalent in romantic relationships. In subsequent research, Bartholomew (1990, 1994) and Bartholomew and Horowitz (1991) developed a four-category classification of adult attachment that corresponds to a two-dimensional model of anxiety and avoidance: secure (low anxiety/low avoidance); preoccupied (high anxiety/low avoidance); dismissing-avoidant (low anxiety/high avoidance); and fearful-avoidant (high anxiety/high avoidance). Although categorical comparisons between the AAI and self-report measures have typically failed to correspond with each other (Bartholomew and Shaver 1998; Crowell, Fraley and Shaver 1999), studies that have related the dimensional coding scales from the AAI to the self-report measures have found that they are significantly related, even if the two categorical typologies were not significantly related (Shaver, Belsky and Brennan 2000).

Formulations of personality disorders from an attachment perspective

Bowlby (1973) believed that attachment difficulties increase vulnerability to personality pathology and can help identify the specific types of difficulties that arise. For instance, Bowlby connected anxious ambivalent attachment to 'a tendency to make excessive demands on others and to be anxious and clingy when they are not met', and linked this presentation to that seen with dependent and hysterical personalities. Bowlby also described how avoidant attachment in childhood – postulated to be a product of caretakers' rebuffing a child's bids for comfort or protection – may be related to later diagnoses of narcissistic personality or 'affectionless and psychopathic personalities' (1973: 14). Thus Bowlby postulated that early attachment experiences have long-lasting effects across the lifespan, and these experiences are among the major determinates of personality organisation and pathology.

Further, virtually all PDs are characterised by persistent difficulties in interpersonal relations (Levy 2005). For example, impoverished relationships are a cardinal feature of both schizoid and avoidant PDs. Those with schizoid pathology appear defensively devoid of any interest in human interaction, whereas the avoidant pathology is typically characterised by a simultaneous desire for, and fear of, close relationships (Sheldon and West 1990). Those with borderline personality disorder (BPD) and dependent PD struggle to be alone and are preoccupied by fears of abandonment and the dissolution of close relationships (Gunderson and Lyons-Ruth 2008). Further, intense and stormy relationships are one of the central features of BPD (Clarkin et al. 1983; McGlashan 1986; Modestin 1987). Those with dependent pathology appear incapable of functioning without the aid of others (Bornstein and O'Neill 1992; Livesley, Schroeder and Jackson 1990).

Integrating Blatt's (1995) cognitive-developmental psychoanalytic theory with attachment theory, Levy and Blatt proposed that within each attachment pattern, there may exist more and less adaptive forms of dismissing and preoccupied attachment (Blatt and Levy 2003; Levy and Blatt 1999). These developmental levels are based on the degree of differentiation and integration of representational or working models that underlie attachment patterns.

In terms of PDs, Levy and Blatt (1999) noted that several PDs (i.e. histrionic, dependent, BPD) appear to be focused in different ways, and possibly at different developmental levels, on issues of interpersonal relatedness. They proposed that preoccupied attachment would run along a relatedness continuum from non-personality disordered individuals to those with BPD. Those without PDs would generally value attachment, intimacy and closeness. Those at the next level would be more gregarious and exaggerate their emphasis on relatedness. At another level below are those with a hysterical style, who not only exaggerate closeness and overly value others but may defend against ideas inconsistent with their desires, and more histrionic individuals who are overly dependent and easily show anger in attachment relationships. Finally, at the lowest level of functioning are those with BPD for whom strong desires for closeness and intimacy coupled with strong interpersonal sensitivity lead to the most chaotic and disrupted patterns of relating to others.

In contrast, another set of PDs (i.e. avoidant, obsessive-compulsive, narcissistic, antisocial) appear to express a preoccupation with establishing, preserving and maintaining a sense of self, possibly in different ways and at different developmental levels. Levy and Blatt (1999) proposed that avoidant attachment would run along a self-definitional continuum from non-personality disordered individuals who are striving for personal development, to those who are more obsessive, to those with avoidant PD, to those with narcissistic PD, and finally – at the lowest developmental levels – to those with BPD and antisocial PD. Levy and Blatt (1999) proposed that BPD would be related to both preoccupied and avoidant attachment, which is now backed up by a host of studies (see Levy 2005 for a review).

Association between attachment and personality disorders

Research has largely supported theoretical assertions of an overlap between PDs and insecure attachment. Much attention in the literature has been given to insecure attachment and BPD (see the Liotti chapter in this volume) and to a lesser extent antisocial personality. There is much less data on attachment variables and other PDs, and what is available tends to compare dimensions of self-reported adult romantic attachment to self-reported PD symptoms (see Rosenstein et al. 1996). Within that literature, while there has been consistency in finding a negative relationship overall between attachment security and personality pathology (Meyer et al. 2001; Meyer and Pilkonis 2005), the relationships between specific PDs and insecure attachment types are less consistent.

Meyer and Pilkonis (2005) evaluated the relationship between adult romantic attachment (using the Experiences in Close Relationships scale) and PD symptoms (using the SCID-II questionnaire) in a sample of 176 college students. Their results indicated that attachment security was associated with an absence of PD features, while a dismissive style was strongly associated with schizoid PD features. A preoccupied style was associated with histrionic, BPD and dependent PD features; and a fearful style was associated with avoidant PD features. Those with paranoid, obsessive-compulsive, narcissistic and schizotypal features fell between the preoccupied and fearful styles.

Meyer and Pilkonis (2005) report similar data in a clinical sample of 152 inpatients and outpatients diagnosed with DSM-III consensus ratings (Meyer *et al*. 2001). In line with the non-clinical study, dismissive style was associated with schizoid PD diagnosis, a fearful style was associated with avoidant PD diagnosis, and a preoccupied style was strongly associated with histrionic, borderline and dependent PD features. However, those with paranoid, obsessive-compulsive, narcissistic and schizotypal features fell more between the dismissive and fearful styles in the clinical sample.

Levy (1993) examined the relationship between attachment patterns and PDs in a sample of 217 college students using Hazan and Shaver's Adult Attachment Questionnaire (AAQ), Bartholomew's Relationship Questionnaire (RQ) and the Millon Multiaxial Clinical Inventory (MCMI). Attachment security was negatively related to the schizoid, avoidant, schizotypal, passive-aggressive and borderline scales. Dismissive attachment was positively associated with paranoid, antisocial and narcissistic personality scales; fearful avoidance was associated with schizoid, avoidant, and schizotypal scales; and preoccupied attachment was associated with schizotypal, avoidant, dependent and BPD scales.

Alexander (1993) examined the relationship between trauma, attachment and PDs in a sample of 112 adult female incest survivors. She assessed attachment using the RQ and assessed PDs using the MCMI-II (Millon 1992). Only 14 per cent of the sample rated themselves as secure, 13 per cent rated themselves as preoccupied, 16 per cent as dismissing and 58 per cent as fearfully avoidant. Preoccupied attachment was associated with dependent, avoidant, self-defeating and borderline PDs. Fearful avoidance was correlated with avoidant, self-defeating and borderline PDs and high scores on the SCL-90-R. Dismissing individuals reported the least distress, most likely due to their proclivity to suppress negative affect (Kobak and Sceery 1988).

Brennan and Shaver (1998) examined the connections between adult romantic attachment patterns (using the RQ) and PDs (using the Personality Diagnostic Questionnaire) in a non-clinical sample of 1,407 adolescents and young adults. Their results indicated that those rated secure with respect to attachment were half as likely to self-rate having a PD, whereas those rated as fearful were four times more likely, those rated as preoccupied were three times more likely, and those rated as dismissive were 1.3 times more likely to self-rate the presence of a PD. Discriminant function analysis was used to predict attachment dimensions based on PD symptoms. Three functions emerged, which differentially predicted attachment ratings on the basis of PD features. The first function, from secure to fearful, was characterised by paranoid, schizotypal, avoidant, self-defeating, BPD, narcissistic, and obsessive-compulsive PDs on the fearful side of the dimension. The second function, from dismissive to preoccupied, was characterised by dependent and histrionic PDs on the preoccupied side of the dimension and schizoid PD on the dismissive side of the dimension. Finally, the third function, characterised by passive-aggressive, sadistic and antisocial PDs, did not correspond to attachment dimensions.

Using the AAI, Rosenstein and Horowitz (1996) found in an adolescent inpatient sample that preoccupied attachment was uniquely associated with avoidant PD, whereas dismissing attachment was uniquely associated with narcissistic, antisocial and paranoid PDs. Similarly, van IJzendoorn and colleagues (1997), in a criminal offender group, found that preoccupied attachment tended to be associated with anxiety related personality disorders (cluster C) and that dismissing attachment was associated with antisocial PD. These findings were confirmed in a meta-analysis examining AAI distributions in clinical samples (Bakermans-Kranenburg and van IJzendoorn 2009).

Despite some differences across studies, for the most part, across both interview and self-report measures and various age groups and samples, the findings converge. Both preoccupied and dismissing attachment are associated with BPD. Generally preoccupied attachment is uniquely associated with the anxiety based PDs such as dependent and histrionic PD, whereas dismissing attachment is associated with antisocial, narcissistic and some of the cluster A PDs, in particular schizoid and paranoid PDs. Fearful avoidance has sometimes been associated with cluster A PDs and sometimes with cluster C PDs.

Clinical features of attachment types in personality disorders

Based on the delineation of Levy and Blatt (1999), and refined by the aforementioned research, the clinical characteristics of several PDs will be discussed in terms of their predominant attachment styles. While some disorders have most often been found to correspond to a preoccupied style (i.e. dependent and histrionic PD), a dismissive style (i.e. schizoid and antisocial PD) and a fearful style (i.e. avoidant PD), others have a less distinctive attachment style (i.e. narcissistic and paranoid PD) but are nonetheless notable for characteristic attachment-related features.

Personality pathology with preoccupied styles

Levy and Blatt (1999) note that PDs characterised by the preoccupied style (i.e. histrionic, dependent, BPD) tend to focus in different ways on issues of interpersonal relatedness. Because such individuals often have a negative model of themselves but a positive model of others (Bartholomew 1990), they are likely to look to the therapist to meet needs that they feel unable to address within themselves. Thus preoccupied individuals are often likely to seek treatment (Levy *et al.* 2012). Such individuals are likely to disclose a great deal of information to the therapist, with evocative descriptions of themselves and others that engage the therapist's attention. However, their discourse often lacks the narrative coherence that would aid in working through the experience or would allow for others to fully join with their experience.

Further, preoccupied individuals with personality pathology are likely to assume that the therapist has more knowledge about them than can be realistically expected, and as a result not explain and contextualise their thinking for the therapist. At best, the therapist may often feel that she is working hard to make links within her own mind between disparate pieces of information, since the patient has not provided such narrative bridges. At worst, the therapist may feel lost in a chaotic, entangled narrative that leads to confusion and frustration. Thus even though the preoccupied patient may eagerly attend and appear to be working very hard in treatment, such work may not translate into a productive dialogue that allows for shifts in the patient's representations of self and others.

> Ms. D, diagnosed with histrionic PD, often began her sessions breathlessly reporting an entangled series of events during the week, with little sequence or structure. Narratives were often pressured and organised around her subjective affective experience, with only cursory anchors in objective events, which prohibited the therapist from following the progression that led to a particular feeling. 'What happened on Monday? I was freaking out, that's what happened on Monday. Why? Because it felt like my guts were being torn out, that's why.' Like the therapist, Ms. D would become lost in her own narratives in ways that she too found destabilising, as she would begin to feel herself drowning in the affect with no structure to grasp on to. Further, efforts on the therapist's part to slow her down and fill in some of the gaps in her narrative would be met with frustration. Given that Ms. D's preoccupation was embedded in pervasive anger at the inconsistent care of attachment figures, this style of expression was also understood to reflect a desire for the therapist to be a completely reliable and omniscient attachment figure who could finally fill her deep well of unmet need states. As a result, the therapist would remark, 'You want me to be completely in sync with you, to know what you are thinking without having to say it. This is why it must be so frustrating for you to be seeing what you are in my face – that I am quite lost in this story and too confused to respond in the way you wish I would'. Over time Ms. D became increasingly aware of the relational impact of her preoccupying anger, as well as the function it served in relation to underlying longings for connection.

The work of Dozier and colleagues (2001) suggests a seemingly contradictory stance on the part of the therapist: to remain securely present with the patient while simultaneously maintaining sufficient distance from becoming entangled in the patient's production. This secure detachment allows the therapist sufficient distance to clarify and confront breaks and omissions in the patient's discourse (Clarkin, Yeomans and Kernberg 2006). Slade suggests that progress is slow-moving with preoccupied patients, and that it is gained through the therapist's 'emotional availability and tolerance for fragmentation and chaos' as they aid the patient in forming less distorted and/or chaotic representations of self and others (Slade 1999: 588).

Personality pathology with dismissive styles

Many with dismissive attachment appear valuing of attachment in their idealisation of caregivers, and yet they are often unable to remember specific events that would corroborate their general event representations. Others can recall negative events with caregivers, but by restricting affect may remain disconnected to the feelings such experiences normally evoke. Finally, many with dismissive attachment are openly derogating of others and the need for relationships that have any dependency attached to them.

Levy and Blatt (1999) note that PDs organised around avoidance (i.e. avoidant, obsessive-compulsive, narcissistic and antisocial PDs) are characterised by a preoccupation with establishing, preserving and maintaining a sense of self. Because individuals with dismissive avoidance often have a positive model of themselves and a negative model of others (Bartholomew 1990), they are unlikely to expect that help from and dependency on others will lead to change. Therefore dismissive patients are less likely to seek treatment of their own accord (Levy *et al*. 2012). When these individuals enter therapy it is often at the behest of another: a significant other who makes it a condition of staying together; an ultimatum from a boss in order to keep a job; a mandate from a court in order to stay out of jail; or a recommendation from a lawyer in order to provide the appearance of remorse. Early in treatment, such individuals often maintain a distance from the therapist, disclose little and express scepticism about the treatment. Though they may appear compliant in relaying personal information, their discourse will often lack the details needed to create vivid, complex and multifaceted images of self and others in the mind of the therapist. At best, the therapist may often feel that she is 'going through the motions' of a treatment with a distant and superficially compliant patient. At worst the therapist may repeatedly feel she has to answer to the criticisms of an individual who continually has 'one foot out the door'.

Therefore the early phases of treatment with dismissive patients often focus on the high threat of drop-out. As with preoccupied patients, this challenges the therapist to balance two seemingly contradictory demands. On one hand, dismissive patients often become more distressed and confused when confronted with difficult issues in treatment (Dozier *et al*. 2001). At the same time, not directly confronting threats to treatment creates an increased risk of drop-out (Clarkin, Yeomans and Kernberg 2006). The capacity of the therapist to emotionally engage herself in a narrative that may not be engaging to begin with, and to bring direct emotional expression to a narrative that often omits complex affects, may provide an optimal space for intervening with such patients. Despite these challenges in engaging and retaining dismissive patients in treatment, when they follow through with treatment they do seem to fare better in terms of outcome (Fonagy *et al.* 1996).

Dismissive attachment tends to be at its most extreme in individuals with malignant narcissism, antisocial PD, and/or sociopathy/psychopathy (Blatt and Levy 2003; Levy and Blatt 1999). These individuals are competitive, aggressive, preoccupied with power and exploitation, and tend to aggress against others or use them for instrumental means. Similarly, Karen Horney (1945, 1950) described a pattern that she characterised as 'moving against people'. The following clinical example illustrates such dynamics.

As is common with those with antisocial PD, Mr. M was court-mandated to treatment. During a public argument he was having with his girlfriend he had pummelled an innocent bystander who he believed was about to intervene. He went into what he described as a blind rage and threw punches at the police officers that were responding to the call for help. Initially he failed to share that he was court-mandated to attend sessions; this information came to light after the therapist questioned his motivation for treatment and suggested that they end their work together. Mr. M's attitude in treatment was generally cavalier, and it was difficult to get him to be serious about his situation or his internal experience. He vacillated between treating therapy as a game and as an imposition forced upon him. He oscillated between seeing the therapist as a naïve fool who was dumb to the ways of the world and seeing the therapist as corrupt and going through the motions of therapy with little interest in his improvement. When he viewed the therapist as naïve, he held him in disdain as weak and unable to help. He berated the therapist as someone who 'just doesn't know', who would be eaten alive in the 'real world', and who probably cried at weddings, funerals and even sad movies. When he saw the therapist as corrupt there was a subtle identification with being both powerful and protected against others' manipulations, but in those moments the therapist was also disinterested, uncaring and dishonest. In these moments, he saw the therapist as 'crying fake tears for the dumb saps who believe that he really cares'. As therapy progressed, the vacillation between these two positions gradually entered the patient's awareness; the motivations for and consequences of each position became more salient and resonate. Although such awareness often angered the patient, it also allowed him to see that his views of the therapist were mental representations and not the actual reality of the therapist or others in the world.

Personality pathology on the fearful to dismissive continuum

As previously discussed, Levy and Blatt (1999) note that those with PDs characterised by avoidance are concerned with creating and maintaining a sense of self, which manifests in a number of ways. Because individuals with a fearfully avoidant style have both a negative model of themselves and a negative model of others (Bartholomew 1990), they are unlikely to expect that they can depend on either themselves or anyone else to improve their circumstances. For example, those with avoidant personality pathology tend to desire intimate relationships but fear that their own inadequacies will become a source of humiliation at the hands of critical others. In contrast, patients with narcissistic and paranoid personality pathology tend to lead with a dismissive view of others, but this stance may be taken to belie some level of attachment anxiety and feelings of vulnerability.

Ms. N, who was diagnosed with narcissistic PD, began her treatment by referring to the therapist's office as 'the nicest broom closet I have ever seen', which was quickly followed by reprimands for a series of perceived failures: he had no water cooler in his office, the office was too far from where she had to park, the weather did not suit her. She was hostile, but it seemed that part of her wanted the therapist to care for her – she wanted him to provide nourishment, intimacy and atmospheric comfort. And even before he said anything more than 'Come in', she was angry for wanting these things from him. If in fact she did want these things from him and was sad that he could not provide them, she was also angry that he had evoked such desire in her. It also seemed that she took great pleasure in knowing that the therapist was incapable of making a water cooler appear or moving the parking garage. And, even if he could get her some water and find her a closer parking spot, he could not change the weather. Thus it was the therapist who was incapable, not her.

Fearfully dismissive patients are likely to alternate between aggression and neediness in the early stages of treatment. Such patients may also vacillate quickly between idealisations and devaluations, leaving the therapist feeling confused and deskilled. Therapists have to be on guard not to over-interpret these behaviours, nor to respond defensively or aggressively, or collude with the pathology through passivity. Avoiding these problematic reactions can be facilitated by the therapist's maintaining his or her own reflective and non-defensive stance, as well as through involvement in some form of supervision or consultation.

Attachment and interventions for personality disorders

From its inception, Bowlby believed that attachment theory had particular relevance for psychotherapy. There are a number of ways in which attachment and psychotherapy may intersect, and many of these connections have been examined empirically (see Borelli and David 2003; Daniel 2006; Levy *et al*. 2011; Obegi and Berant 2009; Steele and Steele 2008 for reviews). Findings from this body of research indicate the clinical importance of accounting for patients' attachment styles and the potential fruitfulness of addressing issues around attachment within treatment. In particular, this work suggests that patient attachment status may be extremely relevant to the course and outcome of psychotherapy for PDs.

Attachment-based interventions

Most existing psychotherapies implicitly employ techniques and principles that are congruous with attachment theory, particularly those concerning the importance of a healthy therapeutic relationship as well as the exploration and updating of mental representations of significant relationships and the self. Until recently, few psychotherapies were directly based on the principles of attachment theory; however, in recent years, attachment-based interventions have been developed for a number of problems (e.g. Johnson 1996) and recently for personality disordered patients. For example, mentalisation-based therapy (MBT: Bateman and Fonagy 1999, 2001, 2008) was designed as a long-term, psychoanalytically-oriented, partial hospitalisation treatment for BPD. This treatment model is based on the idea that patients were not able to develop the capacity of mentalisation (i.e. the social-cognitive and affective process through which one makes sense of intentional behaviour in the self and others by reflecting on mental states) within the context of an early attachment relationship, and that fostering the development of this capacity in turn leads to more stability in terms of the self and relationships with others. This goal of MBT rests on developing a safe attachment relationship between client and therapist to provide a context in which these mental states can be explored. MBT has been demonstrated to be effective over long-term follow-up with regard to reduction of depressive symptoms, suicidality, parasuicidality and length of inpatient stays, as well as improvement in social functioning (Bateman and Fonagy 2009).

Attachment moderating psychotherapy process and outcome

A number of studies have examined how client attachment relates to the process and outcome of psychotherapies for PDs and other conditions. Generally, secure attachment has been associated with better treatment outcomes across psychotherapies for patients with PDs (Meyer and Pilkonis 2005; Strauss *et al*. 2006). Conversely, these studies suggest that clients who are more anxious with respect to attachment may demonstrate different trajectories of treatment engagement and outcome than do more avoidant clients. Given that variation in these attachment styles differentially characterises patients with PDs (Levy and Blatt 1999), these characteristics are useful to consider when making predictions regarding the course of treatment in these individuals.

As noted earlier, clients with PDs who are more anxious with respect to attachment (particularly preoccupied individuals) may initially present as very engaged and interested in pursuing treatment. Empirical studies in this area have indicated that individuals with high levels of attachment anxiety are more likely to perceive distress and seek help for emotional difficulties (Vogel and Wei 2005). Additionally, preoccupied individuals in particular tend to be more frequent users of medical services in general; for example, preoccupied individuals with cluster B PDs report longer medical hospitalisations than do matched individuals of other attachment classifications (Hoermann et al. 2004). Although they may appear more disclosing and dependent on providers, preoccupied clients are not more compliant to treatment recommendations (Dozier 1990; Riggs and Jacobvitz 2002). Additionally, there is evidence that higher attachment anxiety may be especially predictive of poorer treatment outcomes among both preoccupied and fearful-avoidant clients with PDs (Fonagy et al. 1996; Strauss et al. 2006).

By contrast, more avoidant individuals tend to report less distress and help-seeking behaviours (Vogel and Wei 2005), and they tend to be less compliant to treatment recommendations (although in a more subtle manner than preoccupied patients) and exhibit generally weaker therapeutic alliances than other attachment groups (Eames and Roth 2000; Mallinckrodt, Porter and Kivlighan 2005; Satterfield and Lyddon 1998). However, there is some evidence from a mixed sample that included PDs that they may perform better than their anxious counterparts with respect to outcome. For instance, Fonagy et al. (1996) found that dismissive patients were most likely to show improvement during treatment, as compared to patients exhibiting other attachment styles including preoccupied. These findings suggest that while avoidant (particularly dismissing) clients may seem detached, they may be able to effectively utilise treatment; conversely, while preoccupied individuals may seem particularly engaged, they may not be able to use interventions in a helpful way. Of course, these findings may not hold up in PD samples and should be confirmed.

Change in attachment in personality disorders

Some researchers have examined changes in attachment status as a result of treatment for individuals with PDs. Generally, the findings of these studies have suggested that treatment may lead to changes in attachment status for these patients, although this impact may differ depending on the characteristics of treatment (e.g. treatment length). Levy and colleagues (Diamond et al. 2003; Levy et al. 2006, 2007) have examined changes in attachment status as assessed by the AAI in patients diagnosed with BPD. In a pilot study (Levy et al. 2007) of 10 patients in a year-long course of Transference Focused Psychotherapy (TFP) it was found that a third of the patients were classified as secure with respect to attachment post-treatment, and 60 per cent of those previously classified as unresolved with respect to trauma and/or loss were no longer so by the end of treatment. In a randomised controlled trial (Levy et al. 2006), the researchers examined changes in attachment in 90 patients with BPD who were randomised to receive one of three treatments: TFP, dialectical behaviour therapy (DBT), or a modified psychodynamic supportive psychotherapy (PST). After a year of treatment, within the TFP group 7 of 22 patients (31.8 per cent) changed from an insecure to secure attachment classification; this change was not observed within the other two treatment groups. This finding with regard to change in attachment in TFP was recently replicated in an RCT in Munich and Vienna (Buchheim *et al.* 2012). In a chapter publication, Fonagy and colleagues (1995) reported findings from a subset of 35 of the 85 inpatients from the Cassel Hospital inpatient study (described in Fonagy *et al.* 1996). This subset of patients was comprised of individuals from a mixed diagnosis sample, who were mostly characterised as severely disturbed, treatment resistant and personality disordered. All 35 inpatients were classified as insecure during their initial interview; however, 14 (40 per cent) of the 35 inpatients were assigned a secure classification upon discharge, representing a statistically significant increase in the proportion of secure classification. These findings are important because they show that attachment patterns can change as a function of treatment, but neither the specific psychopathology nor the treatment were well specified. Additionally, to date a more detailed description of the changes in AAI status observed in this study has not been published, making reports of these findings difficult to interpret.

Another recent study examined change in attachment following short-term inpatient treatment in a sample of 40 women diagnosed with BPD, avoidant PD, or both disorders. Although patients symptomatically improved over time, there was little evidence of a shift in the proportion of securely attached individuals within this sample. The authors did note that overall ratings for attachment avoidance were higher after treatment, and that a shift from ambivalent to avoidant attachment was associated with better treatment outcomes for patients with BPD. The authors argued that this change was reflective of a de-activation of the attachment system, or a shift away from the enmeshment characteristic of more preoccupied styles. This study suggests that the shifts in attachment that may occur as a result of short-term therapy may be more subtle and that shifts from insecurity to security are less likely in short-term treatment, particularly when compared to the long-term treatments.

Attachment as a process variable in psychotherapy with personality disorders

Some preliminary work has indicated that attachment-related constructs may also be used as a lens through which to examine psychotherapy process. Samstag and colleagues (2008) used the narrative coherence coding system from the AAI to examine psychotherapy process as a predictor of treatment outcome within 48 client–therapist dyads. This sample included clients with primarily cluster C PDs (with comorbid depression and/or anxiety) who were divided into three groups based on outcome: (1) drop-out (termination within first third of treatment);

(2) good outcome (high reliable change); and (3) poor outcome (low reliable change). Coherence was rated for a portion of sessions that were randomly selected from the first third of treatment. Coherence ratings were significantly higher for the good outcome group, as compared with the drop-out and poor outcome groups. These findings suggest that more highly coherent narratives occurring within the context of psychotherapy may be an indication of a particularly fruitful collaboration within the client–therapist dyad. Furthermore, it is possible that patient-level factors, including attachment, may influence the level of narrative coherency, which may in turn influence the course of psychotherapy.

Conclusion

As has been discussed, attachment theory and research provide a robust framework for conceptualising personality disorders. In terms of assessment, evaluating personality disorders in terms of thematic concerns of interpersonal relatedness and self-definition, valence of models of self and others, as well as level of attachment anxiety and avoidance, may inform case conceptualisation and treatment planning. Attachment theory and research also have broad implications for therapeutic interventions with personality-disordered patients. This includes attachment-based treatments for personality disorders such as MBT (Bateman and Fonagy 1999), which specifically target deficits in mentalisation that occur in the context of heightened activation of the attachment system. Change in attachment patterns has also been observed in TFP, a treatment for personality disorders that specifically targets models of self and others. Lastly, attachment research has identified prognostic indicators in psychotherapy as a function of attachment style. Taken together, the clinical utility of attachment theory and research for conceptualising personality pathology is too powerful for clinicians to ignore.

References

Ainsworth, M.S., Blehar, M.C., Waters, E. and Wall, S. (1978). *Patterns of Attachment: a psychological study of the strange situation*. Hillsdale, NJ: Lawrence Erlbaum Associates.
Alexander, P.C. (1993). The differential effects of abuse characteristics and attachment in the prediction of long-term effects of sexual abuse. *Journal of Interpersonal Violence* **8**, 346–62.
Bakermans-Kranenburg, M.J. and van IJzendoorn, M.H. (2009). The first 10,000 Adult Attachment Interviews: Distributions of adult attachment representations in clinical and non-clinical groups. *Attachment and Human Development* **11**(3), 223–63.
Bartholomew, K. (1990). Avoidance of intimacy: an attachment perspective. *Journal of Social and Personal Relationships* **7**, 147–78.
——(1994). Assessment of individual differences in adult attachment. *Psychological Inquiry* **5**, 23–7.
Bartholomew, K. and Horowitz, L.M. (1991). Attachment styles among young adults: a test of a four-category model. *Journal of Personality and Social Psychology* **61**, 226–44.

Bartholomew, K. and Shaver, P.R. (1998). Methods of assessing adult attachment: do they converge? In J.A. Simpson and W.S. Rholes (eds), *Attachment Theory and Close Relationships*, pp. 25–45. New York: Guilford Press.

Bateman, A. and Fonagy, P. (1999). Effectiveness of partial hospitalisation in the treatment of BPD personality disorder: a randomized controlled trial. *American Journal of Psychiatry* **156**, 1563–9.

——(2001). Treatment of borderline personality disorder with psychoanalytically oriented partial hospitalisation: an 18-month follow-up. *American Journal of Psychiatry* **158**, 36–42.

——(2008). 8-year follow-up of patients treated for borderline personality disorder: mentalisation-based treatment versus treatment as usual. *American Journal of Psychiatry* **165**, 631–8.

——(2009). Randomized controlled trial of outpatient mentalisation-based treatment versus structured clinical management for borderline personality disorder. *American Journal of Psychiatry* **166**, 1355–64.

Blatt, S.J. (1995). Representational structures in psychopathology. In D. Cicchetti and S. Toth (eds), *Rochester Symposium on Developmental Psychopathology, Vol. 6: Emotion, cognition, and representation*, pp. 1–33. Rochester, NY: University of Rochester Press.

Blatt, S.J. and Levy, K.N. (2003). Attachment theory, psychoanalysis, personality development, and psychopathology. *Psychoanalytic Inquiry* **23**, 102–50.

Borelli, J.L. and David, D.H. (2003). Attachment theory and research as a guide to psychotherapy practice. *Imagination, Cognition, and Personality*, **23**, 257–87.

Bornstein, R.F. and O'Neill, R.M. (1992). Perceptions of parents and psychopathology. *Journal of Nervous and Mental Disorders* **180**, 475–83.

Bowlby, J. (1973). *Attachment and Loss, Volume 2: Separation: anxiety and anger*. New York: Basic Books.

——(1977). The making and breaking of affectional bonds: I. Aetiology and psychopathology in light of attachment theory. *British Journal of Psychiatry* **130**, 201–10.

——(1982). *Attachment and Loss, Volume 1: Attachment* (2nd edn). New York: Basic Books.

Brennan, K.A. and Shaver, P.R. (1998). Attachment styles and personality disorders: their connections to each other and to parental divorce, parental death, and perceptions of parental caregiving. *Journal of Personality* **66**, 835–78.

Buchheim, A., Hörz, S., Rentrop, M., Doering, S. and Fischer-Kern, M. (2012, September). *Attachment status before and after one year of transference focused psychotherapy (TFP) versus therapy as usual (TAU) in patients with borderline personality disorder*. Paper presented at the 2nd Meeting of the International Congress on Borderline Personality Disorder and Allied Disorders, Amsterdam, The Netherlands.

Clarkin, J.F., Widiger, T.A., Frances, A.J., Hurt, F.W. and Gilmore, M. (1983). Prototypic typology and the borderline personality disorder. *Journal of Abnormal Psychology* **92**, 263–75.

Clarkin, J.F., Yeomans, F. and Kernberg, O.F. (2006). *Psychotherapy of Borderline Personality*. New York: Wiley.

Crowell, J.A., Fraley, R.C. and Shaver, P.R. (1999). Measurement of individual differences in adolescent and adult attachment. In J. Cassidy and P.R. Shaver (eds), *Handbook of Attachment: Theory, research, and clinical applications*, pp. 434–65. New York: Guilford Press.

Daniel, S.I.F. (2006). Adult attachment patterns and individual psychotherapy: a review. *Clinical Psychology Review* **26**, 968–84.

Diamond, D., Stovall-McClough, C., Clarkin, J.F. and Levy, K.N. (2003). Patient–therapist attachment in the treatment of borderline personality disorder. *Bulletin of the Menninger Clinic* **67** (3: Special Issue), 227–59.

Dozier, M. (1990). Attachment organisation and treatment use for adults with serious psychopathological disorders. *Development and Psychopathology* **2**, 47–60.

Dozier, M., Lomax, L., Tyrrell, C.L. and Lee, S. (2001). The challenge of treatment for clients with dismissing states of mind. *Attachment and Human Development* **3**, 62–76.

Eames, V. and Roth, A. (2000). Patient attachment orientation and the early working alliance: a study of patient and therapist reports of alliance quality and ruptures. *Psychotherapy Research* **10**, 421–34.

Fonagy, P., Steele, M., Steele, H., Leigh, T., Kennedy, R., Mattoon, G. and Target, M. (1995). Attachment, the reflective self, and borderline states: the predictive specificity of the Adult Attachment Interview and pathological emotional development. In S. Goldberg, R. Muir and J. Kerr (eds), *Attachment Theory: social, developmental and clinical perspectives*, pp. 233–78. New York: Analytic Press.

Fonagy, P., Leigh, T., Steele, M., Steele, H., Kennedy, R., Mattoon, G. and Gerber, A. (1996). The relation of attachment status, psychiatric classification, and response to psychotherapy. *Journal of Consulting and Clinical Psychology* **64**, 22–31.

Fraley, R.C. (2002). Attachment stability from infancy to adulthood: meta-analysis and dynamic modeling of developmental mechanisms. *Personality and Social Psychology Review* **6**, 123–51.

George, C., Kaplan, N. and Main, M. (1985). The Berkeley Adult Attachment Interview. Unpublished manuscript, Department of Psychology, University of California, Berkeley, CA.

Grossmann, K.E., Grossmann, K. and Waters, E. (2005). *Attachment from Infancy to Adulthood: the major longitudinal studies*. New York: Guilford Press.

Gunderson, J.G. and Lyons-Ruth, K. (2008). BPD's interpersonal hypersensitivity phenotype: a gene-environment-developmental model. *Journal of Personality Disorders* **22**, 22–41.

Hamilton, C.E. (2000). Continuity and discontinuity of attachment from infancy through adolescence. *Child Development* **71**, 690–4.

Hazan, C. and Shaver, P. (1987). Romantic love conceptualized as an attachment process. *Journal of Personality and Social Psychology* **52**, 511–24.

Hoermann, S., Clarkin, J.F., Hull, J.W. and Fertuck, E.A. (2004). Attachment dimensions as predictors of medical hospitalisations in individuals with DSM-IV Cluster B personality disorders. *Journal of Personality Disorders* **18**, 595–603.

Horney, K. (1945). *Our Inner Conflicts*. New York: Norton.

——(1950). *Neurosis and Human Growth*. New York: Norton.

Johnson, S. (1996). *The Practice of Emotionally Focused Marital Therapy: creating connection*. New York: Brunner/Mazel.

Kobak, R.R. and Sceery, A. (1988). Attachment in late adolescence: working models, affect regulation and representations of self and others. *Child Development* **59**, 135–46.

Levy, K.N. (1993, May). Adult attachment styles and personality pathology. New research presented at the 1993 American Psychiatric Association Annual Meeting, San Francisco, CA.

——(2005). The implications of attachment theory and research for understanding borderline personality disorder. *Development and Psychopathology* **17**, 959–86.

Levy, K.N. and Blatt, S.J. (1999). Attachment theory and psychoanalysis: further differentiation within insecure attachment patterns. *Psychoanalytic Inquiry*, **19**, 541–75.

Levy, K.N., Diamond, D., Yeomans, F.E., Clarkin, J.F. and Kernberg, O.F. (2007). Changes in attachment, reflection function, and object representation in the psychodynamic treatment of borderline personality disorder. Unpublished manuscript.

Levy, K.N., Ellison, W.D., Scott, L.N. and Bernecker, S.L. (2011). Attachment style. In J.C. Norcross (ed.), *Psychotherapy Relationships that Work: evidence-based responsiveness*, pp. 377–401. New York: Oxford University Press.

Levy, K.N., Kelly, K.M., Meehan, K.B., Reynoso, J.S., Clarkin, J.F., Lenzenweger, M.F. and Kernberg, O.F. (2006). Change in attachment patterns and reflective function in the treatment of borderline personality disorder with transference focused psychotherapy. *Journal of Consulting and Clinical Psychology* **74**, 1027–40.

Levy, K.N., Temes, C.M., Critchfield, K. and Nelson, S.M. (2012). Differential use of psychotherapy treatment by young adults as a function of sex, ethnicity, religion, and adult attachment style. Manuscript in preparation.

Lewis, M., Feiring, C. and Rosenthal, S. (2000). Attachment over time. *Child Development* **71**, 707–20.

Livesley, W.J., Schroeder, M.L. and Jackson, D.N. (1990). Dependent personality disorder and attachment problems. *Journal of Personality Disorders* **4**, 232–40.

Mallinckrodt, B., Porter, M.J. and Kivlighan, D.M. (2005). Client attachment to therapist, depth of in-session exploration, and object relations in brief psychotherapy. *Psychotherapy: Theory, Research, Practice, Training* **42**, 85–100.

McGlashan, T.H. (1986). Schizotypal personality disorder: the Chestnut Lodge follow-up study IV. Long-term follow-up perspectives. *Archives of General Psychiatry* **43**, 329–34.

Meyer, B. and Pilkonis, P.A. (2005). An attachment model of personality disorders. In M.F. Lenzenweger and J.F. Clarkin (eds), *Major Theories of Personality Disorders*, pp. 231–81. New York: Guilford Press.

Meyer, B., Pilkonis, P.A., Proiette, J.M., Heape, C.L. and Egan, M. (2001). Attachment styles and personality disorders as predictors of symptom course. *Journal of Personality Disorders* **15**, 371–89.

Millon, T. (1992). Millon Clinical Multiaxial Inventory: I & II. *Journal of Counseling & Development* **70**(3), 421–6.

Modestin, J. (1987). Quality of interpersonal relationships: the most characteristic BPD criterion. *Comprehensive Psychiatry* **28**, 397–402.

Obegi, J.H. and Berant, E. (eds) (2009). *Attachment Theory and Research in Clinical Work with Adults.* New York and London: Guilford Press.

Riggs, S.A. and Jacobvitz, D. (2002). Expectant parents' representations of early attachment relationships: associations with mental health and family history. *Journal of Consulting and Clinical Psychology* **70**, 195–204.

Rosenstein, D.S. and Horowitz, H.A. (1996). Adolescent attachment and psychopathology. *Journal of Consulting and Clinical Psychology* **64**(2), 244.

Samstag, L.W., Muran, J.C., Wachtel, P.L., Slade, A. and Safran, J.D. (2008). Evaluating negative process: a comparison of working alliance, interpersonal behavior, and narrative coherency among three psychotherapy outcome conditions. *American Journal of Psychotherapy* **62**, 165–94.

Satterfield, W.A. and Lyddon, W.J. (1998). Client attachment and perceptions of the working alliance with counselor trainees. *Journal of Counseling Psychology* **42**, 187–9.

Shaver, P., Hazan, C. and Bradshaw, D. (1988). Love as attachment. In R.J. Sternberg and M.L. Barnes (eds), *The Psychology of Love*, pp. 68–99. New Haven, CT: Yale University Press.

Shaver, P.R., Belsky, J. and Brennan, K.A. (2000). The adult attachment interview and self-reports of romantic attachment: associations across domains and methods. *Personal Relationships* **7**, 25–43.

Sheldon, A.E.R. and West, M. (1990). Attachment pathology and low social skills in avoidant personality disorder: an exploratory study. *Canadian Journal of Psychiatry* **35**, 596–9.

Slade, A. (1999). Attachment theory and research: implications for the theory and practice of individual psychotherapy with adults. In J. Cassidy, and P.R. Shaver (eds), *Handbook of Attachment: theory, research, and clinical applications*, pp. 575–94. New York: Guilford Press.

Steele, H. and Steele, M. (2008). *Clinical Applications of the Adult Attachment Interview.* New York: Guilford Press.

Strauss, B., Kirchmann, H., Eckert, J., Lobo-Drost, A., Marquet, A., Papenhausen, R. and Höger, D. (2006). Attachment characteristics and treatment outcome following inpatient psychotherapy: results of a multisite study. *Psychotherapy Research* **16**, 579–94.

van IJzendoorn, M.H., Feldbrugge, J.T.T.M., Derks, J., Ruiter, C.D., Verhagen, M., Philipse, M., Staak, C. van der and Riksen Walraven, J.(1997). Attachment representation of personality disordered criminal offenders. *American Journal of Orthopsychiatry* **67**, 449–59.

Vogel, D.L. and Wei, M. (2005). Adult attachment and help-seeking intent: the mediating roles of psychological distress and perceived social support. *Journal of Counseling Psychology* **52**, 347–57.

Waters, E., Merrick, S., Treboux, D., Crowell, J. and Albersheim, L. (2000). Attachment security in infancy and early adulthood: a twenty-year longitudinal study. *Child Development* **71**, 684–9.

Chapter 8

Disorganised attachment in the pathogenesis and the psychotherapy of borderline personality disorder

Giovanni Liotti

Controlled studies suggest that attachment insecurity is a risk factor for Borderline Personality Disorder (BPD), as it is for other mental disorders (for reviews, see Agrawal *et al.* 2004; and Dozier, Stovall-McClough and Albus 2008). Disorganisation of early attachment and associated adult states of mind have been studied in relation to the pathogenesis of and psychotherapy for BPD more than other dimensions and types of attachment insecurity. Quite a number of clinical and empirical research studies suggest that, although it is not a specific risk factor for BPD, attachment disorganisation plays an important role in borderline psychopathology (e.g. Bateman and Fonagy 2004; Buchheim and George 2011; Dozier, Stovall-McClough and Albus 2008; Holmes 2004; Howell 2008; Levy, Beeney and Temes 2011; Liotti 2007, 2011a, 2011b; Lyons-Ruth *et al.* 2007; Morse *et al.* 2009; Steele and Siever 2010). These studies support the idea that the fundamental features of BPD can be explained by a developmental model based on attachment disorganisation. Although we lack conclusive research evidence for the hypothesis that the developmental pathways leading to the disorder begin with early attachment disorganisation in the majority of BPD cases (Levy 2005), two controlled studies suggest that this may indeed be the case (Carlson, Egeland and Sroufe 2009; Lyons-Ruth *et al.* 2007).

Disorganisation of infant attachment and its developmental sequels

About 80 per cent of infants' attachments to the caregivers in low-risk samples can be reliably classified, in the Strange Situation procedure (Ainsworth *et al.* 1978), into three main organised patterns (secure, insecure-avoidant, insecure-resistant). Most of the remaining attachments are characterised by a lack of behavioural and attentional organisation: they are called disorganised attachments. In samples of families at high risk for psychopathology, the percentage of disorganised attachments may be as high as 80 per cent (Lyons-Ruth and Jacobvitz 2008).

Infants with disorganised attachment manifest bizarre and/or contradictory behaviour when reuniting with their caregiver after a brief separation: bizarre behaviour such as freezing, hiding or head-banging, and contradictory behaviour such as trying to approach the attachment figure with head averted or interrupting abruptly a beginning approach to the caregiver by changing direction or collapsing to the ground (Main and Solomon 1990). Unresolved experiences of losses and traumas in the caregiver's Adult Attachment Interview (AAI: Hesse 2008) are a frequent precursor of disorganised attachment in the infants, and are significantly less frequent in the caregivers of infants with organised attachment patterns (for a meta-analysis of research on this topic, see Van IJzendoorn, Schuengel and Bakermans-Kranenburg 1999). An important mediating factor between the caregiver's unresolved state of mind and the infant's attachment disorganisation is that the infant's fear is increased or at least not soothed in the attachment–caregiving interactions. Parental behaviour that is either frightened and indirectly frightening, or aggressive and straightforwardly frightening to the infant has been described in studies of infant attachment disorganisation (Main and Hesse 1990; Schuengel, Bakermans-Kranenburg and Van IJzendoorn 1999). Other adverse influences in caregivers' past attachment experiences have also been evidenced as antecedents of infant attachment disorganisation. These antecedents of early attachment disorganisation are expressed through hostile and helpless states of mind concerning the attachment–caregiving interaction (Lyons-Ruth et al. 2003), and through 'abdication' – assessed with the Caregiving Interview (Solomon and George 2011) – of the responsibility of caregiving in the face of the infant's expression of attachment needs.

Although the type of interaction between the infant and the caregiver plays a key role in infant attachment disorganisation, genetic influences exert a moderating influence (Bakermans-Kranenburg and Van IJzendoorn 2007; Gervai 2009). Attachment may influence the expression of genes related to dysregulation of emotions and impulses (attachment security inhibits the expression of these genes), and conversely these genes increase the risk of developing attachment disorganisation in the presence of fearful and severely misattuned caregiver–child interactions. Given the existing evidence that genetic and temperamental factors play a role, together with attachment experiences, in impulse regulation (Zimmerman, Mohr and Spangler 2009) and in the psychopathology of BPD, the gene-environment interaction in infant attachment disorganisation may contribute to reconciling genetic and attachment-based theories of BPD.

Clinical observations and data from controlled research studies converge in supporting the hypothesis that infant attachment disorganisation is a risk factor for setting into motion dissociative mental processes able to influence cognitive and emotional development (Dutra et al. 2009; Hesse et al. 2003; Liotti 1992, 2004, 2011a; Lyons-Ruth 2003; Main and Morgan 1996; Ogawa et al. 1997). Two longitudinal controlled studies (Dutra et al. 2008; Ogawa et al. 1997) provide robust evidence that children and adolescents who had disorganised attachment in infancy are more prone to dissociative mental processes than their peers who have histories of organised early attachments. Thus it can be argued that dissociated (i.e. multiple, dramatic and non-integrated) representations of self-with-other characterise the Internal Working Model (IWM: Bowlby 1969) of disorganised attachment. The rationale for this hypothesis may be summarised as follows.

An attachment figure who is neglecting, helpless, frightened, or hostile and straightforwardly frightening to the infant, creates a situation in which the source of potential comfort is also, at the same time, the source of fear, even when this caregiver's behaviour is not obvious maltreatment. This situation has been called 'fright without solution' (Main and Hesse 1990), because infants cannot find relief from fear either in flying from the caregiver or in approaching her or him. The experience of fright without solution in infant attachment interactions can be regarded as an early relational trauma (Schore 2009) that causes dissociation among the first representations of self-with-other. The construction of the multiple, dramatic, and non-integrated representations of self and a single attachment figure that characterise the disorganised IWM can be explained as a consequence of these early dissociative processes (Liotti 1992, 2004, 2006, 2009).

In a longitudinal study, the multiple and non-integrated representations of self-with-others that stem from these attachment–caregiving experiences have been shown to mediate between early disorganised attachment and adult BPD symptoms (Carlson, Egeland and Sroufe 2009). This is in keeping with the findings of a study suggesting that 'painful incoherence' (rather than other features such as mood instability) is at the core of BPD symptomatology (Meares *et al.* 2011). The clinical relevance of understanding the developmental trajectory leading from disorganised attachment to 'painful incoherence' and to BPD justifies theoretically informed speculations on the features of the contradictory and non-integrated representations stemming from the disorganised IWM. Liotti (1999, 2004) suggested that they are akin to the three basic roles of the 'drama triangle' (Karpman 1968): the powerful rescuer, the equally powerful but malevolent persecutor, and the powerless victim. Being at least potentially available and willing to help and comfort the infant, parents and other caregivers are perceived by children as rescuers. At the same time, when they are neglecting, subtly hostile, or prone to episodes of aggression, they are perceived as persecutors. Simultaneously, because they express their helplessness, fear and suffering (caused by their own unresolved traumatic memories) while taking care of their infants, the parents of disorganised children are perceived as victims. These reciprocally incompatible representational prototypes are the base for construing the behaviour of self and others during later attachment interactions. Being constructed during the first two years of life, these representations pertain to the non-verbal domain of inner representations – that is, they are 'sub-symbolic' (Bucci 1997) and operate at the implicit level of self-knowledge (Amini *et al.* 1996). In other words, they are aspects of the ongoing implicit relational knowing that characterises the early phases of personality development and persists throughout the lifespan (Lyons-Ruth 1998, 1999). Therefore, throughout the developmental years the multiple and non-integrated representations of the self and of the single caregiver manifest themselves in communication as intersubjective enactments rather than as explicit verbalised structures of memory (Ginot 2007, 2009). No synthesis of them in semantic memory and in fully conscious narratives is therefore possible, at least during childhood. The different, incompatible, simultaneous representations of self-with-other of the disorganised IWM tend to remain compartmentalised throughout the early phases of personality development. Compartmentalisation, it should be remembered, is one of the two basic aspects of dissociation (Holmes *et al.* 2005), the other being detachment (expressed mainly in the symptoms of depersonalisation).

The compartmentalised representations of disorganised attachment, together with the dramatic re-experiencing of fear without solution during later attachment interaction, tend to hamper the higher (conscious and regulatory) mental functions during personality development, so that mentalisation deficits, emotional dysregulation and impulsivity may also follow infant attachment disorganisation (Bateman and Fonagy 2004). It should be emphasised that both dissociation among representations of self-with-other and mentalisation deficits tend to occur during the experience of attachment needs and wishes rather than in moments where interpersonal behaviour is motivated by systems different from attachment (e.g. the competitive, the sexual, the caregiving or the cooperative systems: Liotti, Cortina and Farina 2008; Liotti and Gilbert 2011).

Remarkably, disorganised attachment in infancy develops into rigid, controlling behaviour in middle childhood (Lyons-Ruth and Jacobvitz 2008; Solomon, George and De Jong 1995; Van IJzendoorn, Schuengel and Bakermans-Kranenburg 1999). These controlling strategies seem to compensate for disorganisation in the child–parent interactions: they allow for organised interpersonal exchanges with the caregivers, thus reducing the likelihood of dissociative processes during these exchanges (Liotti 2011a, 2011b).

There is evidence that infants disorganised in their attachments can either become bossy children who strive to obtain dominance by exerting aggressive competitiveness toward the caregiver (controlling-punitive strategy), or become children who invert the attachment relationship and display precocious caregiving toward their parents (controlling-caregiving strategy). A major cause of the controlling-caregiving strategy is the relationship with a vulnerable, helpless parent who encourages the child to invert the normal direction of the attachment–caregiving strategy. A parent who perceives the child as powerful and evil may be one particularly malignant condition for the development of a controlling-punitive strategy (for examples, see Hesse *et al.* 2003). The controlling strategies collapse in the face of events (e.g. traumas, pain, threats of separation) that stimulate intensely and durably the child's attachment system (Hesse *et al.* 2003). During the phases of collapse of the controlling strategies, the child's thought and behaviour suggest that dissociative processes are at work, presumably because of the reactivation of the disorganised IWM (Hesse *et al.* 2003; Liotti 2004, 2011a, 2011b, 2012). It is noteworthy that children with a controlling-punitive strategy are more prone than other children to develop externalising disorders characterised by impulse dyscontrol, while children with a controlling-caregiving strategy tend to develop internalising disorders, characterised by anxiety and depression (Moss *et al.* 2006). It can be hypothesised that a controlling-punitive strategy mediates between infant attachment disorganisation and adult cluster B ('dramatic') personality disorders including BPD, while a controlling-caregiving strategy may be a risk factor for other personality disorders, anxiety disorders and mood disorders.

Research studies conducted with the AAI or with self-report measures of attachment patterns in adults suggest that adult states of mind linked to infant attachment disorganisation are significantly related to a variety of adult mental disorders (Bakerman-Kranenburg and Van IJzendoorn 2009; Dozier, Stovall-McClough and Albus 2008; Levy 2005; Lyons-Ruth and Jacobvitz 2008). It is important to remark that the adult states of mind linked to attachment disorganisation have been called different names according to the different methods for coding the interviews used in the assessment, or according to different self-report measures of adult attachment. The domain of attachment disorganisation comprises AAI adult states of mind classified either 'unresolved as to attachment traumas and losses' (U: Hesse 2008) or 'hostile and helpless' (HH: Lyons-Ruth et al. 2003). Moreover, two other AAI states of mind, called 'preoccupied with traumatic events' (E3: Hesse 2008) and 'cannot classify' (CC: Hesse 2008), arguably are, respectively, the lower and the higher extremes in the dimension of caregiving behaviour related to infant attachment disorganisation. The features of the CC state of mind, in particular, closely parallel those typical of BPD (multiple, contradictory, incompatible and unintegrated working models, often leading to chaotic and mood-dependent interpersonal behaviour). Thus, three AAI codes (E3, CC and HH) should be considered together with the code U when reading reviews of AAI studies on the relation between BPD and infant attachment disorganisation. It is also noteworthy that some of the older AAI studies of borderline patients (e.g. many of those reviewed in Agrawal et al. 2004) did not code the AAI transcripts for the possible E3, U, CC or HH classifications, because these codes were introduced and came to be more widely used only relatively late in AAI research. Finally, it should be noted that other states of mind related to attachment, assessed with self-report measures, may also be related to the domain of disorganisation. For instance, the 'fearful' attachment style, assessed in adults through self-report questionnaires, that is statistically linked to borderline features (Choi-Kain et al. 2009; Scott, Levy and Pincus 2009), may be one expression in adults of the experience of fright without solution that characterises infant attachment disorganisation.

In summary, it is reasonable to conclude that infant disorganised attachment may lead to adaptational vulnerabilities (e.g. a controlling-punitive strategy developed in middle childhood) which, especially as a consequence of further traumatic experiences, can cause BPD. However, disorganised attachment can also be an antecedent of other disorders (Dozier, Stovall-McClough and Albus 2008; Levy 2005). Different mechanisms must be involved in the developmental pathways leading from infant disorganised attachment to other types of adaptational vulnerabilities which in turn are linked to adult disorders different from BPD.

Psychopathology of BPD: a model based on attachment disorganisation

The presence of a disorganised IWM may help to explain the genesis of the fundamental aspects of BPD:

- Poorly integrated (split or dissociated) ego states and the lack of a stable sense of self, involving dissociative processes, is conceptualised as a frequent developmental sequel of the disorganised IWM, especially when later interactions between the child and the family members have been traumatic, as reported by a majority of BPD patients (Carlson, Egeland and Sroufe 2009; Levy, Beeney and Temes 2011).
- Feelings of emptiness, or dissociative blank spells (a subtype of depersonalisation), and a fortiori clear-cut dissociative symptoms can also be explained as a consequence of this dissociative tendency.
- Self-injurious behaviour may be one way of trying to cope with the experience of emptiness and depersonalisation through self-inflicted bodily pain, as Linehan (1993) has convincingly argued.
- Unstable and intense interpersonal relationships, affective lability, impulsivity and the typical bursts of rage can be understood as a consequence of the deficits in mentalising capacities and in emotional regulation – deficits that seem to be characteristic developmental sequels of infant attachment disorganisation (Levy *et al.* 2005).
- Chronic fears of abandonment, intolerance of aloneness, and abnormal sensitivity to feeling intruded upon by well-meaning others, accompanied by mentalisation deficits, may stem from the underlying disorganised IWM (Bateman and Fonagy 2004).

Consideration of the dynamics of the controlling strategies that typically follow infant attachment disorganisation offers potential insights into the immediate interpersonal antecedents of the most disturbing symptoms of BPD patients, and into the threats to the therapeutic alliance that typically plague their psychotherapeutic relationships. The controlling strategies keep a brake on the activation of the attachment system through the activation of interpersonal motivational systems different from the attachment system (notably the ranking system and the caregiving system: Liotti 2011a, 2011b).[1] Thus the interpersonal behaviour and the inner experience of self and others can achieve a sufficient degree of coherence and organisation, even if the cost is a tendency to ranking competitiveness (similar to that observed in narcissistic or antisocial personality) or to compulsive nurturance (similar to that observed in dependent personality). However, events that strongly stimulate the attachment system – such as traumas, separation from the attachment figures and the formation of new affectional bonds – cause the collapse of the controlling strategies and the surfacing of the dissociative processes inherent to the disorganised IWM (Liotti 2011a, 2011b).

On the basis of this hypothesis on the developmental psychopathology of BPD, the most disturbing symptoms (emptiness, dissociative experiences, self-injurious behaviour, fear of abandonment, outbursts of rage) and the typical interpersonal problems linked to split representations of self and significant others will appear or become particularly intense during experiences that involve the activation of the attachment system: the formation of new affectional bonds (including the bond to the psychotherapist), traumas or events reminiscent of past traumas, losses, or impending separations from attachment figures. The dynamics that underpin the typical interpersonal difficulties of borderline patients are linkable both to the activation of the disorganised attachment system (with the multiple and dissociated representations of self and other as rescuer, persecutor and victim), and to the effort of regaining a measure of organisation through the use of a controlling-punitive strategy. The knowledge of these dynamics may be useful to the psychotherapist facing an outburst of unjustified dominant anger in the therapeutic relationship with a borderline patient after a series of sessions where the patient was apparently feeling comfortable in the therapeutic dialogue or even idealising the therapist (for clinical vignettes, see Liotti 2011a, 2012). The clinician may hypothesise that feelings of emotional closeness to the therapist primed the patient's wishes to be helped and soothed, and that these attachment feelings in turn activated a disorganised IWM, with the concomitant experiences of fear without solution and dissociation between dramatic compartmentalised representations of self-with-other (i.e. the role-relationships between rescuer, persecutor and victim of the drama triangle begun to surface in the patient's consciousness as ways of construing the therapeutic relationship). The patient may then have tried to regain control over the relationship and over his or her own inner experiences by resorting to the controlling-punitive strategies he or she developed since childhood to keep a brake on attachment motivations.

This aspect of the psychopathological consequences of early attachment disorganisation and later attachment traumas is usefully captured by the hypothesis that borderline patients, and more generally patients with disorders related to developmental complex trauma (Classen *et al*. 2006; Courtois and Ford 2009), develop opposite and simultaneous phobias of inner feelings related to attachment motives, such as feelings of emotional closeness and feelings of impending losses in the relationship with significant others (Van der Hart, Nijenhuis and Steele 2006). These otherwise normal (and, as far as emotional closeness is concerned, much desired) feelings become, for the borderline patient, forerunners of utter disorganisation of inner experience, of dissociative mental processes and of the surfacing consciousness of fragmented, irrational and dramatic representations of self and others as frightening persecutors and helpless victims. These patients become therefore phobic of such inner forerunners. Psychophysiology (Rockliff *et al*. 2008) and neuroimaging (Longe *et al*. 2009) studies have evidenced the body and brain correlates of the somehow paradoxical fear of much desired emotional closeness and compassionate feelings. Recently developed self-report measures of fear of compassionate feelings provide evidence of the beliefs and attitudes related to the phobia of attachment closeness (Gilbert *et al*. 2011).

Contributions of the attachment-based model to the psychotherapy of BPD

First and foremost, the model of BPD based on the knowledge of attachment disorganisation and its developmental sequels suggests that the clinician should carefully monitor the activation of the attachment system in the patient during psychotherapy. Such activation, if not dealt with properly and promptly, predicts difficulties and dilemmas in the therapeutic relationship that may threaten the alliance and even cause premature interruption of the treatment (Holmes 2004; Liotti 2007, 2011a; Liotti, Cortina and Farina 2008). Especially at the beginning of the treatment, strong and long-lasting activation of the patient's still disorganised attachment system within the clinical exchange may foster unbearable phobias of attachment feelings and dissociative processes. It can also hinder the use of mentalising or metacognitive abilities (Liotti and Gilbert 2011; Prunetti *et al.* 2008).

Different approaches to the problem of dealing with the dilemmas created by the activation of a disorganised IWM of attachment within the therapeutic relationship can be devised by exploiting strategies and techniques of different models of BPD psychotherapy, even if these models do not always consider, at least explicitly, attachment dynamics. For instance, it can be argued that Dialectic Behaviour Therapy (DBT: Linehan 1993) may be instrumental in dealing with the activation of the disorganised IWM in the therapeutic relationship, thanks to the careful attention paid both to the patient's behaviour indicative of feeling the unbearable emotional closeness to the therapist (phobia of attachment closeness), and to the opposite behaviours suggesting fear of the therapist's emotional distance or fear of separation from the therapist (phobia of attachment loss). The DBT therapist is trained to respond to each of these opposite attitudes by dialectically shifting from taking prudent emotional distance from patients, and offering them empathic closeness through validating their emotions or contrasting their tendency to withdraw from the treatment (for a treatise of the compatibility of Linehan's dialectic model with an attachment-based approach to BPD, see Liotti 2007).

Some approaches to dealing with the troublesome consequences of the activation of a disorganised IWM in the therapeutic relationship straightforwardly strive to change it. In compassionate mind training (Gilbert 2009) patients are trained in the ability to imagine idealised soothing others to cope with inner sufferings through compassionate feelings, rather than with phobic avoidance or with punitive aggressiveness directed at others or at the self. In therapies inspired by the theory of structural dissociation of the personality, the same goal of relinquishing both phobic avoidance of soothing and punitive aggressiveness in response to inner suffering is pursued by addressing the opposite simultaneous phobias of attachment closeness and attachment loss through a sort of cognitive-behavioural desensitisation approach (Van der Hart, Nijenhuis and Steele 2006). In schema focused therapy (SFP: Giesen-Bloo *et al.* 2006; Young, Klosko, and Weishaar 2003) the correction of the patients' IWM of attachment is achieved through 'reparenting' by providing corrective relational experiences. Other approaches to the therapeutic revision of patients' disorganised IWMs rely on enhancing patients' capacity to reflect on inner experiences (mentalisation based treatment, MBT: Bateman and Fonagy 2004) and on working with the transference (Yeomans, Clarkin and Kernberg 2002). Indeed, there is emerging evidence that transference focused psychotherapy (TFP) of BPD can change the patient's state of mind concerning attachment in the direction of more organised and more secure patterns (Levy *et al*. 2006).

We can assume that attachment theory informs explicitly or implicitly most current models of BPD psychotherapy, and that there are many different ways of addressing the problems created by a disorganised IWM, in the psychotherapy relationship and any other significant relationships in which borderline patients are engaged. An attachment-based model of BPD, moreover, provides a particularly interesting background for understanding a shared feature of the two diverse types of BPD psychotherapy: DBT (Linehan 1993) and MBT (Bateman and Fonagy 2004). This shared feature is the exploiting of interventions provided by at least two different therapists in at least two separate, albeit integrated, settings. The complex interpersonal dynamics created by parallel integrated interventions may be crucial in explaining why two otherwise so different types of intervention are so remarkably similar in their capacity of reducing the risk of premature interruption of the treatment – a well-known major hindrance in any treatment of BPD.

The benefits of having two therapists (e.g. an individual therapist and a group therapist) working in two parallel and integrated settings may be explained, according to the model of the disorder based on attachment disorganisation. When the patient is guided by an IWM of disorganised attachment in construing the therapist's behaviour, the therapeutic relationship may become so unbearably dramatic, changeable and complex for both partners that serious ruptures of the therapeutic alliance cannot be avoided, or repaired before the patient drops out of the treatment. However, the interaction with two therapists in two separate but integrated settings – 'integrated' means here that the three partners, patient, first therapist and second therapist know, and as far as the two therapists are concerned understand in a similar way, what happens in each setting – prevents overly intense or protracted activation of the attachment system in the patient (Liotti 2004, 2007; Liotti, Cortina and Farina 2008). The contention of attachment theory that explains why having two therapists (working as 'one team': Bateman and Fonagy 2004) may prevent the activation of a disorganised IWM in the therapeutic relationship, or at least allow for a repair of the ruptures in the therapeutic alliance contingent upon it, was originally called 'monotropy' (Bowlby 1958; see also Ainsworth 1982). Monotropy refers to the observation that although from childhood any person can become attached to more than one person, and although the hierarchy of preference for the various attachment figures can change, he or she is biased to be attached especially to one figure at any given moment, so that the other persons in the hierarchy become subsidiary or secondary attachment figures (Bowlby 1969/1982). The implication of monotropy for understanding how a patient becomes attached to two therapists in a parallel integrated treatment is that the patient's attachment system is likely to be active more often and more intensely during the clinical exchanges with one therapist (let us call her or him X) than with those with the other (Y). The untoward consequences of the activation of the disorganised IWM during the clinical dialogue with X (collapses in the metacognitive abilities, surfacing of poorly explicable fear in an until then positive interaction, blank spells and other dissociative symptoms, attempts at re-establishing control over the interaction through punitive strategies) may then be better explored and coped with during the clinical exchanges with Y. Just because the patient's emotional-motivational state is less influenced by the attached system during the dialogue with him or her, Y is in a much better and safer position than X to address the patient's capacity for self-reflection (less undermined by the surfacing of the disorganised IWM than it is during the exchanges with X), and therefore to explore therapeutically fears of attachment and of attachment loss, or the meaning of aggressive and punitive attitudes.

The arguments supporting the idea that deficits in mentalisation ability and in emotion regulation in borderline patients are less trait-like than state-dependent, and that they depend on the activation of attachment (care-seeking) motives, have been summarised by Liotti and Gilbert (2011). A detailed account of other reasons besides monotropy that may explain, in terms of attachment theory, the usefulness of parallel integrated settings in the treatment of BPD may be found in Liotti, Cortina and Farina 2008. Here, space allows only for some summarising and concluding remarks regarding any approach to the psychotherapy of BPD informed by attachment theory and research.

First, such approaches justify on theoretical grounds the importance of paying continuing and close attention from the beginning of the clinical exchange, and even more than in the psychotherapy of any other disorder, to the dynamics of the therapeutic alliance, that is a primary requisite for any successful treatment of BPD (as it is for all the complex trauma-related disorders: see e.g. Courtois, Ford and Cloitre 2009; Van der Hart, Nijenhuis and Steele 2006). The theoretical justification provided by an attachment informed approach is particularly clear: BPD is mainly a disorder grounded in attachment trauma, and the activation of the attachment system in the therapeutic relationship predicts the re-enactment of attachment-related traumatic memories. The more efficient way of limiting the consequences of such activation is to interact with the patient in line with the co-operative motivational system, by building up a therapeutic alliance from the very beginning of treatment (e.g. through careful contracting, as in DBT: Linehan 1993).

Second, any therapeutic manoeuvre aimed at correcting the disorganised IWM, such as working on traumatic attachment memories and phobias of attachment feelings, and providing transference interpretations, should follow the establishment, stabilisation and consolidation of the alliance, and never put it at risk of ruptures. Even the therapist's empathic comments, and those aimed at fostering the patient's mentalising abilities, should be carefully titrated and worded so as to avoid as far as possible the activation of the patient's attachment system, especially in the first phase of the treatment (Prunetti *et al.* 2008).

Third, while aiming at increasing the patient's mentalising abilities and her or his competencies in emotional self-regulation, the therapist should acknowledge, tolerate and respect the possibility that borderline patients have learned to exercise these abilities and competencies through controlling strategies involving either punitive aggressiveness or compulsive care-giving. Any comment of the therapist, in the first phase of the treatment, on the inappropriateness of these attitudes in the present context may create a situation that, from the patient's perspective, is intrinsically contradictory: to be invited to give up their only possibility of tolerating emotional closeness and impending attachment feelings without losing the ability of mentalising or of regulating attachment emotions, and at the same time be invited to mentalise and regulate their affects.

Fourth, as a consequence of all the above considerations, the therapist should be aware that only the prolonged experience of an alternative, secure and rewarding way of relating, based on the cooperative exchanges typical of the therapeutic alliance, can allow borderline patients to reflect on the interpersonal dynamics based on the attachment system and thus begin to explore new and more secure ways of expressing attachment needs and feelings, and of responding to those expressed by significant others.

If readers find that features of the attachment-based approach to treatment are compatible with the main strategies and prescriptions of other models – DBT, MBT, TFP, SFP – then the main aim of this chapter will have been achieved.

Note

1   An outlook on how the different motivational systems selected by evolutionary processes (caregiving, social ranking, sexual bonding and egalitarian cooperation), that alternate normally with attachment (care-seeking) in regulating human interpersonal interactions, may show up in verbal communication during clinical exchanges is provided by Fassone *et al.* (2012). Among these systems, the care-giving and the ranking systems play a key role in the controlling strategies, while the cooperative system is crucial in intersubjective egalitarian exchanges (Cortina and Liotti 2010; Liotti and Gilbert 2011) and in the therapeutic alliance.

References

Agrawal, H., Gunderson, J., Holmes, B.M. and Lyons-Ruth, K. (2004). Attachment studies with borderline patients: A Review. *Harvard Review of Psychiatry* **12**, 94–104.

Ainsworth, M.D.S. (1982). Attachment: retrospect and prospect. In C.M. Parkes and J. Stevenson-Hinde (eds), *The Place of Attachment in Human Behavior*, pp. 3–30. London: Tavistock Publications.

Ainsworth, M.D.S., Blehar, M.C., Waters, E. and Wall, S. (1978). *Patterns of Attachment: a psychological study of the Strange Situation.* Hillsdale, NJ: Erlbaum.

Amini, F., Lewis, T., Lannon, R., Louie, A., Baumbacher, G., McGuinnes, T. and Zirker, E. (1996). Affect, attachment, memory: contributions toward psychobiologic integration. *Psychiatry* **59**, 213–39.

Bakermans-Kranenburg, M.J. and van IJzendoorn, M.H. (2007). Research review: genetic vulnerability or differential susceptibility in child development: the case of attachment. *Journal of Child Psychology and Psychiatry* **48**, 1160–73.

——(2009). The first 10,000 Adult Attachment Interviews: Distribution of adult attachment in clinical and non-clinical groups. *Attachment and Human Development* **11**, 223–6.

Bateman, A.W. and Fonagy, P. (2004). *Psychotherapy for Borderline Personality Disorder: mentalisation based treatment*. Oxford: Oxford University Press.

Bowlby, J. (1958). The nature of a child's tie to his mother. *International Journal of Psychoanalysis* **39**, 350–73.

——(1969/1982). *Attachment and Loss, Volume 1: Attachment*. London: Hogarth Press.

Bucci, W. (1997). *Psychoanalysis and Cognitive Science: a multiple code theory*. New York: Guilford Press.

Buchheim, A. and George, C. (2011). Attachment disorganisation in borderline personality disorder and anxiety disorder. In J. Solomon and C. George (eds), *Disorganized Attachment and Caregiving*, pp. 343–82. New York: Guilford Press.

Carlson, E.A., Egeland, B. and Sroufe, L.A. (2009). A prospective investigation of the development of borderline personality symptoms. *Development and Psychopathology* **21**, 1311–34.

Choi-Kain, L., Fitzmaurice, G.M., Zanarini, M.C., Laverdière, O. and Gunderson, J. (2009). The relationship between self-reported attachment styles, interpersonal dysfunction, and borderline personality disorder. *Journal of Nervous and Mental Disease* **197**, 816–82.

Classen, C.C., Pain, C., Field, N.P. and Woods, P. (2006). Post-traumatic personality disorder: a reformulation of complex post-traumatic stress disorder and borderline personality disorder. *Psychiatric Clinics of North America* **29**, 87–112.

Cortina, M. and Liotti, G. (2010). Attachment is about safety and protection, intersubjectivity is about sharing and social understanding: the relationships between attachment and intersubjectivity. *Psychoanalytic Psychology* **27**, 410–41.

Courtois, C.A. and Ford, J.D. (eds). (2009). *Treating Complex Traumatic Stress Disorder*. New York: Guilford Press.

Courtois, C.A., Ford, J.D. and Cloitre, M. (2009). Best practices in psychotherapy with adults. In C.A. Courtois and J.D. Ford (eds), *Treating Complex Traumatic Stress Disorder*, pp. 82–103. New York: Guilford Press.

Dozier, M., Stovall-McClough, K.C. and Albus, K.E. (2008). Attachment and psychopathology in adulthood. In J. Cassidy, and P.R. Shaver (eds), *Handbook of Attachment: theory, research and clinical applications*, 2nd edition, pp. 718–44. New York: Guilford Press.

Dutra, L., Bureau, J., Holmes, B., Lyubchik, A. and Lyons-Ruth, K. (2009). Quality of early care and childhood trauma: a prospective study of developmental pathways to dissociation. *Journal of Nervous and Mental Disease* **197**, 383–90.

Fassone, G., Valcella, F., Pallini, S., Scarcella, F., Tombolini, L., Ivaldi, A., Prunetti, E., Manaresi, F. and Liotti, G. (2012). Assessment of interpersonal motivation in transcripts (AIMIT): an inter- and intra-rater reliability study of a new method of detection of interpersonal motivational systems in psychotherapy. *Clinical Psychology and Psychotherapy* **19**, 224–34.

Gervai, J. (2009). Environmental and genetic influences on early attachment. *Child and Adolescent Psychiatry and Mental Health* **3**, 25.

Giesen-Bloo, J., Van Dyck, R., Spinhoven, P., Van Tilburg, W., Dirksen, C., Van Asselt, T., Kremers, I., Nadort, M. and Arntz, A. (2006). Outpatient psychotherapy for borderline personality disorder: randomized trial of schema-focused therapy vs. transference-focused psychotherapy. *Archives of General Psychiatry* **63**, 649–58.

Gilbert, P. (2009). Introducing compassion focused therapy. *Advances in Psychiatric Treatment* **15**, 199–208.

Gilbert, P., McEwan, K., Matos, M. and Rivis, A. (2011). Fear of compassion: development of a self-report measure. *Psychology and Psychotherapy* **84**, 239–55.

Ginot, E. (2007). Intersubjectivity and neuroscience: Understanding enactments and their therapeutic significance within emerging paradigms. *Psychoanalytic Psychology* **24**, 317–32.

——(2009). The empathic power of enactments: the link between neuropsychological processes and an expanded definition of empathy. *Psychoanalytic Psychology* **26**, 290–309.

Hesse, E. (2008). The Adult Attachment Interview: protocol, method of analysis, and empirical studies. In J. Cassidy and P.R. Shaver (eds), *Handbook of Attachment: theory, research and clinical applications*, 2nd edn, pp. 552–98. New York: Guilford Press.

Hesse, E., Main, M., Abrams, K.Y. and Rifkin, A. (2003). Unresolved states regarding loss or abuse can have 'second-generation' effects: disorganized, role-inversion and frightening ideation in the offspring of traumatized non-maltreating parents. In D.J. Siegeland and M.F. Solomon (eds), *Healing Trauma: attachment, mind, body and brain*, pp. 57–106. New York: Norton.

Holmes, J. (2004). Disorganized attachment and borderline personality disorder: a clinical perspective. *Attachment and Human Development* **6**, 181–90.

Holmes, E., Brown, R.J., Mansell, W., Fearon, R.P., Hunter, E., Frasquilho, F. and Oakley, D.A. (2005). Are there two qualitatively distinct forms of dissociation? A review and some clinical implications. *Clinical Psychology Review* **25**, 1–23.

Howell, E. (2008). From hysteria to chronic relational trauma disorder: the history of borderline personality disorder and its links with dissociation and psychosis. In A. Moskowitz, I. Schafer and M.J. Dorahy (eds), *Psychosis, Trauma and Dissociation*, pp. 105–16. Oxford: Wiley-Blackwell.

Karpman, S. (1968). Fairy tales and script drama analysis. *Transactional Analysis Bulletin* **7**, 39–43.

Levy, K.N. (2005). The implications of attachment theory and research for understanding borderline personality disorder. *Development and Psychopathology* **17**, 959–86.

Levy, K.N., Beeney, J.E. and Temes, C.M. (2011). Attachment and its vicissitudes in borderline personality disorder. *Current Psychiatry Reports* **13**, 50–9.

Levy, K.N., Meehan, K.B., Reynoso, J., Lenzenweger, M., Clarkin, J.F. and Kernberg, O.F. (2005). The relation of reflective function to neurocognitive functioning in patients with borderline personality disorder. *Journal of the American Psychoanalytic Association* **53**, 1305–9.

Levy, K.N., Meehan, K.B., Kelly, K.M., Reynoso, J., Weber, M., Clarkin, J.F. and Kernberg, O.F. (2006). Change in attachment patterns and reflective function in a randomized control trial of transference-focused psychotherapy for borderline personality disorder. *Journal of Consulting and Clinical Psychology* **74**, 1027–40.

Linehan, M.M. (1993). *Cognitive-behavioral treatment of borderline personality disorder*. New York: Guilford Press.

Liotti, G. (1992). Disorganized/disoriented attachment in the etiology of the dissociative disorders. *Dissociation: Progress in the Dissociative Disorders* **5**, 196–204.

——(1999). Understanding the dissociative processes: the contribution of attachment theory. *Psychoanalytic Inquiry* **19**, 757–83.

——(2004). Trauma, dissociation and disorganized attachment: three strands of a single braid. *Psychotherapy: Theory, research, practice, training* **41**, 472–86.

——(2006). A model of dissociation based on attachment theory and research. *Journal of Trauma and Dissociation* **7**, 55–74.

——(2007). Internal working models of attachment in the therapeutic relationship. In P. Gilbert and R.L. Leahy (eds), *The Therapeutic Relationship in the Cognitive Behavioral Psychotherapies*, pp. 143–61. London: Routledge.

——(2009). Attachment and dissociation. In P.F. Dell and J.A. O'Neil (eds), *Dissociation and the Dissociative Disorders: DSM-V and beyond*, pp. 53–66. New York: Routledge.

——(2011a). Attachment disorganisation and the clinical dialogue: theme and variations. In J. Solomon and C. George (eds), *Disorganized Attachment and Caregiving*, pp. 383–413. New York: Guilford Press.

——(2011b). Attachment disorganisation and the controlling strategies: an illustration of the contributions of attachment theory to developmental psychopathology and to psychotherapy integration. *Journal of Psychotherapy Integration* **21**, 232–52.

——(2012). Disorganised attachment and the therapeutic relationship with people in shattered states. In K. White and J. Yellin (eds), *Shattered States: disorganised attachment and its repair*, pp.127–56. London: Karnac.

Liotti, G. and Gilbert, P. (2011). Mentalizing, motivation and social mentalities: theoretical considerations and implications for psychotherapy. *Psychology and Psychotherapy: Theory, Research and Practice* **84**, 9–25.

Liotti, G., Cortina, M. and Farina, B. (2008). Attachment theory and the multiple integrated treatment of borderline personality disorder. *Journal of the American Academy of Psychoanalysis and Dynamic Psychiatry* **36**, 293–312.

Longe, O., Maratos, F.A., Gilbert, P., Evans, G., Volker, F., Rockliff, H. and Rippon, G. (2009). Having a word with yourself: neural correlates of self-criticism and self-reassurance. *Neuroimage* **49**, 1849–56.

Lyons-Ruth, K. (1998). Implicit relational knowing: its role in development and psychoanalytic treatment. *Infant Mental Health Journal* **19**, 282–9.

——(1999). The two-person unconscious: intersubjective dialogue, enactive relational representation, and the emergence of new forms of relational organisation. *Psychoanalytic Inquiry* **19**, 576–617.

——(2003). Dissociation and the parent–infant dialogue: a longitudinal perspective from attachment research. *Journal of the American Psychoanalytic Association* **51**, 883–911.

Lyons-Ruth, K. and Jacobvitz, D. (2008). Attachment disorganisation: genetic factors, parenting contexts and developmental transformations from infancy to adulthood. In J. Cassidy and P.R. Shaver (eds), *Handbook of Attachment*, 2nd edn, pp. 666–97. New York: Guilford Press.

Lyons-Ruth, K., Melnick, S., Patrick, M. and Hobson, R.P. (2007). A controlled study of hostile-helpless states of mind among borderline and dysthymic women. *Attachment and Human Development* **9**, 1–16.

Lyons-Ruth, K., Yellin, C., Melnick, S. and Atwood, G. (2003). Childhood experiences of trauma and loss have different relations to maternal unresolved and hostile-helpless states of mind on the AAI. *Attachment and Human Development* 5, 330–52.

Main, M. and Hesse, E. (1990). Parents' unresolved traumatic experiences are related to infant disorganized attachment status: is frightened and/or frightening parental behavior the linking mechanism? In M.T. Greenberg, D. Cicchetti and E.M. Cummings (eds). *Attachment in the Preschool Years*, pp. 161–82. Chicago: Chicago University Press.

Main, M. and Morgan, H. (1996). Disorganisation and disorientation in infant strange situation behaviour. Phenotypic resemblance to dissociative states? In L. Michelson and W. Ray (eds), *Handbook of Dissociation: theoretical, empirical and clinical perspectives*, pp. 107–38. New York: Plenum.

Main, M. and Solomon, J. (1990). Procedures for identifying infants as disorganized/disoriented during the Strange Situation. In M.T. Greenberg, D. Cicchetti and E.M. Cummings (eds), *Attachment in the Preschool Years*, pp. 121–60. Chicago: Chicago University Press.

Meares, R., Gerull, F., Stevenson, J. and Korner, A. (2011). Is self disturbance the core of borderline personality disorder? An outcome study of borderline personality factors. *Australian and New Zealand Journal of Psychiatry* 45, 214–22.

Morse, J.O., Hill, J., Pilkonis, P.A., Yaggi, K., Broyden, N., Stepp, S., Reed, L.I. and Feske, U. (2009). Anger, preoccupied attachment, and domain disorganisation in borderline personality disorder. *Journal of Personality Disorders* 23, 240–57.

Moss, E., Smolla, N., Cyr, C., Dubois-Comtois, K., Mazzarello, T. and Berthiaume, C. (2006). Attachment and behavior problems in middle childhood as reported by adult and child informants. *Development and Psychopathology* 18, 425–44.

Ogawa, J.R., Sroufe, L.A., Weinfield, N.S., Carlson, E.A. and Egeland, B. (1997). Development and the fragmented self: longitudinal study of dissociative symptomatology in a nonclinical sample. *Development and Psychopathology* 9, 855–79.

Prunetti, E., Framba, R., Barone, L., Fiore, D., Sera, F. and Liotti, G. (2008). Attachment disorganisation and borderline patients' metacognitive responses to therapists' expressed understanding of their state of mind: a pilot study. *Psychotherapy Research* 18, 28–36.

Rockliff, H., Gilbert, P., McEwan, K., Lightman, S. and Glover, D. (2008). A pilot exploration of heart rate variability and salivary cortisol responses to compassion-focused imagery. *Journal of Clinical Neuropsychiatry* 5, 132–9.

Schore, A.N. (2009). Attachment trauma and the developing right brain: origins of pathological dissociation. In P.F. Dell, and J.A. O'Neil (eds), *Dissociation and the Dissociative Disorders: DSM-V and beyond*, pp. 107–41. New York: Routledge.

Schuengel, C., Bakermans-Kranenburg, M.J. and Van IJzendoorn, M.H. (1999). Frightening maternal behavior linking unresolved loss and disorganized infant attachment. *Journal of Consulting and Clinical Psychology* 67, 54–63.

Scott, L.N., Levy, K.N. and Pincus, A.L. (2009). Adult attachment, personality traits, and borderline personality disorder features in young adults. *Journal of Personality Disorders* 23, 258–90.

Solomon, J. and George, C. (2011). Disorganisation of maternal caregiving across two generations: the origins of caregiving helplessness. In J. Solomon and C. George (eds), *Disorganized Attachment and Caregiving*, pp. 25–51. New York: Guilford Press.

Solomon, J., George, C. and De Jong, A. (1995). Children classified as controlling at age six: evidence of disorganized representational strategies and aggression at home and school. *Development and Psychopathology* 7, 447–64.

Steele, H. and Siever, L. (2010). An attachment perspective on borderline personality disorder: advances in gene-environment considerations. *Current Psychiatry Reports* **12**, 61–7.

van der Hart, O., Nijenhuis, E.R.S. and Steele, K. (2006). *The Haunted Self: structural dissociation and the treatment of chronic traumatisation.* New York: Norton.

van IJzendoorn, M.H., Schuengel, C. and Bakermans-Kranenburg, M.J. (1999). Disorganized attachment in early childhood: meta-analysis of precursors, concomitants and sequelae. *Development and Psychopathology* **11**, 225–50.

Yeomans, F.E., Clarkin, J.F. and Kernberg, O.F. (2002). *A Primer for Transference Focused Psychotherapy for the Borderline Patient.* Northvale, NJ: Jason Aronson.

Young, J.E., Klosko, J. and Weishaar, M.E. (2003). *Schema Therapy: a practitioner's guide.* New York: Guilford Press.

Zimmerman, P., Mohr, C. and Spangler, G. (2009). Genetic and attachment influences on adolescents' regulation of autonomy and aggressiveness. *Journal of Child Psychology and Psychiatry* **50**, 1339–47.

Chapter 9

Starving for affection

Attachment narrative therapy with eating disorders

Rudi Dallos

Introduction

The eating disorders, especially anorexia and bulimia, are among the most dangerous and most difficult to treat of the various mental health problems (Bruch 1973; Ward *et al.* 2001). In this chapter a multi-level perspective will be presented, exploring the experiences of young adults and including a focus on attachment patterns, family relationships and the cultural contexts underlying eating disorders. Though the emphasis will be on anorexia, the model offered is also seen as applicable to bulimia. The discussion will not rely excessively on diagnostic categories and it is suggested that there is often an overlap between restricting and purging forms of eating disorders. These symptoms may also be coupled with depression, anxiety, obsessive compulsive behaviours and even deliberate self-harm (Fairbairn and Brownell 2002). In including a family perspective, it is emphasised that the formulation is not intended to be 'parent blaming'.

The family context

The primary task for the child is how to secure her own attachment needs and this concerns how she learns to turn to others for emotional support and attempts to manage her own feelings. Attachment theory has emphasised that children develop their attachment strategies based on how their parents have responded to their attachment needs (Ainsworth *et al.* 1978; Bowlby 1988; Crittenden 2006). Where parents are able to respond consistently to provide care and comfort to a child when he or she is distressed, then a secure pattern is seen to develop. In cases where the child develops an avoidant pattern, parents are seen to respond consistently but with little care and affection and with a message that encourages the child to become overly self-reliant. In anxious-ambivalent patterns the parents have been found to respond inconsistently, at times not being available and at other times excessively anxious themselves or intruding into the child's activities. Finally, some children develop 'disorganised' or extreme strategies, typically in contexts where the parents have responded in frightening or abusive ways. In these situations the child experiences a severe dilemma in that the person who is meant to provide attachment security may at the same time be a source of threat or distress (Crittenden 2006; Dallos 2006).

A child may develop similar or contrasting patterns to that of their parents. For example, where both parents show anxious-ambivalent strategies, a child may develop an avoidant, emotionally distancing strategy in order to gain some emotional distance from their parents' volatile emotional dynamics. Alternatively, where both parents show insecure avoidant relational patterns, a child may develop exaggerated displays of emotion to mobilise emotional responses in their otherwise unresponsive parents. Where both parents have different types of insecure patterns, the task is more difficult in that the child needs to negotiate a complex task of developing either a pattern of suppressing feelings or exaggerated displays of emotion, or some mixture of the two.

The triadic perspective

The development of affect regulation in attachment theory has predominantly been viewed as a dyadic process, mainly between the child and her mother (Ainsworth *et al.* 1978; Crittenden 2006; Mikulincer, Shaver and Pereg 2003). However, even at a dyadic level, how the mother responds to the infant is influenced by her relationship with the child's father. It is also important to consider that some parents are influenced by the continuing relationship with their own parents, and the grandparents in turn have a relationship with the grandchildren. Some parents are closely tied to, and continually supported by, their own parents. In other families, members may be distant or may even have made a deliberate attempt to avoid, or be completely cut off from, their parents.

The parents' emotional, romantic relationship is evolving alongside the child's development and constitutes a central attachment relationship and emotional context for the child (Hall *et al.* 2003; Hazan and Shaver 1987). If the couple are experiencing conflict, distress or anxiety, for example about possible separation, then the mother is likely to be emotionally distracted and either less available to the child or possibly turning to the child for comfort. The partners need to develop some shared understandings and expectations about how they will meet each other's needs and those of the child (Dallos and Denford 2005; Hall *et al.* 2003). Where each partner brings a history of secure attachment to the relationship, they are able to discuss their positive and negative feelings for each other. They can also develop shared beliefs and avenues of communication about how they will be able to manage anxieties about the relationship and the child's emotions. Where both partners bring a dismissive pattern, this may lead to a shared belief system that they should not burden others with emotional demands and should instead attempt to suppress anxieties, display false positive affect and function at an emotional distance. For partners bringing joint preoccupied patterns, there may be an expectation that they have a right to demand emotional immediacy, to express strong feelings, and to make strong demands and criticisms of others. Where couples hold similar individual attachment patterns, agreements and shared frameworks can develop, albeit with escalating emotional distancing or entanglement. The situation becomes more complex when they bring different strategies in which such agreements are harder to develop and eventually may present a more confusing context for their children. For example, one parent may offer comfort and the other may be critical that the child is being 'spoilt' and needs more discipline and clear boundaries.

A child needs its parents to help manage her own anxieties, but also responds and potentially helps the parents to manage theirs (Dallos 2006). Most parents do not deliberately draw a child into meeting their needs. Instead, a child may evolve a function of regulating the attachment needs of her parents. Byng-Hall (1995) coined the term 'distance regulator' for how a child plays such a stabilising role for a couple. The patterns emerging here are shaped by the interplay of the individual attachment patterns of the parents; where both parents demonstrate preoccupied patterns the child may function to keep the parents apart and to attempt to de-escalate their anxious/angry patterns. Where both have avoidant styles the child may play an important role in enabling some emotional connection between them. In both these patterns, children can establish reasonably consistent roles that can help to regulate their parents' relationship. However, the most difficult may be where the parents have differing attachment strategies. Here the child may need to switch patterns to connect with each parent and to mitigate each parent's strategy, for example calming the mother down or getting the father to say what he feels rather than just to withdraw. This is an incredibly demanding task, especially for a young child. It is possible that, though the onset of eating disorders may be in adolescence, the child has struggled to manage these demands for years. This task may become increasingly unacceptable at adolescence when the young person is also faced with the need to develop their own early romantic relationships.

A triadic perspective offers an important extension to attachment theory, but it also offers a connection to a substantial body of literature in systemic family therapy that points towards a significant role of triadic processes in the development and maintenance of eating disorders (Palazzoli 1974). It has also been observed that families with a young person suffering from an eating disorder frequently demonstrated a pattern of conflict avoidance and enmeshment, and that the parents experienced difficulties in working collaboratively with each other in managing the eating disorder (Minuchin, Rosman and Baker 1978; Ringer and Crittenden 2006). Palazzoli (1974) further suggested that these families were characterised by covert conflicts in which the child with an eating disorder had been triangulated, notably in being conscripted to take sides between the parents. Moreover, she argued that the more this process was secret and disguised the more potentially confusing and problematic it could be for the child.

Corrective and replicative scripts

The concept of attachment scripts (Byng-Hall 1995) introduces the notion of autonomy and choice into attachment theory; corrective scripts involve an attempt to do things differently, better than our parents, for example to be more emotionally available for our children or to have a more affectionate relationship with our partner. Replicative scripts constitute attempts to repeat what we saw as good, desirable features of our childhood experiences with our parents. Family members vary in the extent to which they consciously hold these scripts, but are usually able to articulate them quickly when prompted (Byng-Hall 1995; Dallos 2006).

Corrective and replicative scripts can in some cases have a pendulum quality when there is an extreme swing from one generation to the next. Where this occurs, the intent to do things differently appears to be fuelled by powerful emotions such as anger or disappointment regarding the parents. The concept of a script includes the idea that it contains flexibility and potential ability to adapt itself according to the specific circumstances and changes in the environment (Byng-Hall 1995). In families where there are problematic processes, this flexibility appears to become impeded. Intense experiences or danger and distress experiences in the parents' childhoods may be connected to strong intentions to avoid such experiences in their own families. For example, some parents have a strong desire to be closer to their children, have healthier food and more enjoyable mealtimes. However, without direct experience to draw on from their own childhoods, this corrective script can be an abstract and idealised aspiration which is hard to achieve in reality.

The ability to adapt our scripts to our children also connects with the concept of reflective functioning or mentalisation (Fonagy *et al*. 1991). It is suggested that parents need to accurately reflect back to the infant, the infant's internal emotional states such as distress, anger, sadness, and to communicate simultaneously that these states are manageable and will not overwhelm them. Where parents themselves have not experienced such accurate reflection and containment, they may find it all the harder to adjust and adapt their efforts at corrective scripts for the child. This may add up to a 'double' difficulty in that they perceive themselves as trying to do things better but in fact they are potentially more, not less, confusing for their child than their own experience had been. The child's experience may be that their parent wants to be closer and more sensitive to them, but they are doing it in a way which does not feel consistent with their parents' perceptions. The culmination of this process appears to be a highly frustrating experience for both parents and the child. For the parents: 'I am trying to do it better than my parents, why doesn't she understand?' For the child: 'They tell me they are doing things better and I should be grateful but it does not feel empathetic or sensitive' (Dallos 2006).

A systemic, attachment formulation of eating disorders

The above dynamics are common to a whole range of problems. What may also predispose a family towards a member developing an eating disorder is that there has been a negative or contradictory tradition in the family in relation to food as an attachment experience. Food is one of the earliest and most fundamental forms of pleasure and distress experienced by the infant (Bowlby 1969; Friedman 1996). As adults we can only imagine what it must feel like for an infant to feel the craving for food and drink without conscious awareness that this desperate need will be relieved. At the same time, it can constitute an extremely sensitive and sensual experience of contact with the mother's body and the comforting taste and smell of milk. Bowlby (1969) suggested that the child internalises the mother in terms of whether her breasts provide a consistent and speedy release for the baby from the distress of hunger. In contrast, feeding could also be an unpredictable, frustrating experience that maintains an unpleasant state of distress and anxiety for the baby. In these early interactions mothers vary in how much they are able to manage the intimacy and sensuality of feelings relating to feeding. Some mothers appear to become very anxious and concerned to offer physical contact and others find contact uncomfortable.

Bowlby (1969) argued that food and the resolution of the anxiety generated by hunger provide an important early arena in which these attachment patterns and affect regulation develop. In effect, eating and attachment can become intertwined such that in the avoidant attachment patterns, for example, the experience of hunger appears not to be associated with an anticipation of comfort and pleasure but with attempts to self-regulate and avoid comfort seeking. Avoidant dispositional representations may constitute a move towards a self-reliance regarding food, perhaps as in solitary eating, which does not require dependence on another to provide the release of discomfort from hunger. In more extreme forms, it may be that the avoidance generalises to the extent that comfort itself is avoided. Accounts from people with anorexic symptoms suggest that they do not transcend hunger, but come to tolerate the suffering of intense discomfort (Orbach 2008).

If food is not construed as a positive and pleasurable experience then its cessation may not initially be experienced as a loss of receiving comfort. However, eventually the symptoms resulting from eating problems may elicit concern and attachment responses from the parents (Humphrey 1989). It appears to constitute an 'attachment ambivalence' of being simultaneously both a dismissing and preoccupying process: on the one hand it appears to constitute a dismissive attempt at rejection of comfort through food, but on the other hand, as the illness progresses, it may also elicit and serve to maintain an anxious response from the parents. Hence it can fit with an anxious-ambivalent attachment with the mother or father, or a mixed avoidant-anxious ambivalent pattern between the parents. Hence an important feature of anorexia is that the individual simultaneously (avoidantly) rejects the comfort of food but also elicits anxiety and provision of care (O'Kearney 1996).

The development of a triangulated dynamic in the family in which the young person with the eating disorder has become entangled is not exclusive to eating disorders. It appears that in many families with an eating disorder, there has been both a lack of provision of emotional comfort at times of distress and in turn a lack of a connection between food and comfort. Attachment seeking and response to separation and lack of availability of comfort elicit reactions of both anxiety and protest, but since protest may be discouraged in families with an eating disorder, it becomes expressed through refusal to take in food (Dallos and Denford 2005; Minuchin, Rosman and Baker 1978; O'Kearney 1996). Such protest can represent for the parents a painful sense of failure in their attempts to make a better emotional environment for their children than had been their experience. This may in turn lead to less confidence in responding to the child's distress and their indirect plea for comfort. In turn, anxiety about the child's 'illness' may make it all the more difficult for the parents to work together and to resolve their own attachment needs as a couple.

A focus on attachment and comfort permits some freedom to move away from what can become a relentless and often unhelpful focus on the eating problems. In our experience, the young people presenting with the eating disorder often wish to move away from an exclusive focus on food, whereas the parents are anxious that the problems with eating are not sidelined in the sessions. Our research and clinical experience suggests that insecure attachment patterns operate across the generations. The parents frequently experience dissatisfactions in their attachment relationship with each other as a couple and appear to turn to a child to help meet their own emotional needs. However, this is not simply some selfish sacrificing of their child; it is also driven by a corrective script – an intention to have a closer, more intimate, loving relationship with them than they experienced with their own parents. In some cases this corrective script appears to be fuelled by powerful unresolved traumatic experiences.

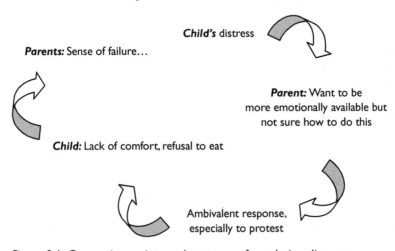

Figure 9.1 Corrective scripts and patterns of escalating distress

Attachment narrative therapy

A broad framework for utilising systemic attachment and narrative ideas – Attachment Narrative Therapy (Dallos 2006) is illustrated below. This employs four key stages in the intervention process:

Creating a secure base

In this stage it is recognised that coming for therapy can be an extremely anxiety-provoking experience for many families. It appears to be especially the case for families where anorexia is the presenting problem. Hence the first session emphasises safety, validation and invites families to comment on the pacing of the work and how comfortable they feel. It indirectly invites attention to their feelings and how these are communicated, and conveys a message that negative or distressing feelings in the session can be commented on and they will be responded to.

Exploration

In this stage the materials for subsequent changes are gathered through a variety of forms of exploration, such as genograms, sculpts with objects, tracking circularities, identifying attachment dilemmas, their explanations of the problems and trans-generational patterns of attachment and comforting. It recognises that such exploration can also provoke anxieties and the emphasis on pacing and commenting on their experience of reflecting and the work is maintained.

Considering alternatives

This stage utilises the material from the exploration and extends these to consider exceptions and unique outcomes, and focuses on the parents' corrective and replicative scripts. Particularly important here is a consideration of what they have attempted to change and whether this has worked. Frequently, families here mention that they have wanted to be more emotionally available than their own parents had been but have experienced a sense of failure in not being able to achieve this.

Maintaining the therapeutic base

In this stage it is recognised that for many families developing a sense of trust with the therapist has been a new and powerful experience. Discussions take place about how the relationship can continue in terms of what ideas and feelings family members will take away and what we will remember about our work with them. This also recognises the need to consider future problems that may arise and to maintain a sense of continuing support by offering a further session if required. In our experience, for many families the potential of future support is sufficient and they do not in fact need to take up further sessions.

Using attachment narrative therapy

Case study 1: The Morrison family

Mary Morrison, aged 19, was attending treatment for anorexia at an eating disorder unit as a day patient following a three-month period as an inpatient. She was living at home with her father (Bill) and older brother Peter. Mrs. Morrison was living with her mother and father nearby, having 'moved out' approximately six months before the start of Mary's anorexia. Mary had gone to university some distance away from the family home about four months after her mother had moved out. She quickly lost weight and had to return home after six weeks and was admitted to a local eating disorder unit. The parents were living separately, with Mrs Morrison visiting the home every day to do the domestic chores. Mary indicated that she felt confused about her parents' relationship and confided that she was very angry with her mother, partly because she thought that her mother had spread a rumour that she and her father might have had an incestuous relationship.

In the initial sessions Mary cried repeatedly and though aware of her distress, neither parent made overt attempts to comfort her. When asked what her sadness was about she repeated that 'People are lying to me, I don't know what is going on'. There appeared to be a shared family belief that 'It's best to avoid difficult feelings' and that 'It's dangerous to express our needs and vulnerabilities'.

Creating a secure base

It was made clear that the purpose of the sessions was not to look for blame and that we might never fully discover the causes. However, we would try to find ways of resisting the problem. The family were also asked how they felt about an approach where we did not spend all of the time in the sessions looking at the anorexia but also spent time on other matters.

Exploring attachment narratives

Mary appeared to be very distressed in the early sessions and repeatedly mentioned feelings that things were 'unreal' and that people were 'lying to her'. Part of this exploration attempted to discuss Mary's difficulties as not just related to the anorexia but as part of 'normal' development; for example, that becoming a young adult, moving away from home and becoming more independent involves difficulties for all families. This led into a discussion, with the aid of a genogram, of how each parent left home, and more broadly into the nature of their relationships with their parents. During this discussion, Mrs Morrison described that she had moved out to start work and that her family had been close and warm. Mr Morrison's story was a stark contrast:

THERAPIST: So can you tell me, Bill, how was it for you, becoming adult, leaving home...?

MR MORRISON: Well I didn't really have a home. I was brought up in various children's homes, it was O.K. I suppose.

THERAPIST: Could you tell me a little bit more about that, where were your parents...?

MR MORRISON: My mother was very ill and in hospital, she died in hospital when I was five. My father drank a lot and carried on with various women. His answer to every problem was to have a drink. I thought it was terrible my mum lying in hospital while he was doing that, but what can you do?

THERAPIST: So what happened when your mother died?

MR MORRISON: His girlfriend moved in with us and she couldn't stand me so I was put in a children's home...

THERAPIST: That must have been pretty tough for you?

MR MORRISON: No, not really, I don't think about it, it doesn't really matter to me. You just have to get on with life ... no point crying about it.

THERAPIST: Have you ever talked to anybody before about these experiences?

MRS MORRISON: He has told me, but I'm glad he is doing it now ... he keeps it all bottled up I think ...

Mrs Morrison explained that her husband's tendency to deny feelings of vulnerability had driven her away. He eventually admitted that he had been hurt by his wife's departure and we hypothesised that possibly Mary had stepped into the role of surrogate wife to meet her father's emotional needs. Mr Morrison denied that he needed emotional support from his daughter but at the same time described a daily ritual of massaging her feet to 'help her to relax'. We were concerned at the potential sexual implications of this ritual and there appeared to be a confusing dynamic for Mary, who may have been aware of her father's need for physical and emotional contact but in providing this was incurring the concern of her mother about possible incest. Mary also appeared to try to deny her own feelings of loss at her mother moving out by taking a critical stance towards her.

Considering alternatives

A number of the following sessions were focused on exploring the possible impact of Mr Morrison's experiences and on the parents' relationship. It was suggested that they might attend as a couple to discuss their own issues, which they agreed to. Mr Morrison was described by his wife as 'working all the time' and was sacrificing himself to look after everybody practically but was not able to do so emotionally. Mrs Morrison indicated that she did want to be back with her husband but that this was hard because he was so emotionally shut off. Eventually, in an individual session and later in a session with the couple, Bill admitted that he still cared for his wife and wanted her back. It seemed that his reluctance to admit this was because he did not want to betray his special relationship with Mary. An attempt was made to monitor the changes in Mary's attachments to her parents carefully and not to go too fast. Gradually Mary was spending more time with her friends, had started to work again and though still struggling with the anorexia she was managing to avoid a readmission to the unit.

Maintaining the therapeutic base

Some significant changes appeared to have occurred in the family, most notably that Mary seemed to be less emotionally triangulated between her parents and was becoming emotionally more independent and more connected to her mother. However, there was a danger that her father was cutting off emotionally too quickly and this was upsetting for her. His history in childhood had been that his needs would not be met and there was a danger that he was feeling this again. Sessions at intervals of six weeks were offered but they agreed that they did not need further sessions since the problems had significantly improved. Considering future issues, the pace of Mary's independence was discussed and the family members agreed that they would monitor this and Mary confirmed that she did not feel emotionally 'pushed out' when her parents spent time together.

Case study 2: Kathy

This case permits more detailed analysis because, as well as therapy, the family took part in our research study. This involved individual semi-structured interviews, Adult Attachment Interviews (AAI) and a family interview.

Kathy, aged 17, had been suffering with an anorexic form of eating disorder for over 18 months. Kathy was the youngest of four children; her three brothers were all over nine years older than her. Her brother Pete had returned to live at home for a while and had been close to Kathy when she was younger. Kathy had suffered with anorexia for over three years and had attended an outpatient unit. Her parents (Dawn and Albert) were living together and had been married for over 30 years.

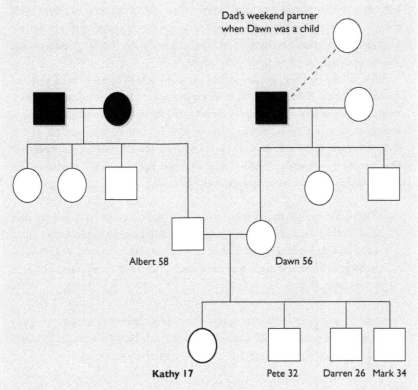

Figure 9.2 Kathy and her family – genogram

Trans-generational patterns

Dawn and Albert confided that their relationship was in difficulty and that Dawn had wanted to leave the relationship, having 'found passion' elsewhere. She described how her mother had 'suffered in silence' while her father had a long-term relationship with another woman and her mother had become depressed and suicidal. The AAIs for Dawn and Albert indicated they had probably each brought insecure attachment patterns to their current relationship: Albert displayed a dismissive pattern in that he avoided talking about his feelings of vulnerability, had forgotten difficult emotional experiences from his childhood, and engaged in largely analytic, intellectualising ways of discussing relationships. He discussed having had a mother who was preoccupied with her own health and not emotionally available and a father with a quick temper. Dawn in contrast displayed considerable emotionality in her interview, became aroused and appeared preoccupied and overwrought by painful memories from her childhood. It was as if she quickly started to relive the experiences, not having found ways to resolve and come to terms with them. These patterns were also revealed in the family sessions where Albert engaged in attempts to rationalise family issues and Kathy's difficulties, whereas Kathy repeatedly became tearful and upset.

Both parents had negative memories of mealtimes, a broad sense of a lack of comfort in their childhoods and little experience of food being used in their past or the current families as a source of comfort, warmth or pleasure. However, it was clear in Kathy's family, as with others, that not all of the children found it difficult to eat. Given Kathy's central role as a connection between her parents, it is likely that she had become finely tuned to the emotional distress between her parents.

> They used to hate each other so much I always used to be so scared that one of them would do something stupid and I would come home and I used to hate coming home just in case something happened. And they've both got the worst tempers, even dad ... dad's is rarely seen but it is really bad ...

It appeared that Kathy had internalised the conflict between her parents such that it was a continual preoccupation. Consequently family mealtimes at home may have started to generalise into being progressively more aversive.

Corrective scripts and unresolved traumas

Dawn said she had resolved not to have the kind of unsatisfactory marital relationship that she had seen her own mother 'put up with'. She also wanted a closer relationship with Kathy than had been possible with her own mother. Likewise, Albert said his own father had been an angry and frightening man at times due to his 'illness' and a demanding physical job. Consequently he had wanted to be a less severe and intimidating father than his own. However, neither Albert nor Dawn appeared to have been able to reflect upon and integrate their early emotional experiences; instead, these appeared to intrude into their relationship with Kathy. At times Albert appeared to repeat some of the angry, dismissing reactions of his father. Similarly, Dawn would at times act in a sullen, childlike, dependent way with Kathy in a reversal of roles, where Kathy was expected to care for and contain her mother's feelings. This appeared to be combined with open expression of sadness and regret about her relationship with Albert and mirroring her own mother's sense of futility and depression.

As Dawn attempted to 'do things differently', for example, be closer to Kathy, it seemed that she could rapidly catastrophise when starting to feel it was not working, and believe that Kathy did not appreciate her. This appeared to lead her to make more emotional demands on Kathy, to become angry with her or to blame Kathy for preferring her father. It was also possible that two opposing corrective scripts were in play for her: wanting to be close to Kathy but also wishing to be an independent woman and not run the risk of being lonely and dependent on her husband as she felt her mother had been. In one family session, Kathy described how nice it was when she was little and her mother was off work for a few days and they had a nice meal together. We noticed a rather dazed reaction from Dawn, as if this voiced her worst fear, namely that the eating disorder was caused by her unavailability as a mother and provider of food.

Triadic relationships and triangulation

It appeared that from birth, Kathy played an essential role for her parents: she represented an opportunity for Dawn to relive and correct her relationship with her own mother and to provide an 'emotional glue'. Albert described Dawn as so happy to have the daughter she had so long wished for that it made their relationship more emotionally and physically intimate. It appeared that Kathy came to recognise that she was significantly important to both her parents and their relationship. However, as the conflicts between her parents resurfaced, Kathy found herself drawn into taking sides. She described her sense of being caught between her parents in the role of emotional regulator for their relationship, and how she needed to keep her symptoms of anorexia in order to promote some stability and calm in the family:

> The only thing I ever hear them talking about is me and if I didn't have this [anorexia] it's kind of like, would everything fall apart, at least it's keeping them talking. And they won't argue while I've got this because it might make me worse. So um ... that's kind of bought, sort of like, I'm not in control as such but I've got more control over the situation that way ...

Kathy demonstrated a pattern of attempting to withdraw emotionally, for example as she described above regarding her father. At the same time, she was often drawn into escalating, tearful patterns of mutual emotional demands and accusations with her mother. These demands to take sides appeared to make it difficult for her to consistently use an avoidant/dismissing style of relating in emotionally tense and difficult moments. Furthermore, the continual sense of imminent threat and catastrophe regarding her parents' relationship also appeared to have contributed to anxious intrusions of feelings and images that disrupted her attempts to self-regulate and calm herself.

Therapeutic interventions

We were able to make connections between comfort, their own histories and the role of food. As part of these discussions, we were able to comment on and share aspects of the parents' childhood experiences in order to help make connections with the family and help reduce a sense of blame or inadequacy. Key family relationships across the generations were discussed and connections made with the current family patterns of relating. For example, how they were attempting to do things differently and the positive intentions they had for their relationship with Kathy. In these discussions Kathy was at points able to validate how her mother had tried to make things better, because at times Dawn was reluctant to consider that she had been able to do anything better and had 'got it all wrong'. The focus of these conversations stayed on their positive intentions rather than digressing into what was not working currently. Gradually both Dawn and Albert were able to identify some aspects of how their intentions had been positive and could be developed further. Kathy's weight increased to normal levels and her emotional state also improved. The positive changes were maintained at 18 months and at an eight year follow-up. Following a number of sessions allowing Dawn and Albert to discuss their marital relationship they decided to maintain their marriage, and their relationship had significantly improved.

Discussion

For both these families, the Morrisons and Kathy's, triangulation was a central issue. Minuchin (1974) has indicated that *all* family members contribute to maintaining the process; for example, when Kathy went away to university she returned frequently, perhaps in part to monitor the well-being of her parents as well as for her own needs. The child's symptoms, their concern about their parents, and the special role they have gained can also make it difficult for a couple to resolve their own issues. Though in both the cases described the couple's relationship was an important focus, and improved considerably, we are not suggesting that anorexia is invariably causally linked to difficulties in the parents' relationship. Typically, in the families we have worked with, there is a counter explanation that the anorexia had caused the problems in the parents' relationship. As with Minuchin's clarification above, a systemic perspective suggests that the causal processes are not simply linear. However, what does seem to be common is that the parents of young people with anorexia (and even of older people with the condition) typically appear to have had difficult and emotionally barren childhood attachment experiences, and alongside this, negative experiences of food and family mealtimes. This appears to leave them at difficulty in dealing with their children's attachments needs and being able to relate attachment needs to eating problems. The central proposition of this chapter is that food is inextricably tied in with comfort and attachment. Though popular magazines and the media talk repeatedly of 'comfort eating' in relation to other eating problems such as obesity, this linking between food and comfort is relatively, and perhaps surprisingly, under-researched (O'Shaughnessy and Dallos 2009). Part of the reason may be that such research can be seen as parent blaming. However, as suggested in this chapter, parents are typically attempting corrective scripts – to do things better than was their experience. It is important to be able to recognise what makes this so hard for the parents to achieve. Recognition of their own difficult attachment experiences offers a compassionate, not a blaming, stance that arguably helps to recognise the frustrations they experience when their efforts to 'do it better' appear to be ineffective or even damaging.

References

Ainsworth, M.D.S., Blehar, R.M.C., Waters, E. and Wall, S. (1978). *Patterns of Attachment: a psychological study of the strange situation.* Hillside, NJ: Erlbaum.

Bowlby, J. (1969). *Attachment and Loss, Volume 1: Attachment.* London: Hogarth Press.

——(1988). *A Secure Base.* New York: Basic Books.

Bruch, H. (1973). *Eating Disorders: obesity and anorexia and the person within.* New York: Basic Books.

Byng-Hall, J. (1995). *Rewriting Family Scripts: improvisation and systems change.* New York: Guilford Press.

Crittenden, P. M. (2006). A dynamic-maturational model of attachment. *Australian and New Zealand Journal of Family Therapy* 27, 105–15.

Dallos, R. (2006). *Attachment Narrative Therapy: integrating attachment, systemic and narrative therapies.* Maidenhead: Open University Press/McGraw Hill.

Dallos, R. and Denford, S. (2005). A qualitative exploration of relationship and attachment themes in families with an eating disorder. *Clinical Child Psychology and Psychiatry* 13, 305–22.

Fairbairn, C.G. and Brownell, K.D. (eds) (2002). *Eating Disorders and Obesity: a comprehensive handbook.* London: Guilford Press.

Fonagy, P., Steele, M., Steele, H., Moran, G.S. and Higgitt, A.C. (1991). The capacity for understanding mental states: the reflective self in parents and child and its significance for security of attachment. *Infant Journal of Mental Health* **12**, 201–15.

Friedman, M.E. (1996). Mother's milk: a psychoanalyst looks at breastfeeding. *Psychoanalytic Study of the Child* **51**, 473–90.

Hall, J., Fonagy, P., Safier, E. and Sargent, J. (2003). The ecology of family attachment. *Family Process* **42**, 205–21.

Hazan, C. and Shaver, P. (1987). Romantic love conceptualized as an attachment process. *Journal of Personality and Social Psychology* **52**, 511–24.

Humphrey, L. (1989). Observed family interaction among subtypes of eating disorders using structural analysis of social behaviour. *Journal of Counselling and Psychotherapy,* **57**, 206–14.

Mikulincer, M., Shaver, P. and Pereg, D. (2003). Attachment theory and affect regulation: the dynamics, development, and cognitive consequences of attachment-related strategies. *Motivation and Emotion* **27**, 77–102.

Minuchin, S. (1974). *Families and Family Therapy.* Cambridge, MA: Harvard University Press.

Minuchin, S., Rosman, B. and Baker, L. (1978). *Psychosomatic Families: anorexia nervosa in context.* Cambridge, MA: Harvard University Press.

O'Kearney, R. (1996). Attachment disruption in anorexia nervosa and bulimia nervosa: a review of theory and empirical research. *International Journal of Eating Disorders* **20**, 115–27.

Orbach, S. (2008). *Fat is a Feminist Issue.* London: Arrow Books Limited.

O'Shaugnessy, R. and Dallos, R. (2009). Attachment research and eating disorders: a review of the literature. *Clinical Child Psychology and Psychiatry* **14**, 549–74.

Palazzoli, M.S. (1974). *Self-starvation: from the intra-psychic to transpersonal.* London: Chaucer.

Ringer, R. and Crittenden, P.M. (2006). Eating disorders and attachment: the effects of hidden family processes on eating disorders. *European Eating Disorders Review* **14**, 1–12.

Ward, A., Ramsay, R., Turnbull, S., Steele, M., Steele, H. and Treasure, J. (2001). Attachment in anorexia nervosa: a trans-generational perspective. *British Journal of Medical Psychology* **74**, 497–505.

Chapter 10

An attachment perspective on understanding and managing medically unexplained symptoms

Robert G. Maunder and Jonathan J. Hunter

Simon is a 37-year-old teacher. He has been referred for psychiatric assessment by his family doctor after three referrals to specialists (gastroenterologist, cardiologist and neurologist) have produced no explanation for a cluster of symptoms, including chest and epigastric pain, intermittent 'pins and needles' in both hands, and diarrhoea. The symptoms have persisted for six months and have been severe enough that he has recently taken a leave of absence from work. He is embarrassed and a little angry that his doctor suggested seeing a psychiatrist, as it is clear that the symptoms 'are real, not just in my head'. His doctor suggested that the symptoms might be due to stress, but Simon notes that he has had a career that is stressful but satisfying for many years without it causing a problem like this. There do not appear to be any obvious changes in his life preceding the onset of pain and the subsequent emergence of diarrhoea and peripheral parasthesia.

Gathering the history of these symptoms is time consuming and somewhat confusing because Simon has trouble organising and completing his thoughts. 'I first had this pain, in the stomach' (he points), 'although I wouldn't call it a pain as much as a twisting feeling at first, and nausea, and ... sharp pain, but I don't eat fibre anymore, just little snacks, and they want me to go back to school, but really, could you work with this sort of pain? I mean I double over, and think of the kids... and the nausea, which, I mean, I don't throw up but I could and I know it isn't a heart attack but you would think that too, at first. And she says "Just relax" like that is something you can just do when you've got a feeling that literally takes your breath away ... I have a cousin with Crohn's disease who had investigations for two years before they figured out what was going on so I know things get missed ...'

Simon's situation is all too common. Physical symptoms that are never adequately explained by organic disease are one of the most common and challenging phenomena in medicine, accounting for about one in three symptoms reported to primary care physicians (Escobar *et al.* 1998; Kroenke 2003) and for most health care visits (Katon, Sullivan and Walker 2001).

The phenomena referred to collectively as medically unexplained symptoms (MUS) are diverse, ranging from a single symptom such as lower back pain to complex functional and psychiatric syndromes. Management of MUS is complicated by lack of certainty about the cause of symptoms, and often by disagreement between patient and clinician as to the role of psychological factors. The likelihood of co-morbid psychiatric diagnosis and of dissatisfaction in patient–provider interaction increases as the number of reported symptoms increase (Simon and Von Korff 1991).

Observational reports of healthy people in the community show that experiencing an unexplained symptom is common, with most people having symptoms every few days, for which they do not seek medical help (Demers *et al.* 1980; White, Williams and Greenberg 1961). MUS may be accompanied by psychological variables (especially a history of childhood adversity and symptoms of depression and anxiety) more often in tertiary care settings than in the community (Smith *et al.* 1990; Talley, Howell and Poulton 2001; Whitehead *et al.* 1988) although the evidence is inconsistent (Locke *et al.* 2004). Problematic MUS are not identified by the nature of the physical symptoms but by multiplicity of symptoms, difficult patient–provider interactions, co-morbid psychiatric syndromes and high utilisation of medical resources (Katon, Sullivan and Walker 2001). Thus, while psychological contributions to MUS are not universal, it remains controversial whether psychological variables are associated with the occurrence of physical symptoms or with medical help-seeking. This chapter focuses on the phenomena that are most challenging to manage, problematic MUS, rather than on the occurrence of symptoms in themselves.

Current approaches to management of MUS

The treatment of MUS is less than optimal. While randomised controlled trials support the value of cognitive-behavioural therapy (CBT) and antidepressants (Kroenke 2007; Sumathipala 2007), the clinical application of these interventions remains problematic. With respect to CBT, evidence supports the value of CBT provided by specialists, but interventions by primary care physicians have had disappointing results (Kroenke 2007). Since the greatest burden of MUS occurs in primary care, this is a major limitation. With respect to antidepressants, trials which demonstrate statistically significant benefits often fail to report the prevalence of side effects, which are a common limiting factor that may account for the high rates of treatment withdrawal in these studies (Sumathipala 2007). The choice of outcome variables in treatment trials has been inconsistent, but reduced psychological distress and reduced medical costs have been more readily achieved than resolution of physical symptoms (Kroenke 2007).

Evidence also supports simpler interventions. Psychiatric consultation followed by a letter to the primary care physician outlining principles of management reduces medical utilisation and improves functional status (Smith, Monson and Ray 1986; Smith, Rost and Kashner 1995). The letter evaluated in these interventions provided a diagnosis (somatisation disorder) and described its chronic relapsing and remitting course and its low morbidity and mortality. It recommended brief regular appointments every four to six weeks and avoiding 'as needed' appointments. Also that every appointment should include a brief physical exam focused on the body system in which symptoms occur and that hospitalisation, diagnostic procedures, surgery and laboratory tests should be avoided unless clearly indicated. Finally, the referring physician was encouraged to avoid telling the patient that symptoms were 'in their head' and instead to assume that the development of symptoms was outside of their conscious control and awareness.

Applying this sound advice is challenging. Problematic MUS raise doubts for most clinicians and introduce conflicts between healthcare providers and patients that interfere with good care. Clinicians are often concerned about missing an occult organic diagnosis; the lack of a medical explanation for symptoms does not mean the impossibility of one. Clinicians may worry about being criticised, or offending a patient with the implication that physical symptoms are not being taken seriously. The limited effectiveness of evidence-based interventions contributes more frustration. Very often, management of MUS requires a capacity to work respectfully and with confidence in spite of diagnostic uncertainty and a patient who actively doubts the value of the interaction.

For all of these reasons, we have found it helpful to formulate the interaction between a healthcare provider and a patient with problematic MUS as a difficult interpersonal interaction, and therefore to use an understanding of interpersonal psychology, specifically attachment theory, as a basis for managing care.

Attachment theory

Attachment theory was described by John Bowlby as a theory of the development of close protective relationships between infants and parents (Bowlby 1969). Attachment theory can be framed in a manner that translates readily into a formulation of problematic MUS, as follows. A primary purpose of attachment relationships is to provide a mechanism for a vulnerable individual to receive protection and solace from a care-providing individual (known as an attachment figure) at times of danger. This goal is achieved through a series of interpersonal signals (attachment behaviours) that are triggered by the perception of danger. These include crying, moving towards the parent and clinging – any of which may elicit an effective response from a care-provider. If the danger is the presence of a predator, the care-providing response might include protective proximity, which provides shelter from the predator and soothing contact. Signals of potential danger can come from within as well as from the external environment; pain and other symptoms of injury and illness are also effective triggers of attachment behaviours.

The pool of attachment behaviours a child is born with is shaped by the amplification of behaviours that are more successful in achieving attachment goals and the relative extinction of behaviours that are less successful. Through this process one internalises a self-image as an individual who is an effective self-regulator of danger and distress, or not. There are marked individual differences between infants in the ease with which expressions of distress are elicited, patterns of approach and withdrawal with respect to the parent, and the effectiveness of contact in reducing distress and providing solace (Ainsworth *et al.* 1978). Interactions between infants and their primary care-providers typically result in stable patterns of attachment behaviours.

Individual patterns of attachment remain identifiable throughout the lifespan, with several important modifications later in life (Mikulincer and Shaver 2007). For adults, the attachment figure is typically a committed romantic partner, or in some cases another close confidante. Adult attachment figures can be identified by three roles that they perform: being the person to whom one most wants to be close, the person one turns to at times of great adversity (a safe haven), and the person from whom one finds the security to go out and explore independently (a secure base) (Hazan and Shaver 1994). The roles are usually transferred from parents to peers and partners in late adolescence or early adulthood (Fraley and Davis 1997).

Individual differences in adult attachment have been classified in several ways, based on theoretical and measurement considerations. In this chapter we describe prototypes that capture the core elements of these patterns, using the system introduced by Bartholomew and Horowitz (1991), who described four categories of attachment: secure, preoccupied, dismissing and fearful. We modify their descriptions to include aspects of insecure attachment drawn from research on attachment 'states of mind' (George and West 2001; Hesse 2008) – specifically, impaired narrative coherence and mentalising. These prototypes and the evidence upon which they are derived are described in more detail elsewhere (Maunder and Hunter 2009, 2012).

Secure

The secure pattern is not commonly associated with problematic MUS (Ciechanowski *et al.* 2002a) and is described to provide contrast with the insecure patterns. Secure attachment is characterised by a positive self-image as resilient, resourceful and capable of eliciting help when warranted. Expectations of others tend to be realistic and, within those limits, positive. Expressions of distress and other behaviours that elicit care from others tend to be proportionate to need and communicated clearly enough to promote a constructive response. While a person with secure attachment may experience intense distress, others are usually able to appreciate and understand both the distress and its relationship to circumstances in a manner that facilitates a constructive response.

Preoccupied

The preoccupied pattern is characterised by a negative self-image as fragile or unworthy of love and caring. This negative self-view is accompanied by intense attachment anxiety, which refers to an exaggerated, fearful expectation of rejection by, or loss of, the attachment figure. Attachment behaviour includes vigilance for the presence and responsiveness of others, frequent expressions of distress, and preoccupation with interpersonal proximity. Although proximity and support are actively sought, they are often insufficient to reduce distress and are perceived to be unsatisfactory. Communication of distress may lack coherence because of intense affect, vague descriptors, a lack of clarity about timelines and individuals in the narrative, and mixed, multiple, fragmentary narrative threads.

Dismissing

The dismissing pattern is characterised by a negative image of others as untrustworthy or disappointing. This is accompanied by attachment avoidance, which refers to a pattern of avoiding intimacy and dependency through interpersonal distance, self-reliance and the devaluation of the importance of intimate or supportive relationships. Expressions of distress are suppressed. The communication of perceived distress is truncated by the omission of detail and the use of conventional or clichéd phrases, and general conclusions about oneself provided in the absence of supportive and contextualising evidence. Attachment avoidance can be understood as a defensive strategy, protecting the dismissing individual from the disappointment and pain that is expected to result from the ineffective responses of others to expressions of need (Shaver and Mikulincer 2002).

Fearful

The fearful pattern is especially relevant to problematic MUS. It is characterised by negative expectations of both self and other and by the combination of prominent attachment anxiety and attachment avoidance. Whereas dismissing attachment appears as a pattern of self-reliance and comfort with interpersonal distance, fearful attachment is characterised by a strategy of maintaining interpersonal distance that does not appear to provide comfort. Distress is communicated in a manner that does not elicit a caring response from the other, or that even actively discourages such a response. If attachment avoidance is understood as a defensive strategy, fearful attachment represents a situation in which avoidant defences are used but fail to protect the individual against negative affect (Shaver and Mikulincer 2002). Fearful attachment represents the pattern of insecure attachment in which insecurity is most severe. Clinically, the opposing pulls of attachment anxiety and attachment avoidance can manifest as inconsistent help-seeking/help-rejecting behaviour, a common feature of difficult patient–provider interactions (Groves 1978).

Simon has a fearful attachment style. His primary method of coping with the recent health challenge has been to try to tough it out on his own. His distress is intense when he discusses his symptoms (a characteristic of attachment anxiety) but he does not welcome gestures of support or sympathy in response. He is mistrustful that he will be accurately understood and expects others to be unhelpful (a characteristic of attachment avoidance). During the psychiatric consultation, his ambivalence about expressing distress and seeking help manifests indirectly as a combination of: (1) overt messages that he does not wish to be there and has very little expectation of practical help; and (2) an implied contrary message that he is reluctant to give up the contact. The latter is demonstrated when his many questions, concerns and objections to the psychiatrist's statement of her understanding of the situation and recommendations lead to an appointment extended much longer than a typical consultation.

An attachment formulation of MUS

The attachment formulation of MUS views the perception of a physical symptom as an internal signal of potential danger; the expression of distress and seeking of medical attention for the symptom as care-seeking attachment behaviours; and the relationship in which care is sought as an attachment relationship in which the healthcare provider is assigned the role of attachment figure (Ciechanowski *et al.* 2002b; Hunter and Maunder 2001; Maunder and Hunter 2004). The attachment patterns that would be predicted to be most strongly associated with problematic MUS are the patterns that feature high attachment anxiety, i.e. preoccupied and fearful. Indeed, the preoccupied and fearful patterns of attachment are associated with the highest prevalence of unexplained symptoms, significantly higher than occurs in secure or dismissing patterns (Ciechanowski *et al.* 2002a; Ciechanowski *et al.* 2002b).

Through established patterns of attachment behaviour, adult responses to physical symptoms are directly linked to general patterns of response to perceived dangers that have occurred throughout life. For example, a person with a new symptom has to choose to do something about it or to ignore it. A symptom must, therefore, meet some personal threshold of concern to result in a medical interaction. A person with a secure attachment might seek medical attention because a symptom is severe or disabling, because it does not fit with previous experiences of benign symptoms, because it is similar to a previous problem that required medical treatment, because it doesn't go away when expected, or because it is combined with other symptoms in a worrisome pattern. In the absence of such signs of special concern, a secure person may choose to tolerate a new symptom and wait for its spontaneous resolution, or may assess and deal with its likely cause (e.g. reducing evening coffee consumption to reduce recent insomnia).

On the other hand, a person with prominent attachment anxiety has had developmental experiences that reinforce the expectation that the likely response to danger (whether from within or from others) will be ineffective, and has not had the opportunity to develop a capacity for affect regulation that would facilitate tolerating uncertainty while waiting to see how seriously to interpret a new danger signal. He or she is thus unlikely to interpret a new symptom as benign and has trouble tolerating distress while waiting for the symptom to subside. Vigilance for signs of danger may result in amplification of mild or nonspecific physical sensations. Anxiety caused by the initial experience of a worrisome symptom focuses attention on the symptom and amplifies it, while further complicating the picture by causing a wide range of physical consequences of anxiety, heightening concern even more. These secondary effects of anxiety include tachycardia, rapid breathing, muscle tension and effects of hyperventilation such as lightheadedness and symmetrical distal paraesthesias.

The primary coping strategies associated with attachment anxiety are to express distress and seek proximity to an attachment figure. In a medical setting, distress may be expressed directly as negative affect, but is often indirectly expressed by reporting symptoms and requesting tests. In the context of this anxiety, reassurance of a benign etiology and other forms of medical support are not effective (because they miss the point that the patient's primary difficulty is feeling insecure), often leading doctors to respond to the persistent distress with extra investigations and consultations with specialists. A doctor who is responsive to physical symptoms and inattentive to psychological distress reinforces a patient's selective focus on MUS.

The anomalies of communication that are associated with insecure attachment add to the difficulty of assessing physical symptoms. People with preoccupied attachment tend to express their concern in a manner that conveys emotional distress much more effectively than it provides medical information. Timelines are often confusing. Relevant characters in the illness narrative may be mentioned without providing explanatory context. Narrative threads are often truncated and interrupted before they reach a logical conclusion, as anxiety drives the narrator to a new thought or topic. Reassurance and understanding is actively and often prematurely sought from the medical practitioner (Maunder *et al.* 2006b).

A clinician's difficulty providing effective reassurance may trigger other unhelpful responses within the clinician, such as anger. Since a person with high attachment anxiety expects rejection, a self-fulfilling interpersonal vicious circle may ensue. The clinician perceives a patient to be excessively anxious and clingy and responds with efforts to truncate the expressions of distress and create greater interpersonal distance. In a medical setting, distancing behaviour by the attachment figure (clinician) may take the form of writing a prescription too quickly in order to terminate the contact, providing a referral to another resource, or offering an appointment far in the future. Such distancing behaviour reinforces a patient's expectation of rejection and their self-image of unworthiness and increases the pressure to maintain contact. Ending the appointment may provoke a crisis, often resulting in unusually long and yet unproductive medical appointments.

Patient–provider interactions are further complicated when a patient with MUS has a fearful pattern of attachment because of the added contribution of attachment avoidance. In the fearful pattern, opposing forces of proximity-seeking and attachment avoidance lead to conflictual help-seeking/help-rejecting behaviour. Communication is impaired by combinations of the excessive detail and vague usages of language that are characteristic of attachment anxiety and the premature truncation of enquiry and interpersonal distancing that are characteristic of attachment avoidance. These complex dynamics likely explain why emergency department physicians, who rarely perceive secure patients to be difficult to deal with, more commonly experience interactions with preoccupied and dismissing patients to be difficult (17–19 per cent of interactions), and very commonly experience interactions with patients with fearful attachment to be difficult (39 per cent of interactions) (Maunder et al. 2006a).

Problematic MUS are associated with multiplicity of symptoms, difficult patient–provider interactions, co-morbid psychiatric syndromes, high utilisation of medical resources (Katon, Sullivan and Walker 2001) and childhood adversity (McCauley et al. 1997). Insecure attachment is also often associated with a history of adverse developmental experience, co-morbid anxiety and depression, multiple somatic complaints and patient–provider difficulty. Since insecure attachment is more common and severe among those who have experienced major childhood adversity (Alexander et al. 1998; Lyons-Ruth and Block 1996), an attachment formulation of MUS may help to explain why a history of childhood adversity is so common among patients with problematic MUS. As well, insecure attachment is consistently found to be a risk factor in itself for anxiety and depressive disorders (Bifulco et al. 2002a; Bifulco et al. 2002b). Thus there is a close homology between expected patterns of symptom presentation in insecure attachment and the characteristics of problematic MUS. Adopting a developmental formulation of MUS, based on attachment theory, may help clinicians to maintain an empathic and compassionate response to patients whose behaviour can otherwise elicit unhelpful frustration.

An attachment-informed approach to the management of MUS

The attachment formulation views an interaction between a clinician and a patient with MUS as a dynamic interpersonal system in which the goal is to restore a patient's feeling of security. This perspective can help to reframe an interaction in which exclusive attention to the goals of investigation, diagnosis and treatment of a physical symptom frequently leads to unsatisfactory outcomes. The ways in which the clinician and patient can restore a patient's sense of security are: (1) for the clinician to provide external regulation of a patient's distressing affect; (2) for a patient to enhance his or her capacity for self-regulation of distressing affect; and (3) to enhance access to other sources of support and improve their effectiveness.

Providing external regulation

Two of the primary functions of someone serving (even temporarily) as an attachment figure are to provide a safe haven that shelters an individual from perceived threats and a secure base from which to reassess resources and challenges. Needless to say, in order for a clinician to provide a calming base for an anxious patient, the clinician must first be feeling reasonably calm him or herself. Problematic MUS may provide a challenge to the clinician's sense of security because of concerns about missing an occult organic diagnosis or about conflict with a patient. Having a familiar formulation of the problem may in itself serve to mitigate unnecessary anxiety on the clinician's part.

Several evidence-based strategies for managing problematic MUS can be understood as serving a helpful attachment function. Validating a patient's symptoms and providing an explanatory model[1] reassures a patient that their suffering is being taken seriously and that they are being kept 'in mind'. Providing such an understanding is an example of the attachment figure's capacity to mentalise (i.e. the ability to reflect upon the mental life of others and of oneself), which is a powerful contributor to security. (Although a discussion of mentalising is beyond the scope of this chapter, see Allen 2003 and Fonagy and colleagues 1991 for a description of the development of mentalising and its relationship to attachment security, and Bateman and Fonagy 2009 for evidence of its role in psychotherapy). A clinician's diagnostic and therapeutic conservatism not only reduces the risk of iatrogenic harm and excessive costs but also conveys a sense of calm and rational evaluation of the magnitude of the risks signalled by the MUS. Reliability and responsiveness are characteristics of an attachment figure that promote security (Belsky 2008). A clinician can provide a reliable, predictable and responsive interaction by scheduling frequent (even if brief) appointments during which full attention is paid to the MUS as well as their context.

Beyond predictability and responsiveness, regularly scheduled appointments (rather than ad hoc crisis appointments) serve an additional, important role in problematic MUS by disrupting the contingency between reporting symptoms and receiving support. A vicious circle can occur in which distress (expressed as symptoms) promotes attentive contact, reinforcing the value of the medicalisation of distress as an attachment behaviour, which leads to more symptom reporting, increasingly frustrating medical interactions, more intense insecurity and so on. Regularly scheduled appointments make attentive care predictable and reduce the value of additional symptom reporting as an attachment behaviour.

Enhancing self-regulation

Improving a patient's ability to feel more secure by self-regulating distress is even more important than efforts to provide external support. This begins during the initial history taking, which should include an enquiry into previous health problems and major stressors and how a patient responded to these. Very often this enquiry into preferred modes of coping will reveal personal strengths and experience with effective affect management that can be highlighted and reinforced. Even while first hearing their story, a clinician can remind a patient with MUS about personal strengths that are forgotten or under-emphasised. Additionally, preferred modes of coping that are ultimately counter-productive (such as substance use) can be identified as targets for change.

Education in skills that enhance self-regulation of distressing affect, such as various relaxation techniques, is often valuable both because it gives a person with MUS tools to reduce distress and because it bolsters their sense of self-control and mastery, which are important contributors to feeling secure.

Optimising other sources of support

Preoccupied and fearful patterns of attachment are consistently associated with ineffective social support (Mikulincer and Shaver 2007), which may perpetuate problematic MUS. The fearful expectation of invalidating and rejecting responses from others often leads to a self-fulfilling prophecy. A communication style that emphasises distress but interferes with a coherent understanding of the person's situation compromises the ability of others to understand, sympathise and remain available. Clinging and otherwise excessively dependent requests for support may make others feel overwhelmed and prone to withdrawal. Insisting on attention to physical symptoms (which others may be unable to reduce), rather than difficulties that confidantes may be able to address more effectively, further impairs the value of interacting with others.

Much of modern medical care takes place within the context of a multi-disciplinary team. This can be an ideal model for a patient with MUS, as it distributes the inevitable frustration across several individuals, thus preventing any single practitioner from burning out. However, it requires excellent intra-team communication, and a commitment to 'staying on message'. Otherwise a patient with MUS may come to focus idealistically on one member, while devaluing the input of others. This may eventually result in the team structure and communication becoming as chaotic as the patient's internal world. A team that is cohesive and communicates well, on the other hand, provides affect-regulating structure that a patient can internalise to create greater order. Thus regular, consistent meetings in which a clear care plan is developed and reviewed, and in which team members are encouraged to articulate their experiences – asking for team resolution of new requests, for instance – will allow the clinic to maintain its 'secure base' function for the patient.

The same risk of miscommunication and unintended conflict occurs in the broader health network. Many patients with MUS have involved a wide array of professionals and non-professionals in their care, ranging from medical specialists and generalists to providers of alternative care and spiritual support, friends and family. Given the nature of the presentation of problematic MUS and the difficulties with effective treatment, much advice will be received that is ineffective and in conflict with guidance from other sources. The drive for obtaining comfort through proximity to others means that contact with ineffective sources of care is likely to be perpetuated because the individual will be reluctant to give up any contact, even while new 'experts' are sought. Few of these contacts will be well-informed as to what is happening in the other interactions. As with the systemic chaos that can occur in a clinic team, this pattern of 'fragmentation of the agents of care' (as originally described by Donald Winnicott (1989)) is even more difficult in the broader community. Thus one of the important tasks of a healthcare provider assuming primary care of a person with MUS is to try to bring order and clear communication to a fragmented network of care providers. Emphasising the importance of communication between these individuals and seeking a patient's permission for open communication is an important first step. Over time, encouraging a patient to retain sources of care who are making a unique and valuable contribution and to limit contact with those whose care is being perpetuated 'just in case' will help to bolster the quality of support received within the healthcare system.

Similarly, one also seeks to facilitate the interactions of a patient and their closest family members and confidantes. The goal here is to improve their perception of the quality of support they receive in all regards, not only with their MUS. Thoughtful, non-blaming couple- or family-based sessions can clarify a plan for dealing with the patient's distress when it is expressed within the family, with a goal of containing anxiety. Explication of the interpersonal circumstances that exacerbate feelings of insecurity – and thus amplify MUS – may lead to a different familial interaction that provides support and structured reassurance.

The psychiatrist explains to Simon that unexplained symptoms such as his are a common problem and that very often an underlying disease is not identified. She suggests that while she does not know what is causing Simon's symptoms, it is obvious that the pain is real and it would be helpful to discuss how to limit its impact on his life. Taking the extra time required to work through Simon's objections and concerns, the psychiatrist offers him a plan that focuses on three goals: (1) preventing unintentional complications by avoiding unnecessary tests and excessive consultations with specialists; (2) maintaining regular, scheduled contact with a consistent, trusted healthcare provider every 4–6 weeks to monitor his symptoms and discuss practical steps to limit their impact; and (3) learning techniques that aid in reducing the distress that the symptoms are causing and sometimes help to reduce pain. They discuss resources available to learn relaxation techniques and mindfulness meditation. Although Simon is not interested in pursuing cognitive-behavioural therapy, the psychiatrist describes its potential value and offers to pass on information about its availability to the family doctor in her consultation letter, for Simon's future reference. Simon is disappointed that the plan is not designed to eliminate his symptoms, but feels that his concerns have been heard and have not been minimised. He leaves the office feeling cautiously optimistic.

Summary

Medically unexplained symptoms are a common yet vexing problem that often leads to intense resource utilisation. The most investigated therapeutic interventions, such as CBT, are often ineffective in creating change. An attachment formulation is a parsimonious means of understanding problematic MUS as a social communication of need and insecurity, within the context of a preoccupied or fearful insecure attachment pattern. The goal of the MUS is understood as communicating an ongoing need for proximity to those who can provide solace – in this case a healthcare worker.

Typical medical interventions designed to reduce symptoms, and thus make ongoing contact unnecessary, are unconsciously resisted by patients who are both highly invested in the need for personal validation and support and disadvantaged by the withdrawal of medical support that would accompany a 'cure'. The resulting conflict in which medical intervention can appear to be both sought and rejected contributes to frustration and hopelessness in clinicians. Pre-emptively addressing the attachment needs of a patient, with consistency across time and between clinic personnel, may provide additional benefits in the effort to reduce the distress and frequent presentations associated with MUS, increase recognition of the role of emotion and relationship issues in the quality of life of patients with MUS, and reduce the costs of healthcare.

Note

1   The most appropriate explanatory model varies depending on circumstances and on finding a model that both clinician and patient can agree is valuable. Typically, the most useful 'model' is not complex and is sufficiently flexible to simply provide an acceptable vocabulary for enquiry – it may involve the physiological effects of stress or of anxiety, anger or depression, or simply be a mutual agreement on relevant issues that are secondary to having MUS, such as conflict with doctors, unhelpful patterns of help-seeking, or ineffective social support.

References

Ainsworth, M., Blehar, M., Waters, E. and Wall, S. (1978). *Patterns of Attachment: a psychological study of the strange situation.* Hillsdale, NJ: Erlbaum.

Allen, J.G. (2003). Mentalizing. *Bulletin of the Menninger Clinic* 67, 91–112.

Alexander, P.C., Anderson, C.L., Brand, B., Schaeffer, C.M., Grelling, B.Z. and Kretz, L. (1998). Adult attachment and longterm effects in survivors of incest. *Child Abuse and Neglect* 22, 45–61.

Bartholomew, K. and Horowitz, L.M. (1991). Attachment styles among young adults: a test of a four-category model. *Journal of Personality and Social Psychology* 61, 226–44.

Bateman, A. and Fonagy, P. (2009). Randomized controlled trial of outpatient mentalization-based treatment versus structured clinical management for borderline personality disorder. *American Journal of Psychiatry* 166, 1355–64.

Belsky, J. (2008). Precursors of attachment security. In J. Cassidy and P.R. Shaver (eds), *Handbook of Attachment: theory, research and clincal applications,* 2nd edn, pp. 295–316. New York: Guilford Press.

Bifulco, A., Muran, P.M., Ball, C. and Bernazzani, O. (2002). Adult attachment style. I: its relationship to clinical depression. *Social Psychiatry and Psychiatric Epidemiology* **37**, 50–9.

Bifulco, A., Muran, P.M., Ball, C. and Lille, A. (2002). Adult attachment style. II: its relationship to psychosocial depressive-vulnerability. *Social Psychiatry and Psychiatric Epidemiology* **37**, 60–7.

Bowlby, J. (1969). *Attachment and Loss, Volume 1: Attachment.* New York: Basic Books.

Ciechanowski, P., Katon, W.J., Russo, J.E. and Dwight-Johnson, M.M. (2002a). Association of attachment style to medically unexplained symptoms in patients with hepatitis C. *Psychosomatic Medicine* **43**, 206–12.

Ciechanowski, P., Walker, E.A., Katon, W.J. and Russo, J.E. (2002b). Attachment theory: a model for health care utilization and somatization. *Psychosomatic Medicine* **64**, 660–7.

Demers, R.Y., Altamore, R., Mustin, H., Kleinman, A. and Leonardi, D. (1980). An exploration of the dimensions of illness behavior. *Journal of Family Practice* **11**, 1085–92.

Escobar, J.I., Waitzkin, H., Silver, R.C., Gara, M. and Holman, A. (1998). A bridged somatization: A study in primary care. *Psychosomatic Medicine* **60**, 466–72.

Fonagy, P., Steele, M., Steele, H., Moran, G.S. and Higgitt, A.C. (1991). The capacity for understanding mental states: The reflective self in parent and child and its significance for security of attachment. *Infant Mental Health Journal* **12**, 201–18.

Fraley, R.C. and Davis, K.E. (1997). Attachment formation and transfer in young adults' close friendships and romantic relationships. *Personal Relationships* **4**, 131–44.

George, C. and West, M. (2001). The development and preliminary validation of a new measure of adult attachment: the adult attachment projective. *Attachment and Human Development* **3**, 30–61.

Groves, J.E. (1978). Taking care of the hateful patient. *New England Journal of Medicine* **298**, 883–7.

Hazan, C. and Shaver, P.R. (1994). Attachment as an organizational framework for research on close relationships. *Psychological Inquiry* **5**, 1–22.

Hesse, E. (2008). The Adult Attachment Interview: protocol, method of analysis, and empirical studies. In J. Cassidy and P.R. Shaver (eds), *Handbook of Attachment: theory, research and clinical applications,* 2nd edn, pp. 552–98. New York: Guilford Press.

Hunter, J.J. and Maunder, R.G. (2001). Using attachment theory to understand illness behavior. *General Hospital Psychiatry* **23**, 177–82.

Katon, W., Sullivan, M. and Walker, E. (2001). Medical symptoms without identified pathology: relationship to psychiatric disorders, childhood and adult trauma, and personality traits. *Annals of Internal Medicine* **134**, 917–25.

Kroenke, K. (2003). Patients presenting with somatic complaints: epidemiology, psychiatric comorbidity and management. *International Journal of Methods in Psychiatric Research* **12**, 34–43.

——(2007). Efficacy of treatment for somatoform disorders: a review of randomized controlled trials. *Psychosomatic Medicine* **69**, 881–8.

Locke, G.R., III, Weaver, A.L., Melton, L.J., III and Talley, N.J. (2004). Psychosocial factors are linked to functional gastrointestinal disorders: a population based nested case-control study. *American Journal of Gastroenterology* **99**, 350–7.

Lyons-Ruth, K. and Block, D. (1996). The disturbed caregiving system: relations among childhood trauma, maternal caregiving, and infant affect and attachment. *Infant Mental Health Journal* **17**, 257–75.

Maunder, R.G. and Hunter, J. (2004). An integrated approach to the formulation and psychotherapy of medically unexplained symptoms: meaning- and attachment-based intervention. *American Journal of Psychotherapy* **58**, 17–33.

——(2009). Assessing patterns of adult attachment in medical patients. *General Hospital Psychiatry* **31**, 123–30.

——(2012) Prototype-Based Model of Adult Attachment for Clinicians. *Psychodynamic Psychotherapy* **40**, 549–74.

Maunder, R.G., Lancee, W.J., Nolan, R.P., Hunter, J.J. and Tannenbaum, D.W. (2006a). The relationship of attachment insecurity to subjective stress and autonomic function during standardized acute stress in healthy adults. *Journal of Psychosomatic Research* **60**, 283–90.

Maunder, R.G., Panzer, A., Viljoen, M., Owen, J., Human, S. and Hunter, J.J. (2006b). Physicians' difficulty with emergence department patients is related to patients' attachment style. *Social Science and Medicine* **63**, 552–62.

McCauley, J., Kern, D.E., Kolodner, K., Dill, L., Schroeder, A.F., DeChant, H.K. and Bass, E.B. (1997). Clinical characteristics of women with a history of childhood abuse: unhealed wounds. *Jama* **277**, 1362–8.

Mikulincer, M. and Shaver, P.R. (2007). *Attachment in Adulthood: structure, dynamics, and change*. New York: Guilford Press.

Shaver, P. R., and Mikulincer, M. (2002). Attachment-related psychodynamics. *Attachment and Human Development* **4**, 133–61.

Simon, G.E. and Von Korff, M. (1991). Somatization and psychiatric disorder in the NIMH epidemiologic catchement area study. *American Journal of Psychiatry* **148**, 1494–1500.

Smith, G.R., Monson, R.A., and Ray, D.C. (1986). Psychiatric consultation in somatization disorder: A randomized study. *New England Journal of Medicine* **314**, 1407–13.

Smith, G.R., Rost, K. and Kashner, T.M. (1995). A trial of the effect of a standardized psychiatric consultation on health outcomes and costs in somatizing patients. *Archives of General Psychiatry* **52**, 238–43.

Smith, R.C., Greenbaum, D.S., Vancouver, J.B., Henry, R.C., Reinhart, M.A., Greenbaum, R.B., Dean, H.A. and Mayle, J.E (1990). Psychosocial factors are associated with health care seeking rather than diagnosis in irritable bowel syndrome. *Gastroenterology* **98**, 293–301.

Sumathipala, A. (2007). What is the evidence for the efficacy of treatments for somatoform disorders? A critical review of previous intervention studies. *Psychosomatic Medicine* **69**, 889–900.

Talley, N.J., Howell, S. and Poulton, R. (2001). The irritable bowel syndrome and psychiatric disorders in the community: is there a link? *American Journal of Gastroenterology* **96**, 1072–9.

White, K.L., Williams, T.F. and Greenberg, B.G. (1961). The ecology of medical care. *New England Journal of Medicine* **265**, 885–92.

Whitehead, W.E., Bosmajian, L., Zonderman, A.B., Costa, P.T., Jr. and Schuster, M.M. (1988). Symptoms of psychologic distress associated with irritable bowel syndrome. Comparison of community and medical clinic samples. *Gastroenterology,* **95**, 709–14.

Winnicott, D.W. (1989). Psycho-somatic disorder. In C.Winnicott, R. Shepherd and M. Davis (eds), *Psycho-analytic Explorations*, pp. 103–18. Cambridge, MA: Harvard University Press.

Section 3

Specific populations

Chapter 11

Bringing a gendered perspective to attachment theory in therapy

Susie Orbach

This chapter argues that understanding the gendered aspects of attachment is of value. Many current mental health issues, from violence against self, aggression towards others, body dysmorphias, eating problems and sexuality concerns to insecurity in relationships and in parenting, arise out of the gendered prescriptions that mark our child rearing and psycho-social relationships. An awareness of the inflections of gender on the clinician and on the patient is important in providing understanding at a sufficiently complex level.

Attachment theory offers itself as gender neutral. Not exactly gender blind, for there is much in the work that relates to the attachment style of the mother.[1] But like a good deal of psychological and psychoanalytic theory, the meaning of the mother's gender, how it will inform her psyche, her social practice, the woman's own understanding of the significance of her gender and that of the baby, the context into which she parents and so on, is left absent. It is as though, because we are deemed to share certain assumptions, these assumptions do not need to be questioned.

Bowlby's work was one of questioning and deconstruction in the process of theory making. He looked, he observed, he studied. He took apart things that were taken for granted – sometimes the most obvious – and in recasting the basic mechanisms of infant and child development as an attachment paradigm, he gave us the means by which to see the significance of the early relational style between mother and infant-toddler as indicative of the emotional security or insecurity of the child and later the adult. Missing from Bowlby's work (Bowlby 1969, 1973, 1980), but of interest to later generations who have found a resonance with the attachment paradigm, has been attention to gender and the ways in which conscious and unconscious apprehension of gender shape the mother's self experience and the ways in which she relates and attaches to children of different genders.

Gender and infancy

Gender is not a given (Fine 2010; Hare-Mustin and Marecek 1990). It is a psychological and social outcome of biological interpretation. A baby is anticipated in gendered categories. There is no such thing as a non-gendered baby. There are babies with male sexual characteristics, with female sexual characteristics and with hermaphroditic sexual characteristics. The latter are commonly assigned the more 'appropriate' gender at birth and historically fingers were crossed that secondary sexual characteristics of the opposite gender will not emerge at puberty and that medical interventions to support the assigned gender will be relatively trouble free.

It is well-nigh impossible to ask a new parent about the baby without reference to gender. The conversation stops. Enquiries about the health and the weight of the baby only take one so far. We need to know whether we are speaking of a baby girl or a baby boy because sets of behaviours, attitudes, meanings, feelings and expectations are unconsciously influenced by gender. Without our recognising it, the constructs of masculinity and femininity prompt us in both obvious and subtle ways. These prompts always relate to the social, temporal, class and cultural circumstances of what it means to be a girl or a boy. Just over a hundred years ago, a boy would be dressed in pink and a girl in blue. Today we would find it hard to dress the baby boy in pink (although it would be alright for the baby girl to wear blue) and the reason is because, following the designation of gender, how we hold, how we feed, how we potty train, the register of our voices, the fantasies we have about how to treat the baby and relate to its well-being, depend on gender. Pink on a baby boy transgresses the felt experience of gender. We are not used to it. It will incline us to relate to that particular boy and his mother in a way that is out of kilter to present cultural norms. It is not a neutral curiosity that he is dressed that way. If or when we encounter this kind of 'gendered' discordance we come up with explanations to explain it to ourselves.

Gender transmission is unconscious and conscious

On average, we breast feed boys for longer than girls (Belotti 1977). Each feed is lengthier than for girls. Weaning is more gradual than it is for girls. Potty training comes later than for girls. Holding is more frequent than it is for girls (Belotti 1977). These observable and the not so observable behaviours are part of the attachment environment. They are not separate from it but are woven into the very texture of relating. They shape the mother's experience of her mothering in explicit and subtle ways, inflecting both her sense of herself and her sense of the new baby to whom she is relating. Her conscious and unconscious feelings and knowledge about gender are central to the mother–baby couple. Consider for a moment, then, the emotional implications of the use of the word greedy in relation to a hungry girl infant versus the use of the word eager in relation to a hungry boy. These adverbs describe the infant's appetites in ways that range from a (mild-ish) criticism of the infant's appetite to an embrace and enjoyment of it. The word is not value free. Maybe the mother admires the girl baby's 'greed'. Maybe she fears for a daughter with a robust appetite. Most likely, she will project on to her daughter feelings she has about her own appetite. These will include her hopes and her fears which in themselves will encode the cultural values seen to be intrinsic to femininity. Whatever the mother's response, it is set inside a matrix of familial and social beliefs that inevitably direct aspects of her own femininity called forth by her conceptions of mothering. They form part of the attachment nexus.

The transmission of attachment styles: from mother to baby and from baby to mother

Feeding, holding and potty training are behaviours that are visible and easily amenable to observation. If we reflect on the often less visible gender-led instructions that coalesce around issues of nurture, dependency, agency and separation, we will see that these important aspects of development, so apparent in childhood, adolescence and adulthood, have their roots in the very early relating between mother and child. More on this presently.

The basis of secure attachment emerges out of the experience of having one's needs attended to in a relatively consistent manner. It involves being seen as an individual – as both separate and connected to intimate others. The sense of being an individual, that is to say, one's own person, emerges from being recognised and seen.

Recognition is the outcome of interpersonal relating. As one responds to and initiates the various emotional and physical repertoires of infancy and early toddlerhood, one inhabits a sense of being. Being seen and being responded to and showing that one has been, make up the intersubjective field between the mothering person and the baby. This interplay provides the basis of secure selfhood.

The nature of the relationship that is offered will come to constitute the emotional bedrock of what organises the notion of 'relationship' in the baby's internal structure. The human infant is dependent on its caregiver and its own idioms and desires will be honed in relation to those needs that the mother is able to meet. Because the human infant is dependent outside of the womb for survival, the baby is not able to turn away from the relationship with mother that to an outsider looks negative and destructive. It cannot leave and find a more satisfactory one. Even if it could, the journey from neonate to the kind of human being one is going to be is formed through the relationship that is offered. If the baby experiences a relationship which is negative and destructive, this will form part of the baby's developing sense of self. What the baby receives and what is received back from the baby in the complex dialogue between mother and baby will be the bedrock psychological foundation for the baby's identity, its place in relation to mother and it will form the template for future relationships.

Secure attachment

Attachment theory shows high correlation between a mother's attachment profile and that of her offspring (Fonagy *et al.* 1995; Steele and Steele 2008). This makes sense. The secure mother conveys confidence in her own being. She is thus able to offer the baby a relationship of safety – one in which the baby will be accepted, enjoyed and can thus thrive. The concerns of infancy – early feeding, sleeping, walking and so on – are experienced as an aspect of mothering, not as a stimulus to incapacity or extreme worry. The baby's responsiveness to the mother reinforces in the mother her sense of herself as an adequate mother. This is important. The mother makes the baby and the baby makes the mother and they reciprocally influence one another's emotional states.

Anxious attachment

The anxiously attached mother will find the needs of her infant more perplexing and anxiety provoking. Out of her own history and the experience of being attended to in an anxious manner, she will engage with her infant with a certain hesitancy and nervousness and this in turn will be the emotional ambience that her infant will absorb. The infant will then feed back this hesitancy and nervousness to the mother, creating an emotional loop between them that is authenticated by each of them through this felt sense of anxiety.

Avoidant dismissive attachment

The avoidant dismissive mother who is unused to close emotional contact in her own emotional history may offer her infant a relationship that encodes this way of being. She may treat the infant as though he or she were detached and should 'get on with it', feeding, changing and putting the baby down in a mechanical manner. Emotional dependency is refused and the mother–infant dyad is characterised by missing and ambivalence.

Disorganised attachment

The disorganised mother, too, will convey in her actions and affect the jitteriness which marks her relation to self and others. Her infant will know this as the fundamental form of relating and it will imprint her own relation to self and be part of what makes up the relationship between mother and herself.

All these different attachment styles[2] show themselves in the therapy relationship. They are an important dimension of the clinical situation and provide useful information for the therapist and, in time, for the patient.

Culture and attachment styles

Woven into the attachment styles will be the beliefs and customs governing gender (and other crucial social markings). Psychological femininity and psychological masculinity become quasi material structures in the minds and bodies of individuals.[3] Just as babies are related to with reference to gender, so the individual relates to her or himself with regard to the social practices of gender.

The question for psychoanalytic gender theorists is how the psychological forms of being that signify gender are apprehended and played out.

We have seen that the very different treatment accorded to boy infants and girl infants vis-à-vis feeding and potty training are an important aspect of gendering. I have also suggested as an example that the language with which the child's appetite is described is gendered (there are many more I could use). How then do the equally profound and deeply felt issues of dependency, autonomy, competition, longing, envy, anger and sexuality, issues that are saturated by gender at many levels (although perhaps not all), come to be enacted in the attachment relationship? What is the primary parent or parental substitute doing in order to ensure that girls become psychological girls and boys become psychological boys?

Girls have been historically raised to provide for the dependency needs of others (Eichenbaum and Orbach 1982, 1983). This includes looking out for their children and their intimate relationship as well as their parents. Boys have been historically raised to provide for the economic shelter of others. In the old deal, women looked after the men emotionally in return for the legitimacy of their sexuality and for economic protection. While a woman's activity was being a midwife to the desires of others and she gained her sense of femininity in the enactment of these behaviours, men were raised to be protective in a warrior-like sense and to take on identities that encoded a narrative of the valiant, the independent, the heroic.

While these stark realities have become muted, the vestiges of these gendered imperatives continue, nowhere so manifest as in regard to issues of emotional dependency. It is still the case that girls are directed to take care of the emotional and dependency needs of others and to meet their own needs for nurture in the service of caring for others (while appearing to be the dependent ones). Boys meanwhile are still raised to expect that their dependency needs will be attended to without them having to notice it, and that their sense of independence will rest on the implicit knowledge that there is someone there for them (while appearing to be need-free). While girls are schooled in the language of emotional initiative, boys are schooled in the language of independence.

Girls and women bond together through identification and an affiliative stance that reaches for the common and familiar. Their sense of self is reinforced in relationships of confirmation and empathy. Boys and men bond through competition and challenge. They feel themselves to exist as boys and men as they differentiate. While these descriptions may sound unrefined, they reflect the felt experience of femininity and masculinity today. This has significant implications for heterosexuality, for girls' and boys' psychology, the psychological transactions between women and men, for women and men's sexuality, and of course for the therapy relationship.

How can we make use of this in the therapy relationship?

The gender conscious therapist will observe that while women and men both come to therapy in need, they show this differently. I am not making an argument that disagrees with Bowlby, rather I am proposing that the forms of attachment and the defence structures developed can additionally be seen through the gender lens. For the therapist to find the words to enable the individual to understand the ways in which their desires and motivations emerge is helpful. One does not say to a patient: you are doing this because you are a woman and therefore you feel x. Nor does one say, you feel this because you have a disorganised attachment. Neither of these kind of statements would be therapy. However, it is helpful for therapists to be able to understand gender phenomena that are woven into the attachment paradigm. It is equally helpful for individuals to understand the complexity of the ways in which their behaviours and desires are structured – what they imagine they want, what gets in the way, the means by which they inadvertently trip themselves up and so on.

In regards to women, there are a cluster of issues that come up frequently whatever the specifics of the attachment structure. These include: a fear of dependency; a tendency to give to the other in ways that might be quite driven; a difficulty with receiving and digesting the care and attention that comes towards one; a hyper-criticality towards their own physical sense of self that negatively affects sexuality and body acceptance.

These themes emerge in the therapy and they are often enacted within the therapy relationship within the transference–countertransference dynamic. If one is a woman working with a woman, one's own identification with these struggles needs to be addressed in supervisory and seminar settings so that there is not an unconscious collusion with the difficulties that are being presented (Eichenbaum and Orbach 1982). When we started The Women's Therapy Centre three and a half decades ago, it was noticeable how, after about six sessions, women would say that they felt so much better and that they were ready to stop therapy. This sentiment was accurate on many levels but the persistence with which it emerged encouraged us to reflect. In our study groups, we came to understand that this was almost like a built-in protection – a defence – against a woman's longing for attachment and dependency. The dilemma was that having felt listened to – which went against her experience – she felt compelled to put a lid on her desire for contact. The wish to stop came from fears of being too vulnerable, too much in need, too attached. Engaging with this issue and being aware of the tendency towards collusion with the woman's disdain and reluctance around her dependency and attachment needs, as well as her longing for that attachment and the difficulties with acceptance, was and is crucial. It opens the way to productive therapies (Orbach 1990; Orbach and Eichenbaum 1986).

If one is a man working with women, a different but equally collusive aspect may be evoked in relation to the woman's hesitancy about dependency. Men can be as uneasy as women about women's dependency needs. They may concur with the patient's criticism of her own longings as being 'too needy' and read the defence as the real issue instead of understanding it as the woman's unconscious fear of her own desires for deep attachment. Beyond this, the therapist may not understand the difficulty with receiving that can be a challenge. In the absence of being able to receive, women can become caught up in giving and in reassuring the therapist how well he is doing. This points to another aspect that the male therapist needs to be alerted to: the woman's tendency to divert away from her own conflicts and desires. For a male therapist to notice and challenge his own gendered prejudices is important.

If we turn now to the ways in which masculinity is woven into attachment, then we can address the issues that need addressing in general in the therapy. The gendered prejudices that are brought to masculinity are no less troublesome than those brought to femininity and it is important for therapists to be aware of the gendered expectations they carry and the ways in which these can ill service their patients. A common issue for men in the initial stage of therapy is hesitancy with showing their emotions, but when they are encouraged to do so, there is little reluctance to staying in therapy. Their difficulty is with the premise of a process that is not immediately solution based. It is not that men need to be coaxed into being helped, but sometimes there is a need for a form of psycho-education in which the links between feelings, behaviours and repressed conflicts require explication in order for the man to feel sufficiently comfortable to make use of the therapy.

Men can also disdain attachment needs. They may do this through flirting in the session, by showing a strength that is supposed to nullify need and, commonly, by making their own needs to be about the other's neediness (often ascribing them to their sexual partner). Teasing out and endeavouring to enable the individual to recognise his own needs for attachment and dependency can be an important aspect of the therapy. This may mean receiving them in the therapy relationship and helping him to risk the recognition of his desire for attachment. This is a tricky process. Part of socialisation, and woven into the attachment pattern towards boys, is that a boy's/man's needs will be met (by a woman) without them being exposed. The attention to men's emotional states is something that can happen surreptitiously – I do not mean this in an underhand sense but in the sense that women feel it to be essential to their own identity to look after others, and attending to men/boys is part of that. Thus, a man may not know about his attachment and dependency needs unless they are not being met. If he has suffered the loss of a partner or a relationship is in difficulty, the withdrawal of the other can highlight the importance of an attachment/dependency need that boomerangs back on him. When these needs land back they can be quite frightening, for the man may not be accustomed to them. This is in distinction to the woman, who knows and is frequently ashamed of these needs in herself.

Delicacy is required on the part of the therapist. Male therapists have to work hard not to share the prejudices of the man who may scorn the needs that now beset him. And women therapists have to work hard not simply to meet them but to address with their patient how he can acknowledge this important aspect of who he is. Meeting them in the therapy relationship without discussing what is occurring reproduces the original disavowal and does not enable a man to feel a confidence about his own acceptance of his needs.

Summary

In this chapter I am highlighting in general terms the differing ways attachment needs can emerge, can be missed and can be addressed in therapy. Of course there are many subtleties to the ways in which attachment and gender play out and the manner in which the attachment and gender binaries occur within couples (hetero- and homo-sexual couples) other than the therapeutic couple (Orbach 1993, 2007). My aim in this chapter has been to remind us of how profoundly gender shapes our deepest sense(s) of self and our relation to others, and the consequent shape of our defences against the most private longings and needs for attachment that humans carry. In paying attention, rather than skirting over such defences, we enable ourselves and our patients to enter into a deeper humanity in which, instead of disavowal and shame, the recognition of attachment can be known, held and acted on.

Notes

1   I use the term mother to describe the primary relationship between caregiver and child. This person is most commonly female whether she is the mother, grandmother, nanny or other substitute. Obviously there are extremely interesting consequences for the emotional impact of gender when children are reared by two parents and the gender of these parents will affect the attachment milieu in profound ways. This chapter restricts itself to the impact of gender when the primary parent is a woman.
2   Of course for most people relational structures are not neatly packaged but contain elements of perhaps two or more categories; nevertheless, they are a useful grid.
3   Obviously in some cases these are actually material but I use the term to describe the obduracy of felt experience that structures the individual's experience of being a girl or a boy, a woman or a man.

References

Belotti, E.G. (1977). *Little Girls*. London: Writers and Readers.
Bowlby, J. (1969). *Attachment and Loss, Volume 1: Attachment*. New York: Basic Books.
——(1973). *Attachment and Loss, Volume 2: Separation: anxiety and anger*. New York: Basic Books.
——(1980) *Attachment and Loss, Volume 3: Loss: sadness and depression*. New York: Basic Books.
Eichenbaum, L. and Orbach, S. (1982). *Understanding Women: a feminist psychoanalytic approach*. London: Penguin Books.
——(1983). *What do Women Want?* London: Michael Joseph.
Fine, C. (2010). *Delusion of Gender*. New York: Norton.

Fonagy, P., Steele, M., Steele, H., Leigh, T., Kennedy, R., Mattoon, G. and Target, M. (1995). The predictive validity of Mary Main's adult attachment interview: a psychoanalytical and developmental perspective on the transgenerational transmission of attachment and borderline states. In S. Goldberg, R. Muir and J. Kerr (eds), *Attachment Theory: social, developmental and clinical perspectives*, pp. 233–78. Hillsdale, NJ: The Analytic Press.

Hare-Mustin, R.T. and Marecek, J. (1990). *Making a Difference: psychology and the construction of gender*. New Haven: Yale University Press.

Orbach, S. (1990). Gender and dependency in psychotherapy. *Journal of Social Work Practice* **4**, 1–15.

——(1993). Women, men and intimacy. In C. Clulow (ed.), *Rethinking Marriage: public and private perspectives*. London: Karnac.

——(2007). Separated attachments and sexual aliveness: how changing attachment patterns can enhance intimacy, *Attachment* **1**, 8–17. (Reprinted in C. Clulow [ed.], 2009: *Sex, Attachment and Couple Psychotherapy: psychoanalytic perspectives*; London: Karnac).

Orbach, S. and Eichenbaum, L. (1986). Separation and intimacy: crucial practice issues in working with women in therapy. In S. Ernst and M. Maguire (eds), *Living with the Sphinx*. London: The Women's Press.

Steele, H. and Steele, M. (2008). Early attachment predicts emotion recognition at 6 and 11 years. *Attachment and Human Development* **10**, 379–93.

Chapter 12

Attachment in African Caribbean families

Lennox K. Thomas

Understanding attachment behaviour and its role in the life cycle is important when working across cultures. This chapter focuses on therapeutic work with people from Caribbean communities and what needs to be considered when using attachment theory. Beginning with the history of attachment and loss, the chapter moves on to consider mental health in Caribbean communities. A case study of a Caribbean man is used to identify attachment based practice. Being without ethnic frontier, attachment theory is useful if we can understand its adapted styles in different communities. Studies conducted by Ainsworth (1967) in different countries with a variety of parents and infants from different cultural backgrounds focused on child-rearing styles and attachment. From studies in Uganda and the USA, Ainsworth developed and categorised the Attachment Styles – Secure, Avoidant and Resistant/Ambivalent – on the basis of how the infant responds to a series of separations and reunions with their mother. Main and Weston (1982) and Hesse and Main (2000) later described the category of infants who displayed a Disorganised attachment style. Despite the establishment of these 'cross-cultural' systems of classifications of individual differences in attachment, observations of caregivers and infants have demonstrated a range of different attachment behaviours and caregiving practices across cultures, including multiple caregiving and the suckling of other mother's babies (Marvin *et al.* 1977). In an interesting study based on attachment patterns in the USA and Japan, Rothbaum and colleagues (2000) consider the cultural difference that skews findings in attachment research. The authors found that descriptors such as autonomy and independence are linked to Western individualism, which would affect the lens through which attachment theorists see behaviour. Attachment theory, they believe, is infused with Western assumptions. Whilst attachment is a basic human behaviour, adaptation is dependent on cultural, economic and social factors (Thomas 1996). In order to work effectively across cultural and ethnic boundaries, a close view of the context is therefore always important.

A history of broken attachments

It would be difficult to have a discussion about psychological treatment of Caribbean people without talking about attachment separation and loss. The region has a long history of separations and the breaking of family bonds. Without the context of their enslavement and the patterns that developed during that time, such as the separation of men and women and the anonymous fathering of children, there will be little understanding of current family structure.

> Basically, the system used separation of mothers from their babies, of loving couples from each other, as a conscious and unconscious method of creating anxiety, depression and hopelessness. Under this system the development of togetherness in families was foreclosed.
>
> (Fletchman-Smith 2011: 49)

People of the colonies had taken up arms to defend the empire during both world wars. After the Second World War, West Indians were asked again to assist the mother country in peacetime by the ministry of labour recruiting in the West Indies. This led to large-scale postwar separations. The novelist Andrea Levy (2004) charts the movement of a young Jamaican couple in her book *Small Island*. Like many young people they saw their opportunities in the United Kingdom for work, a new life and support for their families back home. Some parents did not expect to stay away for long, having left spouses and children behind. Many children saw their mothers leave to join dad and, in time, these children would leave grandparents to join their parents in the United Kingdom (Arnold 1975, 1997; Feldman and Marriott 1969). These separations seem to have been accepted as a way of life and echoed plantation separations. The children of Windrush parents who arrived between the late fifties and the sixties were separated from all that was familiar to them and in many cases faced difficulties. One might ask how this history relates to attachment and the lives of people that are now seen by therapists and social workers.

Whilst the patient's collective history of separation might be an unpleasant truth, keeping it outside the scope and boundaries of therapy will not help their emotional development. Tracking family patterns of broken attachments is important in order to help them to understand what might have been set up for them long before they were born, and which they are at risk of repeating. Separation is a big part of Caribbean history and this became something to which the people of the region were desensitised. The harshness of attitude to separation and loss came to be seen as strength because to really experience such loss would destroy the soul. Being able to support a family often meant leaving its youngest and eldest members behind. Reunion of these families was generally smooth but some children had difficulties settling down with their parents. Eve, a former patient, described meeting with her mother at a UK airport after a separation of six years. Eve was told that it was her mother, but she had been convinced that when the ship with her mother on board had disappeared off the horizon in the Caribbean Sea, her four-year-old mind told her that the ship had sunk. This lady who was hugging her at the airport in London must then have been a new mother whom she and her sister came to refer to as 'the lady'. It took some weeks for them to be convinced that it was the same mother with whom they had had a loving relationship and whose leaving was experienced as a death. This young girl settled well and was able to recognise in the lady the loving aspects of the mother who was a distant memory to her.

Not all reunions went well and many children who joined parents at a later age had greater difficulty making a loving connection. Some could not accept the authority of people they hardly knew and demanded to be sent back home to their grandparents. Many people had lived with parents in extended family groups, so young parents who had left children behind hid their pain of separation by putting a brave face on it, assured that their children were in the safe care of their grandmothers. That they were missed and loved was not often shared with the children who arrived from the Caribbean, because parents had often found it difficult to revisit their emotional partings from them. Feeling unwanted and not thought about in their absence led in turn to these young people keeping their feelings of hurt to themselves.

The mass evacuation of British city children during the Second World War and the emotional difficulties experienced by both mothers and children seemed to merit study. Prompted by the work of Bowlby, James and Joyce Robertson and Claire Winnicott, a study was conducted by Elaine Arnold (Robertson) (1975) with young Caribbean children who came to join their parents in the United Kingdom. Dr Arnold followed up cohorts of these children as they moved into adulthood, parenthood and now grandparenthood (Arnold 2012). When breakdown in these relationships threatened the fabric of the family, many older children were accommodated in children's homes. With hindsight, social workers might not have been so ready to take these children from their families without some attempt at addressing the problems and trying to repair the fractured relationships. There had been a variety of reasons for difficulties; in some cases there were new young siblings born to parents in the UK. Some children were unable to engage because of the loyal bonds they had developed with grandparents and were afraid of risking this through closeness with parents in the UK. Others could not cope with the change of circumstances and came to see their parents as preventing them from returning to their beloved grandparents. Because time had lapsed, and in some cases parents separated under the strain of being in the UK, children came to a step-parent who they did not get on with.

Children's institutions presented them with a culture shock and differed considerably from the almost Victorian system of order and physical discipline that many were accustomed to in the Caribbean. In many cases institutional care further served to distance these young people from their family, because they often absorbed the attitudes and customs of those around them. In some cases incurring a third or fourth separation, some of these young people became closed off emotionally or volatile and unhappy about the way they felt treated. This degree of separation and loss is traumatic but was not always recognised and not appropriately dealt with by the social care and probation services. Post Traumatic Stress Disorder as a result of multiple separations, and its contribution to family breakdown, was not entirely understood.

Mental health and Caribbean communities

There were many factors that contributed to mental ill-health in the new migrants from the Caribbean. In addition to the many social problems, there were the difficult messages of racism and feeling unwanted in the cold mother country. Children were equally exposed to these harsh experiences. On beginning school many Caribbean children were assessed as educationally subnormal (Coard 1971). At a later date in the United Kingdom black professionals questioned the degree to which racism played a part in the diagnosis of subnormality in Caribbean children. Bernard Coard began the debate in 1971 about the cultural biases in psychological testing and how this played against black children. This is explored in the publication *How the West Indian Child is made Educationally Subnormal by the British School System*.

The issue of racist attitudes among white British professionals had not yet been considered as a factor in the labelling of black children, which was coupled with issues of the children's identity and self esteem. In the United States, however, African American psychologists were commissioned to study identity issues in school children, and racial prejudice featured highly in this (Clarke and Clark 1947). This study was later conducted in the United Kingdom by Davey and Norburn (1980) in a similar enquiry about children in British schools. The findings of these studies seemed to ask many questions about the prevalence of prejudiced attitudes among school children, absorbed from the society around them. An important outcome was the question of the degree to which black children had internalised negative self identities and how false self issues had affected them. If developing attachment relationships is a lifelong activity and children move into trusting relationships outside the home, how does racism affect this? In a society that can be openly discriminatory, how does this locate black children in relationships outside the home, in the nursery or school? Some black children employed a 'proxy self' for psychological protection against racism in their dealings with white people in order to secure a sense of themselves. Assuming a false self-presentation as described by Winnicott (1964/1986), they could get by in the short term, but this could ultimately lead to psychological splits, incurring later damage (Thomas 1995). Whilst identification by proxy can be a useful childhood defence that affords the child some ability to function, the inability to separate this from the real self can, as Winnicott indicated, lead to mental health problems in adolescence and adulthood.

Both GPs and school psychological services were reluctant to refer black people for therapy and many were treated with anti-psychotic medication or were sectioned under the Mental Health Act. Littlewood and Lipsedge (1997) had found from figures collected in 1977 that West Indian men and women were more than two and a half times more likely to be admitted to hospital for schizophrenia than people of English and Welsh backgrounds. Eaton and Harrison (2000) found this figure to be between two and eight times more likely in parts of the United Kingdom. The over-representation of Caribbean people in the mental health statistics led to suspicions of discrimination. Black people's mistrust of the medical establishment was at its height after the exposure of the Tuskegee syphilis experiment (Jones 1981). In order to understand the progress of the disease, medical practitioners left over 300 African American men untreated without their knowledge for over forty years. Consequently many died, wives were infected and children born with congenital syphilis. That such unethical practices should be conducted with white subjects was unthinkable to many. Other debates into the 1980s about intelligence and black people maintained suspicion of white psychology. The effect of racism and discrimination in the UK, and other issues they met with, played their own part in the difficulties faced by some families.

From research in the early eighties, Kareem and Littlewood (1992) identified dedicated intercultural psychotherapy and counselling services that showed promising results (Acharyya *et al*. 1989). Prior to Kareem's work there had been little interest in the poor showing of ethnic minorities in psychotherapy and talking therapy in the United Kingdom. Psychiatrists Burke (1984) and McKenzie (2006) have considered that the experience of racism and the daily grind of stress play some part in the high numbers of African Caribbean people presenting with what appear to be serious mental illness. The provision of culturally sensitive psychotherapy played an important part in prevention and recovery for some of these patients. Separation and broken attachments are an unmentionable truth in the history of African-descended people and its ubiquity is such that it has gone unrecognised for many years. Repeated separation and loss as a result of migration might have impacted on psychological wellbeing (Thomas 2010). Understanding attachment behaviour is not only important for understanding its role in the patient's life cycle but also for understanding affective responses to loss.

Using attachment theory

Before Bowlby's (1951, 1958) observations of what took place between infants and their caregivers, Melanie Klein (1951) had moved the locus of interest in psychoanalysis from a one- to a two-person psychology. Seeing the patient in relationship to another and being interested in the context of the developmental history widened the scope for therapy.

Technique used in attachment therapy has been developed for use in all relationship-based therapies, with individuals, couples and families. The practice of attachment based psychotherapy is relatively new and has come about in the light of developmental findings by attachment specialists and the work done by psychotherapists on early development such as Winnicott (1960), Spitz (1945), Fraiberg (1980) and latterly, relational psychotherapists.

From neuroscience, Schore (2002) teaches about the importance of reciprocal bonds between infants and their primary caregivers, which act to 'switch on' important brain functions for the baby. Early bonding with babies begins before they are born and develops with feeding, holding and attunement to the babies' cries. Infants in secure attachment relationships with caregivers have pre-verbal 'conversations' with them that help with the co-construction of their personality and with their ability to make sense of the world around them. This is part of their lifelong quest for understanding others, themselves, and themselves in relation to others.

Beyond the biologically determined need of bonding for survival, the infant's connection with its primary carer cements their relationship and is the first opportunity for the child's learning. Generally, families transmit attachment and child-rearing styles and, of course, this is set in a cultural context. Therapy is relationship focused and lends itself well to the work of social workers, psychologists, psychotherapists and others. Attachment based therapies do not just rely on making what is unconscious conscious, but endeavour to repair the individual's relational systems that might have led to difficulties in their emotional or psychological functioning. The experience of the therapist as an accessible, sympathetic figure will be helpful to the patient in engaging with their past and the process of change. Transference and countertransference resemble an object relations use of the concepts, covering the broad span of both the patient's developmental and contemporary relationships.

The following case explores the difficulties that arose between a teenager and his mother when he came to join her in the United Kingdom after a separation of nine years. Steve had been in the care of his parents and grandparents until he was left in the care of grandparents at the age of three years. The case illustrates the usefulness of the attachment skills employed by the psychotherapist in helping the patient to deal with his despair and isolation. He began therapy after developing mental health problems many years later.

Steve, a very formal 42-year-old hospital lab technician, came to therapy. His depression had resulted in absences from work. He was given sick leave and the phone number of a therapy organisation by human resources. Suspicious of therapy, he felt that it was important to attend because he was sent by work. He told Jan, the therapist, that he had recently separated from his partner and children and had experienced a death in his family. Steve began to tell his story to Jan. He was born in the Caribbean to professional parents and raised by paternal grandparents when his parents left for the United Kingdom. He said that he had a good life, enjoyed school, church and the small town life. He remembered that his mother arrived one day to take him to England when he was 12. His grandfather told her that he needed permission from his son to allow this to happen. It was a very unpleasant incident and it was not until that point that he learnt that things were not good between his parents. He made his reluctant farewells two days later and said that his 'first' meeting with his mother gave him the impression that she was an unfeeling person. In

London he met a younger brother, an infant sister and a new father. A capable student, he settled well in school and he got on well with his stepfather, who played cricket and took Steve with him to matches. He was not happy to be in England and wanted to go back to St Vincent. When Steve was 16 his grandfather died and he felt a mixture of sadness and anger. He had an argument with his mother and she threw him out of the home. Steve slept in the park for several nights until a friend's parents allowed him to stay so that he could complete 'O' levels. After 18 months he left the Gilberts, shared a flat for some years and attended night school. He had become very close to the Gilberts who had taken him in and was very affected by the death of Mr Gilbert just a year before he began therapy. He was never reconciled with his mother but secretly saw his step-brother, who had attended school a short bus ride from Steve's place of work. At 26, Steve moved in with his girlfriend and they had two sons. For many years until he left the home he found that he and his girlfriend were incompatible. His depression and loneliness had grown in these past few years and he moved into a studio flat. Jan realised quite early in her work with Steve that he had numerous losses and broken attachments in his life and wrote a formulation along these lines.

Progress of the therapy

Steve came to therapy because he had been isolated and depressed, his relationship had broken down and he had lost someone a year earlier who had been in a fatherly role to him. He had not made connections with his separations, lost relationships and his general distress. His referral was to a service that was well known for working with black and ethnic minority patients. He settled well with Jan, his white female therapist, after an uneasy start. Steve was asked if he had a preference of gender or ethnicity of therapist. He said that he had none, but he was surprised that he was not given a Black or Asian therapist. Never openly questioning her ability to help him, Steve was just cautious in the early sessions with Jan. He was very aware of Jan's whiteness and wondered both about her degree of experience and knowledge of working with Black people and about how racist she might still be. It was only after she asked him about his relationships at work and whether or not he had any difficulties with racism from colleagues in the past, that he decided she was an 'OK person'. This acknowledgement helped Steve to feel appreciative of his therapist and helped him to begin to explore his past relationships.

Steve was cared for by his grandparents. He knew that his parents lived in London but their absence did not have a great deal of meaning to him and he did not remember the event. He felt loved, and was happy with his life in St Vincent. On arriving in London, Steve felt that his mother expected him to be grateful for giving him a new life in England. He regretted not making it difficult by crying or refusing to leave his grandparents. He wondered if it was his curiosity about London that had made him comply with the arrangements that left such a hole in his emotional life. He said that after leaving the Caribbean he was never hugged and nobody wanted to know how he felt. His mother, he said, had no time for him and his father, who lived not too far away, made little effort to have a relationship with him. He felt that his stepfather took an interest in him but he could not comment on his mother's decisions in the home. He said that coming to England was the worst thing that had ever happened to him. He later came to understand that leaving his grandparents was his second broken attachment. Jan told Steve that he seemed to have lost trust in relationships with others and had increasingly found it difficult to let people into his life. He agreed, saying that he had learned to be a self-sufficient person over the years but was not always this way. Jan explained that sometimes being in therapy might feel uncomfortable and he might feel that she was intrusive because he had become so self-reliant.

Being taken in by his friend's parents was a very positive experience for Steve and the death of Mr Gilbert had affected him in an unexpected way. He described the family, their two sons and daughter as loving and warm. Steve wondered what it was about his family that made them so very different from the Gilberts, who were also a Caribbean family. They were affectionate, jolly and interested in what their children were doing at school. He said that his recurrent dream since coming to England, of rushing to catch a plane or train only to see it pull away, had gone away whilst living with the Gilberts. Steve had not been able to understand this dream, which always left him feeling sad on waking and recalling it. From his work with his therapist he came to understand this as a preoccupation with loss. Jan had avoided making interpretations and waited to understand the feelings that dreams evoked in Steve. Mrs Gilbert had encouraged him to keep in contact with his family and was keen for his mother to ring. Steve said angrily, 'Not once did my mother ring to check that I was OK, or how my exams went'. He believed that his mother was more affectionate to the younger children, but from his contact with his brother learnt that she continued to rule with an iron fist. He said that he could never understand his mother, as if she was unreadable, and that when she looked at him she saw someone else.

Jan and her supervisor were left to speculate on Steve's early attachment with his mother. After she left the Caribbean he seemed to have had a secure relationship with his grandmother, she was an early attachment figure. It is not uncommon in some communities, particularly in developing countries, to find examples of multiple attachments (Thomas 1996). Infants in these circumstances have their needs met by more than one member of their household or kinship group. This evolved style, developed centuries earlier in human development, was clearly important during the period of enslavement for survival of the infant in the event of permanent separation or maternal death. Steve had become attached to his grandparents with whom he had an uninterrupted relationship until reluctantly leaving them at 12.

Steve came to a session and said that he realised that all that had happened to him had made him unhappy. He said that his emotional state had left him stuck in a corner and he could not respond to his partner's kindness and warmth. He feared that his unhappiness might be passed on to his sons and he did not want them to live with the emptiness that he felt. He wanted to get better and to be more involved with them. Steve's description of being stuck in a corner reflected his temporarily lost ability to self-sooth. Jan's constancy enabled him to work through the difficult feelings of abandonment and rage. As well as her reliable presence, Jan provided Steve with a sounding board for feelings that he had dared not express before. The therapeutic relationship is unique, co-constructed, and is a foundation to engage with what will take place in the therapy. Childhood incidents, or emotional wounds that could not be understood or thought about, can be powerfully enacted in therapy (Wallin 2007).

From his good relationships with his grandparents and the Gilberts, it seemed that Steve had been capable of secure attachment. Jan took care to be an emotionally available person in order to help him to talk about those first months in London when he so missed his grandfather and grandmother. Loss of Mr Gilbert was experienced as twofold, echoing the loss of his grandfather and the row that led to his leaving home. Jan helped him to construct a coherent narrative out of confusing and damaging experiences in his life.

Indications of attachment issues do not only rely on the fact that the patient has problems making and keeping relationships, but also having false self presentations (Winnicott 1960, 1964/1986). 'Ego distortion in terms of true and false self' describe what happens when there are problems with very early bonding and the infant gives up on getting what they need and develops a caretaking part of themselves. Whilst this can be an indicator of very early disturbance in the developmental relationship, it is more likely to be observed in the patients with avoidant dismissing attachment styles. This was not an aspect of Steve's early life; his withdrawal occurred later in his life when he had bricked up his feelings. His ability to engage well with Jan offered some corroboration of her view that Steve had experienced a secure early relationship. Jan was very aware of working at Steve's pace to avoid the risk of him leaving therapy to regulate emotional proximity to her. For the first time he was able to ask somebody what it was about him that made him unlovable to his mother and father. As a secure base, Jan was able to help him to explore his past to find an understanding of the course his life had taken and the relationships that have shaped it. After some time, Jan was able to ask Steve if his mother had ever spoken to him about how it was for her to have left her three-year-old son behind in St Vincent. He replied that neither one of them ever made reference to their leaving, but both behaved as if it was he who had left her.

With attachment problems, the therapist is actively involved in helping the patient to restructure their proximity to others. With the alleviation of his depression and improved relationships, therapy helped with the modification of Steve's internal working models. The therapist becomes an important figure by picking up a similar role previously occupied by primary caregivers. Through the experience of a good therapeutic relationship, the patient will begin to resume some functions of self-care and self-soothing, following the cues of the therapist. From this position Steve was able to repair his relationships. He had made good progress in his therapy and was able to return to work to deal with his losses and to re-establish good relations with friends and his children, and develop an appreciation for his former partner.

Conclusion

Attachment based psychotherapy is a relatively new therapeutic modality with adults and families. The value of this approach lies in its ability to trace problematic relationship footprints in families and to help patients to consider their options to repair and not repeat. Professionals who have closely observed infants will attest to the importance of good early attachment. A child's bond to its parents is important to it, as we have frequently seen in child protection cases where abused and neglected children will repeatedly give their parents chances for them to get it right. It is important for professionals and policy makers to make the connection between early parent–child relationships and adult psychopathology. Working therapeutically can help in many ways by assisting the patient to connect up problems from early life with adult relationships and functioning. Attachment techniques in therapy lend themselves well to working with family relationships and what happens between family members over several generations. In the case of Caribbean people, this poses a particular challenge to mental health professionals. Change would entail remembering and discovering generations of damaging separations and loss. People of African descent from the Americas and the Caribbean have endured significant trauma and survived. The cost of survival has been significant not only to individual wellbeing but also to the group as a whole, and different challenges face each generation. Therapists and clinical social workers in the USA have been drawing attention to how help can be provided for those caught up in the cycle of social failure. Many of the social and psychological problems of black people often represent the maladaptive behaviour of a people who are still in the process of surviving the pernicious effects of slavery. Working with attachment and loss will help patients from Caribbean backgrounds to appraise present problems and relationships, and how these have been affected by past family attachment styles. Professionals are required to be sufficiently trained and skilled to recognise traumatic loss or attachment disorder that has been transmitted from one generation to another. By breaking these damaging patterns, therapeutic work can help to prevent difficult relationships from blighting the lives of future family members.

References

Acharyya, S., Moorhouse, S., Kareem, J. and Littlewood, R. (1989). Nafsiyat psychotherapy centre for ethnic minorities. *Psychiatric Bulletin* **13**, 358–60.

Ainsworth, M. (1967) *Infancy in Uganda and the Growth of Love*. Baltimore: Johns Hopkins University Press.

Arnold, E. (Robertson) (1975). Out of sight but not out of mind: a study of West Indian mothers living in England separated from their children through leaving them behind when migrating and subsequently reunited. Unpublished MPhil thesis, Sussex University.

Arnold, E. (1997). Issues of reunification of migrant West Indian children in the United Kingdom. In J.L. Roopnarine and J. Brown (eds). *Caribbean Families: diversity among ethnic groups*, pp. 243–59. Greenwich, CT: Ablex.

——(2012). *Working with Families of African Caribbean Origin*. London: Jessica Kingsley.

Bowlby J. (1951). *Maternal Care and Mental Health, (WHO monograph series no. 2)*. Geneva: World Health Organization.

——(1958). The nature of the child's tie to his mother. *International Journal of Psychoanalysis* **39**, 350.

Burke, A. (1984). Is racism a causatory factor in mental illness? *The International Journal of Social Psychiatry* **30**, 1–2.

Clarke, K.B. and Clark, M.P. (1947). Racial identification and preference in Negro children. In T.M. Newcomb and E.L. Hartley (eds), *Readings in Social Psychology*. pp. 169–78. New York: Holt, Rinehart and Winston.

Coard, B. (1971). *How the West Indian Child is Made Educationally Subnormal in the British School System*. London: New Beacon Books.

Davey, A.G. and Norburn, V. (1980). Ethnic awareness and difference in primary school children. *New Community* **8**, 51–60.

Eaton, W.W. and Harrison, G. (2000). Ethnic disadvantage and schizophrenia. *Acta Psychiatrica Scandinavica* **102**, 1–6.

Feldman, H. and Marriott, J.A.S. (1969). Effects of parent/child separation in Jamaica. Diagnostic patterns and child/parent separation in children attending the Jamaican child guidance clinic. *Newsletter of the Jamaican Psychiatric Association* **1**, 1.

Fletchman-Smith, B. (2011). *Transcending the Legacies of Slavery*. London: Karnac.

Fraiberg, S. (ed.) (1980). *Clinical Studies in Infant Mental Health: the first year of life.* New York: Basic Books.

Fraiberg, S., Adelson, E. and Shapiro, V. (1980). Ghosts in the nursery: a psychoanalytic approach to the problems of impaired infant-mother relationships. In S. Fraiberg (ed.), *Clinical Studies in Infant Mental Health: the first year of life.* New York: Basic Books.

Hesse, E. and Main, M. (2000) Disorganised infant, child and adult attachment: collapse in behavioural and attentional strategies. *Journal of the American Psychoanalytic Association* **48**, 1097–1148.

Jones, J. (1981). *Bad Blood: the Tuskegee syphilis experiment*. New York: Free Press.

Kareem, J. and Littlewood, R. (1992). *Intercultural Therapy: themes, interpretations and practice*. Oxford: Blackwell.

Klein, M. (1951). *Love, Guilt and Reparation*. IPA Library: Hogarth Press.

Levy, A. (2004). *Small Island*. London: Hodder Headline Books.

Littlewood, R. and Lipsedge, M. (1997). *Aliens and Alienists, Ethnic Minorities and Psychiatry*, 3rd edn. London: Routledge.

Main, M. (1990). Cross cultural studies of attachment organisation, recent studies, changing the methodologies and the concept of conditioned strategies. *Human Development* **33**, 48–61.

——(2000). The organised categories of infant child and adult attachment: flexible vs. inflexible attention under attachment related stress. *Journal of the American Psychoanalytic Association* **48**, 1055–96.

Main, M. and Weston, D. (1982). Avoidance of the attachment figure in infancy: descriptions and impressions. In C.M. Parkes, and J. Stephenson-Hinde (eds), *The Place of Attachment in Human Behaviour*, pp. 31–60. London and New York: Tavistock Publications.

Main, M., Kaplan, N. and Cassidy, J. (1985). Security in infancy, childhood, and adulthood: A move to a level of representation. *Monographs of the Society for Research in Child Development* **50**, 66–104.

Marvin, R.S., Van Devenker, T.L., Iwanaga, M., Le Vine, S. and Le Vine, R.A. (1977). Infant caregiver attachment among the Hausa of Nigeria. In H.M. McGurck (ed.), *Ecological Factors in Human Development*, pp. 247–60. Amsterdam: Holland Publishing Company.

McKenzie, K. (2006). *Mind Your Head: improving the mental wellbeing of men and boys*. Wembley Conference Presentation UK.

Robertson, J. and Robertson, J. (1971). Young children in brief separation: a fresh look. *Psychoanalytic Study of the Child* **26**, 264–315.

Rothbaum, F., Weisz, J., Pott, M., Miyake, K. and Morelli, G. (2000). Attachment and culture, security in the United States and Japan. *American Psychologist* **55**, 1093–1104.

Schore, A. (2002). Advances in neuropsychoanalysis, attachment theory, and trauma research: implications for self psychology. *Psychoanalytic Inquiry* **22**, 433–84.

Spitz, R. (1945). Hospitalism: genesis of psychiatric conditions in early childhood, *Psychoanalytic Study of the Child* **1**, 53–7.

Thomas, L.K. (1995). Psychotherapy in the context of race and culture: an intercultural therapeutic approach. In S. Fernando (ed.), *Mental Health in a Multi-ethnic Society*, pp. 172–80. London: Routledge.

——(1996). Multicultural aspects of attachment. Paper delivered to the annual conference of The Centre for Attachment Based Psychotherapy. RACE Journal, British Association Counselling.

——(2010). Relational psychotherapy: the significance of father, *Psychodynamic Practice* **16**, 61–75.

Wallin, D.J. (2007). *Attachment in Psychotherapy*. New York: Guilford Press.

Winnicott, D.W. (1960). Ego distortions in terms of true and false self in the maturational process and the facilitating environment. IPA Library: Hogarth Press.

——(1964/1986). The concept of the false self. In D.W. Winnicott (ed.), *Home is Where We Start From*, pp. 65–70. Harmondsworth: Pelican Books.

Chapter 13

Meeting the mental health needs of older adults using the attachment perspective

Cecilia Yee Man Poon

Attachment theory has been recognised as a relevant conceptual framework for clinical practice with older adults for more than a decade (Bradley and Cafferty 2001). Clinical work with older adults may be informed by the attachment perspective for several reasons. Firstly, theory and research have both emphasised the enduring and powerful impact of attachment across the lifespan. Secondly, late adulthood is filled with experiences of separation and loss that may activate the attachment system. Finally, attachment security is associated with better psychosocial adjustment among older adults. This chapter illustrates how the attachment perspective may inform geriatric mental health care. A brief review of attachment across the lifespan is followed by a discussion on how attachment influences the treatment process. Specific aging-related challenges are presented to illustrate the usefulness of the attachment perspective when working with older adults and their caregivers.

Attachment across the lifespan

Bartholomew and Horowitz (1991) conceptualised four attachment styles along two continuous dimensions of anxiety and avoidance: secure, dismissing-avoidant, preoccupied-ambivalent, and fearful-avoidant. With low attachment anxiety and avoidance, secure older adults may possess more psychosocial resources, such as greater self-esteem and effective help-seeking skills, to cope with stress. Dismissing older adults low in anxiety and high in avoidance may minimise their attachment needs and be overly self-reliant. Preoccupied older adults high in anxiety and low in avoidance may be excessive care-seekers. Fearful older adults high in both anxiety and avoidance may withdraw from others due to fear of rejection.

Despite some methodological limitations, a growing body of research supports Bowlby's claim that the influence of early attachment may last 'from the cradle to the grave' (1969/1982: 208). For example, individuals who were separated from their families or experienced poor family nurturing in childhood because of World War Two were more likely to report an insecure attachment style in late adulthood in a British sample (Rusby and Tasker 2008). Although research suggests that attachment styles are quite stable in adulthood, some aging-related and cohort-based differences have been observed. In a community sample of young adults aged 18 to 34 and older adults aged 60 to 94, older adults were less likely to report a fearful or preoccupied style compared to younger adults, possibly because of better emotion-regulation in late life and social norms that discourage the expression of negative emotions among earlier-born cohorts (Segal, Needham and Coolidge 2009).

Regardless of one's prevailing attachment style, the attachment system is more likely to be activated in times of perceived threat (Bowlby 1969/1982). Many individuals in old age will experience the threat of losing their functional abilities or their loved ones due to illness and death. Instead of regarding the ensuing emotional turmoil and interpersonal difficulties merely as signs of personal defect or pathology, the attachment perspective can help frame these problems as manifestations of a universal need for proximity to protection and care in times of distress. Rather than encouraging an absolute reliance on oneself and treating the acceptance of help from others as a sign of weakness, the ability to trust and to ask for assistance are considered to be indicators of secure attachment. By framing older adults' increasing dependency in a positive light and legitimising their attachment-related concerns, interventions informed by attachment theory may be less stigmatising and more appealing.

Despite having a weaker influence on psychotherapy outcomes among older adults than with younger adults (Levy *et al.* 2011), attachment style continues to be an important concept in treatment because of its association with various psychosocial outcomes in late adulthood (Bradley and Cafferty 2001). In one study, Israeli older adults with secure attachment reported less ageism against themselves and better quality of life (Bodner and Cohen-Fridel 2010). In an ethnically-diverse sample in the United States, the positive impact of emotional support was much stronger among securely-attached older adults (Merz and Consedine 2009). Therefore, by examining older clients' attachment history, beliefs, behaviours and needs as part of the intervention, therapists may promote better psychosocial outcomes in late adulthood.

Therapeutic relationship as a foundation of treatment

The attachment perspective brings to light the interpersonal dynamics between therapists and their older clients, thus allowing the therapeutic relationship to be a powerful stage for their respective attachment styles to play out and engender change. An awareness of ongoing attachment processes in older adults, family members and treatment providers may strengthen the therapeutic relationship at every stage of treatment, sustaining older clients' willingness to remain engaged.

Conceptualisation

Older adults who are referred for mental health treatment often have a myriad of concerns that are not explicitly interpersonal in nature, such as recurring panic attacks post-surgery, or depressive symptoms associated with physical disability. When therapists decide to formulate a case from the attachment perspective, they have to evaluate how the presenting problem is related to themes of separation, loss and dependency; how one's internal working model of self and others, and existing attachment behaviours, may contribute to the problem; and how one's attachment is shaped by past and current relationships within a specific sociocultural context.

Assessment

To establish rapport, therapists may intersperse the assessment process with empathic validation of their older clients' distress and psychoeducation on the basic tenets of attachment theory. For example, an older client stepped into the first session expressing a desire to acquire coping skills to manage her health problems but spent most of the time venting about her daughter. The therapist reflected on the client's concerns and gently moved towards an assessment of the client's attachment history:

> 'Major illnesses often make us feel vulnerable and helpless. It is only normal that you want someone to reassure you that you will be cared for. What seems to upset you the most is that you don't believe you're getting any support from your daughter. You feel that the more you call, the less concerned she sounds. I understand that you'd like to learn to cope with your illness. For many people, social support is an important coping resource. I wonder if you could tell me how you've coped with situations that made you feel vulnerable in the past, and whether someone was there to support you …'

Some clients have been ignored or rejected by their attachment figures when they expressed their emotional needs. By acknowledging the legitimacy of older clients' concern and normalising their desire to be protected, therapists may nurture a different kind of attachment experience in the therapeutic relationship.

An assessment of the attachment style of older clients' current attachment figures will also inform treatment. Preoccupied clients may have a greater need for support from their attachment figures. Their constant need for reassurance may create a much bigger challenge with a dismissing spouse. Conversely, dismissing clients may be less aware of their partners' emotional needs and become frustrated if they have to deal with someone who demands excessive reassurance. Although the attachment style of older clients' significant others may not be the focus of intervention in individual therapy, clients will benefit from psychoeducation on how attachment style influences behaviours in relationships. Clients may come to appreciate the common and intrinsic need for safety within them and their partners, in spite of differences in their overt attachment behaviours. They may develop greater empathy for their significant others and become more ready to adapt accordingly.

Sociocultural considerations

Older adults' beliefs and behaviours are shaped by their sociocultural experiences, which may in turn influence the treatment process (Knight and Poon 2008). The activation of attachment behaviours may vary across cultures. When working with older clients from a different cultural background, therapists have to be mindful of the presence of within-culture differences in attachment history, beliefs and behaviours. Within the United States, some ethnic minority older adults may be more likely to endorse a dismissing attachment style because of their experience of socioeconomic hardship in childhood (Magai 2008). Their parents may have been less physically available as they had to work very long hours away from home to support the family. Thus, these individuals may have become extremely self-reliant. In general, active intervention may not be necessary when an older person's level of dependency or emotional distancing is within the limits of what is culturally sanctioned and is not causing subjective distress or objective impairment.

Older adults from certain cultures may be more sceptical and weary of the discussion of early attachment. Psychotherapy has previously been portrayed by the media as a way to blame one's parents for every problem in life. In many cultures this goes against the social norm of revering one's elders, especially among earlier-born cohorts. Therapists may introduce the concept of attachment to their older clients by highlighting how it may inform treatment, while emphasising that the goal is to change the present, not blame the past.

Therapists are encouraged to guard against trivialising or pathologising non-traditional attachment relationships that may become more common in late life after the deaths of same-age partners, siblings and elderly parents. To replace lost attachment ties, older adults may identify their adult children, deceased loved ones, God and animals as attachment figures (Cicirelli 2010). An examination of these relationships may facilitate the assessment of current attachment needs. A smaller social network in old age does not always warrant immediate intervention. Research has shown that securely-attached older adults were able to maintain their most-valued social relationships and experienced less depression during life transitions, despite having a smaller social network than younger adults (Gillath *et al.* 2011). Instead of assuming that all older clients who endorse feeling lonely need to expand their social network, therapists may focus on how these clients' attachment style has kept them from experiencing adequate affection in existing relationships.

Intervention

Just as an older person is not defined by his or her attachment style, treatment is not dictated by attachment theory alone. When the presenting problem is primarily poor self-esteem and feeling unworthy of love, an appreciation of how one's attachment experiences have influenced one's view of self may inform case conceptualisation. Specific strategies can then be flexibly drawn from different approaches. Cognitive-behavioural strategies may be used to highlight faulty expectations about oneself, and how these beliefs may influence attachment behaviours. Taking an attachment perspective does not negate other ways of approaching a presenting problem. For example, instead of dismissing the role of neurobiological and psychosocial changes in the development of post-stroke depression, attachment-informed treatment may focus on helping older clients cope with these changes by examining and potentially changing maladaptive attachment behaviours with their family caregivers and healthcare providers. This may result in better adherence to pharmacological interventions and a greater willingness to engage in behavioural activation and rehabilitation.

Regardless of how case conceptualisation is informed by the attachment perspective, an understanding of basic attachment concepts will strengthen the therapeutic relationship. There are parallels between the roles of parents and therapists, in that caregivers who promote secure attachment may enhance care recipients' desire to engage in physical and cognitive exploration (Bowlby 1988). When therapists are consistent and responsive, older clients may be more ready to participate in therapy. As attachment is built upon a mutual relationship, a healthy awareness of therapists' own attachment needs may also reduce the likelihood of problematic countertransference in treatment.

Consistency

The ability to remain consistent in the therapeutic relationship contributes to the development of trust. One practical way to maintain consistency is to schedule appointments at a regular time as much as possible. Cancellations and changes in scheduled appointments should be brought up in a neutral manner, with the intention of reassuring the older client of the therapist's availability. During a session, insecurely-attached older adults may suddenly become hostile or withdrawn to protect themselves from emotionally-charged topics, or to test their therapists' reliability and competence. When therapists remain empathic and supportive despite their clients' inconsistencies, it will promote trust and facilitate change.

Responsiveness

Therapists' ability to respond appropriately to their older clients' emotional needs is important within and across therapy sessions. Some anxiously-attached older clients may be reluctant to open up because they have been maintaining their attachment relationships by being excessive caregivers. Their tendency to take care of everyone first may fuel a desire to protect their therapists by not overburdening them with strong emotions. Older clients' reluctance to share their thoughts and feelings may be expressed in a subtle manner. They may suddenly jump from topic to topic or repeatedly tell a specific personal anecdote. Although the possibility of dementia is a valid concern, disinhibition and perseveration may be a way to mask one's attachment insecurity and avoid discussing an attachment concern.

One way to work through these situations is the use of process comments. Therapists who do not work with older adults on a regular basis may find this to be challenging at first, because interrupting an older person may be viewed as a form of disrespect in many cultures. Judicious use of non-judgemental process comments may prove to older clients that their therapist is actively listening. Passively allowing older clients to digress may undermine the perceived emotional presence and responsiveness of the therapist. Because insecurely-attached older adults may have a tendency to interpret process comments as threatening, it may be prudent to ask for permission at the beginning of therapy and regularly discuss how they feel about these comments. A similar strategy to highlight the therapist's responsiveness is to have an ongoing discussion on therapy goals and progress. An emphasis on goal-setting and progress-monitoring may help older clients realise that their therapist is mindful of their improvement and evolving needs.

Counter-transference

Therapists' attachment style can help or hinder psychological interventions. Counter-transference may be a normal reaction to an older client's attachment behaviours, or a reflection of the therapist's unresolved attachment needs. Clinical staff's personal experiences with aging and caregiving responsibilities may set off counter-transference that interferes with assessment and intervention. It is not uncommon for long-term care staff to become angry at family members for not doing more for their elderly relatives, especially when staff are dealing with similar situations at home. Consultation, referral or supervision may be necessary for clinical staff who are confronting personally challenging aging-related circumstances.

Some therapists may have difficulty approaching therapy termination because of the assumption that their older clients will be lonely when therapy ends. Although treatment termination may amplify the fear of abandonment, most older clients are quite resilient and glad to find out that they have made sufficient progress and no longer need therapy. When reviewing an older client's treatment progress, therapists have to consider whether their own attachment needs are distracting them from a realistic appraisal of their client's readiness to leave therapy, or from the need to refer a client to another provider for a different level of care such as medication management. If an older client does present with mild concerns about being rejected by other providers, the therapist may problem-solve with the client during the pre-termination phase and practise initiating contact with new providers.

Separation, loss and dependency in late adulthood

In the following section, several aging-related experiences that may heighten one's personal vulnerability and fear of dependency are presented to illustrate how treatment may be informed by the attachment perspective in different clinical settings.

Physical illness and decline

Major illness often results in potential loss and separation, thus triggering greater attachment needs even among older adults who have been previously well-adjusted. Decline in physical functioning may result in a need to rely on others for assistance. This may be particularly challenging for dismissing individuals because of their reluctance to seek help. Psychoeducation on human beings' innate need for security may flow from an expression of strong attachment emotions, such as fear of abandonment.

Bill was an older widower who had recently had a stroke. Despite regaining most of his physical and mental functioning, he could no longer return to his job as a factory manager. He experienced profound hopelessness and attempted suicide. His physical and emotional condition stabilised soon after he was admitted to the psychiatric unit. When the attending psychiatrist evaluated Bill for possible discharge, Bill admitted that he could not find any purpose or meaning in life and would continue to look for ways to kill himself. Bill decided to give therapy a try only because 'There's nothing else to do on the unit'.

Based on reports from the psychiatrist and staff, Bill appeared to have a dismissing attachment style. Given his perceived lack of purpose in life and hopelessness, life review was used as a tool to keep him engaged in therapy by allowing him to reflect on his personal accomplishments and how he might find meaning in his life again. The use of life review also generated a discussion about Bill's childhood attachment experience. Bill shared that after his father left, his mother was so busy with his younger siblings that she had no time for him. He explained that he was 'always very independent anyway'. As Bill described his self-reliance to overcome adverse situations in the past, his tendency to minimise his relationship needs was also brought to the surface.

Because of the huge age difference between Bill and the therapist, as well as his dismissing attachment style, Bill often questioned the therapist's abilities by making belittling or patronising comments. The therapist used these examples to help Bill explore his attitude towards concepts such as weakness, dependency and trust. It dawned on Bill that he had a strong desire to be invincible because he did not trust that anyone would be capable of helping him. As an adult, his suspicious attitude encouraged others to keep a distance from him, thus strengthening his belief that nobody was available to help him. During one session, Bill reported that therapy was a 'pleasant surprise', as he had never imagined how good it would feel when someone actually listened to him as a person, especially after he became 'crippled' and unemployed. Bill began to embrace the possibility of establishing some social relationships. He later wrote to the therapist that although he still preferred to spend most of his time alone, he had begun to volunteer at a local school several hours per week. He found it quite fulfilling to mentor students from immigrant families who yearned to be heard and accepted.

Relocation

Physical illness, caregiving responsibilities and financial difficulties often force older adults to leave their home. Whether it is moving to an adult child's home, a long-term care facility or another part of the country, relocation may represent a major loss and intensify one's sensitivity to potential danger. For those who have already experienced multiple losses, relocation may trigger a fear of becoming completely helpless. Cognitive restructuring and problem-solving techniques may be useful in these situations, such that the older person may learn not to catastrophise the situation, and to take practical steps to establish new relationships.

Linda was feeling overwhelmed about managing the five-bedroom house she had lived in since she was born. When her son suggested that she move to a retirement community, Linda became extremely resentful, accusing him of scheming to steal her property. Linda was reluctant to enter therapy because of a fear that information shared with the therapist would be used against her. When the therapist commented on Linda's mistrust of people and wondered out loud with Linda why anybody could be trusted at all, Linda became more engaged in therapy and went on a tirade about how her son left home two days after his high school graduation and never came back until his father's funeral.

Behind Linda's suspicion and hostility was an intense fear that she would not be able to adjust to a new environment on her own, especially when she had little faith that people in the community would be willing to help her. The therapist challenged Linda's rigid expectations by helping her identify experiences that did not support her mistrust in others. Linda finally agreed to visit a few retirement communities. She was surprised by her pleasant encounters with residents and staff. In the meantime, Linda continued to wonder if others would be willing to help her in the future.

Treatment then focused on Linda's strengths in managing her life in the past seven decades and how she might be able to manage her new environment through a combination of self-reliance and help-seeking. To prepare for the relocation, help-seeking was role-played in therapy and later practised in real life when she spoke to her son. As Linda became more confident in herself and others, she gradually realised that her resentment was driven by a sense of extreme helplessness. This allowed Linda to work through her experience as a child abuse survivor, achieve greater inner peace, and become more forward-looking as she prepared for the move.

Long-term care settings

Older adults often have to depend quite heavily on the assistance of staff in most institutional settings. Constant shift changes and staff turnover may heighten feelings of insecurity. Mental health professionals may assist clinical staff in creating an environment that supports secure attachment, as well as teaching insecurely-attached residents how to effectively express their needs to minimise staff burnout. An awareness of counter-transference and its impact may help staff develop more positive interpersonal relationships with residents. An awareness of residents' attachment styles may prepare staff for potential behavioural challenges and encourage the use of person-centred interventions to manage these behaviours.

Anne lost her husband of 50 years a month after he was diagnosed with cancer. When Anne moved to a nursing home because she could no longer take care of herself and her husband's farm, she presented with extreme anxiety. She was hypervigilant that she was in danger. Efforts to reassure Anne soon became emotionally draining to staff. Attempts to walk away from her only exacerbated her anxiety.

An examination of Anne's life history revealed a longstanding preoccupied attachment style. Her husband was the only one who was able to withstand her anxiety and reassure her that she could turn to him for help. The therapist brought up how Anne had framed herself as an 'eternally vulnerable' individual who needed constant protection. Instead of punishing or pathologising any clingy behaviours, the therapist normalised these behaviours as Anne's reaction to her attachment needs. Treatment focused on refining Anne's behaviours and challenging her feelings of extreme vulnerability. Whenever Anne exhibited ineffective attachment behaviours, such as crying incessantly and accusing the therapist of being uncaring to turn down her request for more frequent sessions, the therapist would highlight Anne's desire to feel taken care of, while encouraging Anne to ponder on whether her behaviours had brought others closer to her or drawn them away in the past.

Anne eventually calmed down when she realised that the therapist remained responsive and supportive despite standing firm with her professional boundaries. The therapist met with staff to discuss Anne's attachment style and the importance of consistency in staff behaviours. A fixed schedule of staff-initiated 10-minute interactions with Anne after each meal was proposed. Appropriate help-seeking behaviours were praised. When Anne calmly requested and waited for staff to fill out a form for her, instead of demanding everyone in the hallway to help her immediately, staff would compliment her for being patient. Staff were encouraged not to promise to meet with Anne or perform specific chores for her unless they were certain they would be able to honour the promise. As staff's behaviours became more predictable, Anne reported less anxiety. She began to develop a more positive sense of self that made her more self-reliant. Staff became more empathic and confident in their ability to deal with Anne's dependency and reported a much better relationship with her.

Caregiving

Secure attachment has been associated with a less subjective sense of burden and a greater commitment to provide care among the adult children of ailing parents (Crispi, Schiaffino and Berman 1997), whereas avoidance and anxiety have been associated with lower levels of wellbeing (Perren *et al.* 2007). When individuals assume the role of caregivers to an attachment figure, such as their elderly parents, anticipatory grief and previously unresolved grief may exacerbate their attachment needs because of an augmented feeling of helplessness and vulnerability. Some caregivers may minimise or dismiss their care recipient's concerns to guard against these negative feelings. Others may engage in excessive caregiving because of an intense fear of separation and loss.

Insecurely-attached older care recipients may impose filial responsibilities on family caregivers to preserve their relationship with their adult children, combat feelings of poor self-worth, and fulfill their need for reassurance and validation (Karantzas, Evans and Foddy 2010). Preoccupied older adults may be more demanding to their caregivers as a result, whereas dismissing older adults may be unwilling to seek help because of conflict-avoidance. It may be confusing when care recipients express their attachment needs through rejection, hostility or paranoia.

Although it is not always possible to change a family caregiver's prevailing attachment style when the intended client is the older adult, therapists may help caregivers become more aware of their own attachment needs. It is important to help caregivers recognise how insecure attachment may influence their understanding of their loved one's end-of-life care wishes. In one study, individuals with attachment-related avoidance or anxiety made less accurate prediction of their loved ones' wishes for life-sustaining treatment (Turan *et al.* 2011). Therapists may intervene by normalising caregivers' tendency to become overwhelmed or withdrawn, before addressing how this may affect the quality of care given to the care recipient.

Raul had been caring for his terminally ill 90-year-old mother for several years. Despite his own failing health, Raul continued to travel a long distance to visit his mother daily. Raul would make multiple requests that were inappropriate given his mother's medical condition, thus alienating support from staff. After a family conference, a therapist mentioned how common it was for caregivers to experience great fears about their own future when a loved one was dying. Raul broke down in tears and stated that his mother was the only reason for him to live. Although the therapist only briefly touched upon Raul's fears about losing his last surviving attachment figure, the opportunity for Raul to vocalise his fears helped him reconsider whether he was making the best decision for his mother and himself. He warmed to the idea of in-home hospice care. With encouragement from the therapist, Raul agreed to join a caregiver support group to address his attachment needs and anticipatory grief.

Dementia care

Dementia does not only strip individuals of their memory but also of their identity, making it a terrifying experience of loss of control over a once familiar world. As stated in an earlier section, the attachment system is activated when there is perceived threat in the environment (Bowlby 1969/1982). While a secure pre-morbid attachment style has been shown to predict more positive emotions after the onset of dementia (Magai 2008), less securely-attached individuals are more likely to express their attachment needs through agitation, aggression, panic and paranoia (Perren *et al.* 2007). The attachment perspective may shift caregivers' attention from overt behavioural challenges to underlying attachment needs of comfort and security. This may increase caregivers' empathy and ability to maintain a soothing presence when interacting with someone afflicted with dementia. Caregivers' attachment avoidance has been found to be associated with more behavioural problems among care recipients (Perren *et al.* 2007). The less anxious or angry the caregiver is, the more likely it is that the person with dementia will be able to calm down. Behavioural interventions that promote consistency, structure and the availability of familiar figures, such as the use of previously recorded voices of familiar individuals (Browne and Shlosberg 2006), may foster a sense of security and reduce agitation.

After being diagnosed with dementia, Julia moved in with her daughter Carol. When Carol had to move to another country for work, she planned to move Julia to a nursing home. To promote a smooth transition, they visited with residents and staff several days per week a month before the move. Carol provided staff with family photos, items Julia had used for decades, and a list of her favourite activities. To maintain a sense of consistency in the mother–daughter attachment, Carol continued to call Julia on a regular basis. Being securely-attached, Julia was usually easily soothed when she became disoriented and began to wander. Staff would ask Julia what was bothering her in order to understand the emotional meaning of her agitation, reassure her that she was in a safe place, redirect her to participate in her favourite activities, or invite Julia to talk about a familiar object such as her wedding photo. Because staff responded to Julia's distress in a prompt and calm manner, a sense of security was fostered. To manage staff's potential frustration towards difficult residents, the nursing home regularly scheduled training to highlight the attachment needs of individuals with dementia, to elicit greater empathy and to discuss behavioural strategies that could enhance attachment security. The facility also obtained behavioural observation data to illustrate the benefits of being responsive, consistent and calm when dealing with challenging behaviours. Although Carol encouraged staff to call her if Julia remained agitated, staff seldom had to call Carol for help.

Concluding comments

This chapter illustrates how the attachment perspective can inform conceptualisation, assessment and intervention when working with older adults and important individuals in their social network. Aging-related challenges in late adulthood are often characterised by separation, loss and increasing dependency, making the attachment perspective an appropriate conceptual framework in clinical practice with older adults. An examination of older clients' attachment history, beliefs, behaviours and needs can strengthen the therapeutic relationship and promote change. Interventions that are informed by the attachment perspective allow for a flexible selection of strategies from different approaches.

Clinical work with older adults often involves a diverse range of professionals, settings and interpersonal systems. One of the most important contributions of the attachment perspective is that it accentuates a common and universal need for protection and care in times of distress and danger. Its intuitive appeal renders it a relatively simple concept to teach and accept. There may be a greater readiness to empathise and collaborate among older adults, family members and service providers when this common pursuit of comfort and safety is emphasised, thereby fostering successful aging and personal growth even in the face of multiple aging-related challenges.

Note: All examples are informed by the author's experience but do not concern specific individuals in real life.

References

Bartholomew, K. and Horowitz, L.M. (1991). Attachment styles among young adults: a test of a four category model. *Journal of Personality and Social Psychology* **61**, 226–44.

Bodner, E. and Cohen-Fridel, S. (2010). Relations between attachment styles, ageism and quality of life in late life. *International Psychogeriatrics* **22**, 1353–61.

Bowlby, J. (1969/1982). *Attachment and Loss, Volume 1: Attachment.* New York: Basic Books.

——(1988). *A Secure Base: clinical applications of attachment theory.* London: Routledge.

Bradley, M. and Cafferty, T.P. (2001). Attachment among older adults: current issues and directions for future research. *Attachment and Human Development* **3**, 200–21.

Browne, C.J. and Shlosberg, E. (2006). Attachment theory, ageing and dementia: a review of the literature. *Aging and Mental Health* **10**, 134–42.

Cicirelli, V.G. (2010). Attachment relationships in old age. *Journal of Social and Personal Relationships* **27**, 191–9.

Crispi, E.L., Schiaffino, K. and Berman, W.H. (1997). The contribution of attachment to burden in adult children of institutionalised parents with dementia. *The Gerontologist* **37**, 52–60.

Gillath, O., Johnson, D.K., Selcuk, E. and Teel, C. (2011). Comparing old and young adults as they cope with life transitions: the links between social network management skills and attachment style to depression. *Clinical Gerontologist* **34**, 251–65.

Karantzas, G.C., Evans, L. and Foddy, M. (2010). The role of attachment in current and future parent caregiving. *Journal of Gerontology: Psychological Sciences* **65**, 573–80.

Knight, B.G. and Poon, C.Y.M. (2008). Contextual adult life span theory for adapting psychotherapy with older adults. *Journal of Rational-Emotive Cognitive-Behavioral Therapy* **26**, 232–49.

Levy, K.N., Ellison, W.D., Scott, L.N. and Bernecker, S.L. (2011). Attachment style. *Journal of Clinical Psychology* **67**, 193–203.

Magai, C. (2008). Attachment in middle and later life. In J. Cassidy, and P. Shaver (eds), *Handbook of Attachment*, 2nd edn, pp. 532–51. New York: Guilford Press.

Merz, E-M. and Consedine, N.S. (2009). The association of family support and wellbeing in later life depends on adult attachment style. *Attachment and Human Development* **11**, 203–21.

Perren, S., Schmid, R., Herrmann, S. and Wettstein, A. (2007). The impact of attachment on dementia-related problem behavior and spousal caregivers' well-being. *Attachment and Human Development* **9**, 163–78.

Rusby, J.S.M. and Tasker, F. (2008). Childhood temporary separation: long term effects of the British evacuation of children during World War II on older adults' attachment styles. *Attachment and Human Development* **10**, 207–21.

Segal, D.L., Needham, T.N. and Coolidge, F.L. (2009). Age differences in attachment orientations among younger and older adults: evidence from two self-report measures of attachment. *International Journal of Aging and Human Development* **69**, 119–32.

Turan, B., Goldstein, M.K., Garber, A.M. and Carstensen, L.L. (2011). Knowing loved ones' end-of-life health care wishes: attachment security predicts caregivers' accuracy. *Health Psychology* **30**, 814–18.

Section 4

The organisation and the individual practitioner

Chapter 14

Four pillars of security

Attachment theory and practice in forensic mental health care

Gwen Adshead and Anne Aiyegbusi

John Bowlby's first published study was a forensic one: a study of the early attachment histories of juvenile thieves (Bowlby 1944). Forensic psychiatry did not then exist as a clinical speciality, only emerging in the UK during the last thirty years. In that time, extensive research based on attachment theory, in both clinical and non- clinical populations, has produced data that has proved valuable to forensic practice, both theoretically and clinically (Pfäfflin and Adshead 2004).

In this chapter, we explore four key areas of research and practice from attachment theory that are relevant to forensic mental health care. They are:

- Attachment theory, the development of the personality, and disorders of personality
- The relevance of attachment insecurity to the risk of violence
- Attachment and thinking about victims
- Attachments within residential care: relational security and insecurity between staff and patients.

We suggest that a thorough understanding of these domains provides theoretical 'pillars' of knowledge that can underpin the 'secure bases' that are essential to forensic practice. We also discuss implications for training and supervision. Throughout, we refer mainly to male patients; not because there are no female offender patients, but because they are a minority of service users. We are also linguistically explicit about the nature of the psychological challenges faced by the patients; especially the struggle to master the feelings of cruelty and violence that have resulted in their offences. Everyone struggles with such feelings from time to time, but forensic patients have acted on them and have to live with the consequences.

Attachment theory, the development of the personality and disorders of personality

Attachment theory is useful not only for understanding how personality develops but also for understanding how personality disorders develop. This is particularly relevant in forensic services where the prevalence of personality disorder diagnoses is 60–80 per cent, which is considerably higher than the community prevalence of 4 per cent (Coid *et al.* 2006; Duggan and Howard 2009).The most common type of personality disorder in forensic practice is 'anti-social': i.e. a personality that lacks the qualities of the 'social mind' that allow us to interact fruitfully with others in groups (Dunbar 2003).

We assume a basic knowledge of categories of attachment style derived from research. These categories are not types of people or 'symptoms' of disorder, but rather ways that people think about attachment relationships. Bowlby (1969) theorised that insecure attachment representations are based on internal working models (IWMs) of relationships that are built up in the mind over time. These models develop in response to attachment-related stressors and are (in effect) 'defences' (cognitions and affects) that help to reduce arousal and distress. These IWMs have both conscious and unconscious elements and may be revealed in behaviour and language (Hesse 2008).

Children who are exposed to high levels of attachment distress may develop an avoidant/dismissing attachment IWM, which reduces distress through hypo-arousal and reduced affect; *or* they may develop an ambivalent/enmeshed attachment IWM, which is associated with hyper-arousal and unstable, high amplitude affect states (Schore 2001, 2003). Children exposed to chronic fear and chaotic home environments may develop a 'disorganised' IWM, which is characterised by rapid oscillations between different states of mind with regard to attachment, and odd behavioural manifestations of anxiety (van IJzendoorn and Bakermans-Kranenburg 2003). Insecure and disorganised attachment styles tend to persist into adolescence and adulthood, and are associated with more interpersonal dysfunction and severe clinical disorders (Dozier, Stovall-McClough and Albus 2008; Sroufe *et al.* 2005; Steele and Steele 2009; van IJzendoorn and Bakermans-Kranenburg 2003).

Early childhood attachment insecurity is highly influential on the development of the 'Big Five' personality traits or dispositions that also seem to develop in childhood and then persist into adulthood (Bartholomew, Kwong and Hart 2001; Mikkelson, Kessler and Shaver 1997; Shiner and Masten 2002). Early attachment experience is likely to be as influential as genetic vulnerabilities or other environmental stressors in terms of risk of developing personality dysfunction (Brennan and Shaver 1998; Dozier, Stovall-McClough and Albus 2008) and early attachment insecurity is an established risk factor for the development of personality disorder (Bartholomew, Kwong and Hart 2001; Crawford *et al.* 2006, 2007; Livesley 1993). We argue that personality disorder might be best understood as the adult sequelae of profound attachment disorder in childhood. Such an approach is supported by those researchers who argue that personality disorders should be redefined as 'relational disorders' or disorders of interpersonal function (First *et al.* 2002; Skodol *et al.* 2011).

The studies of the influence of early attachments on personality dysfunction would suggest that forensic clinical assessment of people with personality disorder will be incomplete without a detailed developmental attachment history, one that provides a clear account of the attachment environment in which the forensic patient grew up and his or her first behavioural or affective responses to stress, threat or perception of threat. Detailed attachment histories will allow us to make much better predictions of the type of emotional responses our patients will make under stress; especially stress that arises in the context of relationships, both personal and professional (Sarkar and Adshead 2006).

Mentalisation based therapies help patients manage negative emotions when they are activated by attachment-related situations, such as perceived threat, abandonment or unmet need. Mentalisation based therapies have been used to good effect with personality disorder in non-forensic settings, and are the focus of current treatment trials in forensic settings (Bateman and Fonagy 2008).

The relevance of attachment insecurity to the risk of violence

There have been a variety of studies of attachment insecurity in a range of violent offenders; including rapists, sex offenders, child abusers, homicide perpetrators and offenders who score highly on psychopathy (Adshead and Bluglass 2001; Bogaerts, Vanheule and Declerq 2005; Frodi *et al.* 2001; Levinson and Fonagy 2006; Marshall, Serran and Cortoni 2000; van IJzendoorn *et al.* 1997).

It is worth noting the low prevalence of attachment security compared to non-clinical populations. It is also worth noting that some offenders appear to have secure attachment representations, which suggests that security of mind with respect to attachment is therefore *not* an indicator of safety (Bakermans-Kranenburg and van IJzendoorn 2009; Van IJzendoorn and Bakermans-Kranenburg 1996). This data serves as a reminder that every act of violence is a complex phenomenon, and attachment security (or lack of it) is only one of a number of risk factors that may be operating at the time of a violent act.

There is evidence that the dismissing style is over-represented in forensic populations (Adshead and Bluglass 2001; Frodi *et al.* 2001; Levinson and Fonagy 2006). If the excess of the dismissing style is a valid finding, then this suggests that the conscious psychological attitudes characteristic of the dismissing style are risk factors for the commission of violence. As described in the Adult Attachment Interview manual (AAI; George, Kaplan and Main 1994), these include:

- claims of personal strength and normality
- denial of need for help
- denial of pain or suffering
- dismissing of distress (in self or others) as not of interest or concern
- active derogation or contempt for distress.

A lack of concern or compassion for the self is likely to be associated with a similar lack of concern and compassion for others, because there is a relationship between self-reflective function and empathy (Fonagy and Target 1997; Fonagy *et al*. 1997). If your own neediness or pain is not of interest to you, then you are unlikely to be interested in others' pain, and this feature alone will make the inflicting of harm more psychologically possible and less ego-dystonic. Dismissing attachment is also associated with avoidance of social relationships and social isolation; a known risk factor for violence (Estroff and Zimmer 1994).

'Active derogation' is described as a sub-category of the dismissing style (George, Kaplan and Main 1994). These individuals are not just dismissive about distress or neediness, they are actively derogatory about it. The AAI manual states that this classification is rare in normal populations, but presumably will be more common in populations where dismissing attachment is generally more prevalent. A derogatory and contemptuous attitude towards the distress of others would make violence easier to commit: it also closely resembles those 'callous' and 'mean' states of mind that are characteristic of personality profiles associated with high risks of violence (Hare 1999; Patrick, Fowles and Krueger 2009).

An excess of dismissing attachment has implications for clinical forensic practice. Patients with a dismissing attachment style are harder to engage in treatment and less likely to be treatment compliant (Dozier *et al*. 2001). Large sub-groups of forensic patients are also known to be non-compliant and reluctant to engage; and it is easy for professionals to see such behaviour as a feature of antisocial attitudes, not a psychological issue about trust and avoidance of distress that needs to be addressed through attempts to develop relationships and encourage the expression of affect at a gradual pace.

Attachment and thinking about victims

Attachment figures are people in our lives on whom we depend, or who depend on us: people we go to when distressed or who come to us seeking relief from distress and comfort (Weiss 1991). They typically include parents, children, siblings, friends and emotional/sexual partners; and can also include professional care-givers (Adshead 1998, 2010).

However, perpetrators of violence often attack those to whom they have had some emotional attachment. The second most common form of violence in England and Wales is between people who are in an intimate relationship. Of homicide or rape perpetrators, 60 per cent are well known to their victims. Nearly all (90 per cent) of adults who kill children are either parents or in a parenting role; and most child abuse is carried out by family or peers (Smith and Flatley 2010). Mental illness makes very little difference to the general risk of violence in society but is a significant risk factor for family violence (Estroff *et al*. 1998). Therefore, assessment of an individual's attachment relationships may be highly relevant to the assessment of their risk.

In a vulnerable person, loss or potential loss of an attachment relationship can be a powerful trigger for violence because the pain and fear of loss stimulates defensive anger (Bowlby 1984). An angry mental state, which is then further aroused by substance misuse or affected by the reality-distorting effects of psychosis, is a potent risk factor for violence (Fazel *et al.* 2009). Vulnerable individuals include those who rely on the attachment figure to regulate their own feelings, i.e. what is sometimes described as co-dependence on the attachment figure. If the attachment figure leaves (or appears to be leaving), this stimulates intense anxiety, then panic, and then rage, which can be manifested as violence. Such unstable violence in response to perceived abandonment by an attachment figure is characteristic of borderline personality disorder, and has been commonly described in perpetrators of intimate partner violence (Holtzworth-Munroe *et al.*1997).

There are other forms of toxic attachments that give rise to violence, such as highly abnormal care-giving behaviour (as found in Factitious Illness by Proxy behaviours). Mothers who perpetrate such atypical and risky care-giving behaviours on their children have high levels of insecure attachment patterns (Adshead and Bluglass 2001). In addition, it is plausible to speculate that toxic attachments exist in those families where a father (or rarely, a mother) kills their children and then themselves, usually after the break-up of the parental relationship.

It is also important to consider paranoid attachments that may result in stalking behaviour. The most famous example of this is the case of Tatiana Tarasoff, who was killed by a young man who had formed a psychotic attachment to her and killed her in response to a perceived rejection. We know now that anyone who has a paranoid attachment to another presents a risk to them, and the size, degree and time-span of the risk may be hard to assess.

Finally, attacks on professional caregivers can be understood as a form of dysfunctional attachment behaviour. To recap, attachment theory states that when in distress, the securely attached child elicits care from their attachment figure, who is then able to give care successfully. However, there are sub-groups of psychiatric patients who attack caregivers, either psychologically or physically, on a regular basis. Such attacks may represent maladaptive attachment behaviour in response to perceived rejection or neglect and/or an attempt to get attention for distress. Some patients seek care, but then are hostile to it, or seem to be unable to make use of the care that is offered (Norton 1996). Serious and repetitive attacks on healthcare staff quickly result in admission to higher and higher levels of security; with huge associated costs; there is anecdotal evidence that one third of admissions to high security are as a result of severe violence to staff in medium security. However, little attention is paid to the attachment histories of these patients, or the exploration of how and why a professional attachment figure should provoke such rage and distress. It would seem sensible to add routine questions about attachment relationships, both in childhood and adulthood, to risk assessment, both in terms of clinical enquiry and formal assessment tools.

Attachments within residential care: relational security and insecurity between staff and patients

An awareness of attachment issues can help staff establish therapeutic relationships that really act as a 'secure base' for therapeutic engagement and clinical improvement. Engagement is a particular problem for forensic patients (Glorney *et al.* 2010), so understanding that insecure patients may appear dismissing or demanding because of their attachment disturbance helps staff not to react inappropriately, but to tailor their interventions accordingly.

We assume that any professional who delivers long-stay residential psychiatric care is effectively in an attachment role with patients because of: (a) the length of time; and (b) the dependence and intensity of the contact between staff and patients in this context. Unlike community or general in-patient work, where the length of stay is measured in weeks, forensic patients may stay more than five years on a forensic ward and may be 'living' with the same nursing staff all that time.

One of the authors has been involved in qualitative research exploring the attachment narratives of nurses working in secure settings, and their therapeutic relationships with patients, especially those with personality disorder.[1] Below are themes arising from the complexity of relationships between nurses and patients in these settings, some of which are supported by quotes from this study.

Childhood history and help seeking

Insecure attachment representations mean that forensic patients may not know how to make use of the staff care; and they may find it hard not to repeat dysfunctional attachment behaviours or to relate to the staff as dangerous carers from the past. Given that most forensic patients have histories of abuse at the hands of carers, they are naturally suspicious of authority figures, or those who claim to be carers. In most forensic services, each ward may have as many as fifteen or twenty people like this, but perhaps only six nurses to manage their needs and prevent them from harming themselves or each other.

Nursing staff report that patients often secure care by behaving in a disturbed way and are also unable to accept care when it is offered. Here is an example of a patient rejecting care when offered:

> And there is a particular patient who when they are very distressed, they will say 'I don't need you' when they really need you … so by not understanding the communication that is coming from them you are more likely to miss out certain important things … So it's a bit like working opposite, like taking their no as a yes.

This relational pattern, in attachment terms, suggests ambivalence about asking for help and is due to prior experiences of rejection when vulnerable (Adshead 1998; Fonagy 1998).

Understanding attachment-related aggression

In some patients, the anxiety about asking for help may be so great that the patient becomes aroused, angry and aggressive, and may then act out in a threatening manner that can often alienate those who might be able to care. Disorganised attachment experiences in early life are particularly associated with later controlling behaviours towards carers. Using an attachment approach, staff can understand the arousal and hostility as a hyper-aroused response to threat and the experience of being in need. The nurse can acknowledge how difficult it sometimes is to ask for help, and gently but firmly remind the patient that hostility tends to make it difficult for others to help effectively. Such an approach can disconfirm patients' negative expectations; and can lay the foundation for a more 'secure' nurse–patient relationship.

Nurses' ambivalent feelings about relationships

Within these complex relationships, nurses also report that they may have to manage ambivalent feelings about the patient, who can simultaneously elicit both caring and angry, fearful and rejecting feelings in staff, as described below by a nurse:

> She evoked in me quite a lot of mixed feelings. She was a fragile woman who wanted to be taken care of. At the same time I was always quite wary: she was a woman who on some occasions could be quite rigid in her views and racist and that to me threw me back to the environment that I grew up in at the time in [country].

Managing fear

Managing fear is a key issue for forensic nursing staff. Children who have been abused by their caregivers face an intolerable dilemma because they are frightened by the very person from whom they are meant to seek help (Fonagy 1998). As discussed previously, many forensic patients are profoundly fearful of seeking help from caregivers on whom they depend, often for their most basic needs. At the same time, the nursing staff may also fear the patient; either directly because of the way they present or because of their offending history.

> Oh, oh dear. For starters she scares me, she scared me a great deal, she really did scare me a great deal. Erm … on a lot of occasions I avoided having one to ones with her, I avoided confronting her. She could be very kind, very considerate, certainly considerate but it was almost, it was her menacing way, that was the most difficult, it is certainly almost impossible to have a relationship with someone you are afraid of and working with someone who has those kind of defences.

Sexualised attachment

A particular type of problematic attachment in forensic settings is a sexualised or eroticised attachment (Thomas-Peter and Garrett 2000). A significant sub-group of forensic patients have experienced sexual abuse as children; and a further sub-group are admitted for sexual offending, i.e. breaking legal boundaries around sexual behaviour. It is therefore not surprising to find that a sub-group of forensic patients (male and female) see the nursing staff in sexual terms and eroticise the nurse–patient relationship.

Forensic patients may openly compare notes with each other regarding who has the best or nicest primary nurse and sometimes behave in a way that suggests they are infatuated with members of nursing staff, including primary nurses. Through projection, patients may wrongly perceive that the primary nurse or other member of the nursing staff is attracted to them or even loves them, proclaiming that if they had met under different circumstances a romantic attachment would develop between nurse and patient.

These highly idealising attitudes are characteristic of the dismissing attachment style. They are defensive because they do not admit that the loved object has any weaknesses or flaws. Nurses who are the object of an idealised attachment by a patient are at high risk of being the victim of assault when they (inevitably) disappoint the patient, or if the patient fears to lose them (as described above in the section about victims). Highly idealised or enmeshed attachments can also lead to sexual boundary violations by staff in forensic settings (Thomas-Peter and Garrett 2000). Female staff have been found to be at risk of engaging in sexual boundary violations with male patients; possibly because they are targeted by predatory male patients; but if they are experiencing personal difficulties at home this can also make them vulnerable to 'special' attention from a patient (Gabbard 1989).

A key feature of relational security is the making and maintaining of professional boundaries in the relationships between staff and patients. Understanding everyone's need for attachments at times of stress may help senior staff and managers to understand why staff who are undergoing personal loss or stress at home might behave inappropriately with patients or colleagues. Sexual boundary violations are also known to commonly involve patients with histories of sexual abuse in childhood; suggesting that these patients may be particularly vulnerable to this maladaptive attachment pattern (Kluft 1990).

Professional and personal boundaries

Attachment theory may also aid understanding of other, more egregious, failures in residential forensic care. All professionals working in these settings will themselves have IWMs of attachment that affect their own care-giving and care-eliciting behaviour, and the normative data from non-clinical populations would indicate that insecure attachment representations will be found in as much as 40 per cent of the workforce (Bakermans-Kranenburg and Van IJzendoorn 2009; see Adshead 2010 for review).

Therapist attachment style has an impact on the outcome of therapy (Rubino *et al.* 2000) and has been shown to influence therapeutic relationships in forensic care (Zegers *et al.* 2006). Staff with insecure attachment styles may (without realising it) become hyper-aroused and agitated when faced with threat or need; or may become avoidant or hostile to patients. They may also be at increased risk of stress reactions, burn out, sexual boundary violations and other types of inappropriate relationship.

For example, we may consider the two different sets of inquiries into institutional failure of care in Ashworth hospital (Department of Health 1990; Fallon Report 1999). In the first Ashworth Inquiry, there was evidence that staff had been physically abusive to patients; in the second it became clear that staff had either colluded with patients in rule-breaking behaviour, turned a blind eye to it, or not noticed it.

These might seem like different kinds of problem, but in reality they are not. They are sad examples of how the IWMs of attachment that are present in both staff and patients can be activated by the stresses of life in long-term residential care. The activation of IWMs in staff results in conscious emotional reactions to the patients, such as hostility, rage, contempt and fear, which may be difficult enough to manage. But activation of these models can also trigger unconscious reactions to the patients, derived from unresolved distress from past traumatic relationships with the patients or someone else from their personal history.

In the incidents mentioned in the first Ashworth inquiry, we can guess that the staff must have perceived the patients as especially provocative and threatening; given that they used violence against patients (as opposed to organised restraint or some other socially sanctioned response). It may be that there was something about the presentation of the patients that unconsciously triggered in staff fears about their own capacity to become disorganised; and anxiety about their capacity to contain the patients. It seems likely that the attachment relationships between staff and patients were highly insecure, with the patients looking to the staff to contain anxiety and the staff feeling increasingly anxious about their capacity to do so. As anxiety rose, the staff seem to have adopted a dismissing style in which they rejected the neediness of the patients and responded with derogation and anger. They may also have become angry and abusive in response to their own distress and fear that they were not in control.

If in reality staff numbers are down, or the ward is particularly stressed, then the chance of staff feeling helpless and panicky is increased, which in turn may increase the risk of staff acting in a hostile way to patients. None of the above is an excuse for unprofessional behaviour, but it does provide a framework for understanding what happened and how it might be prevented.

Conversely, in the set of incidents recorded in the second inquiry, we might speculate that the attachment relationship between staff and patients was an enmeshed one, in which there was an abolition of boundaries between staff and patients and some degree of role reversal. Such enmeshment may be a defence against feeling overwhelmed and helpless in the face of the patients' capacity for cruelty and hopelessness. It is possible that staff failed to notice what was going on and/or failed to take action because they felt there was no point in noticing or acting. In this way, they may have unconsciously identified with the victims of their patients and also the victim part of each patient's history. Victims of violence characteristically 'freeze' and become passive in the face of danger; they can also experience overwhelming hopelessness and helplessness, which further increases passivity (van der Kolk 1989).

What happened in Ashworth were examples of violations and erosion of professional boundaries as a result of highly disorganised attachment relationships between staff and patients. The staff lost sight of their therapeutic goals by the gradual erosion of their professional identities. Boundary violations happen in all forms of health care, but they are particularly common in places where staff and patients have to engage in long-term relationships. The point here is not that the staff in Ashworth were 'bad apples' who need to be rooted out. Rather, we would argue that what happened at Ashworth is a professional hazard of long-stay residential forensic care. Forensic institutions need to face this head on and make working with these issues part of everyday clinical practice.

Implications for training and supervision

Attachment theory is an accessible theory of psychological development and interpersonal functioning that provides a useful base for the training and support of forensic nursing staff (Aiyegbusi and Clarke-Moore 2008) and other professionals such as occupational therapists and psychologists. Much traditional mental health training may leave staff unaware of the interpersonal aspects of their relationship with patients (especially if those relationships are difficult), and with a tendency to attribute relational problems to 'mental illness', personality disorder or 'evil' (Bowers 2002). It may be hard for staff to appreciate that medication may improve symptoms of mental illness but does little to change attitudes to caregivers. They may also be unprepared for the fact that they will experience emotional reactions to the patients, both positive and negative, which may be evoked in them by the patient's attachment behaviour. Attachment based 'supervision' can provide a space for reflection on the emotional demands of the job (Winship 1995) and the complexities of relating to people whose attachment history is highly insecure. Identification of a vulnerable sub-group of staff with insecure attachment styles could lead to the provision of extra support; but could also place staff at risk of stigma and unfair employment practice.

Conclusion

In this chapter, we sought to set out why attachment theory is of particular practical relevance to services for forensic patients, whether in prison or secure mental health settings. We described the impact of attachment on the development of personality and how insecure attachment patterns can increase risk for the development of personality disorders. We have described the high prevalence of insecure attachment styles in forensic populations, compared to non-clinical populations; and the impact this may have on risk assessment. We have also considered how attachment figures can be potential victims of violence and how threats of loss of attachment figures can trigger violence. Finally, we have also explored how insecure attachment patterns in both patients and staff impact on therapeutic relationships in long-stay residential secure care; and looked at ways of managing interactions to help people become more psychologically 'secure'.

Note

1   Aiyegbusi, A. (2011). Managing the nurse – patient relationship with people diagnosed with personality disorders in therapeutic community and secure mental health settings. Unpublished doctoral thesis, Middlesex University, Tavistock Clinic.

References

Adshead, G. (1998). Psychiatric staff as attachment figures. *British Journal of Psychiatry* **172**, 64–9.

——(2010). Becoming a care giver: attachment theory and poorly performing doctors. *Medical Education* **44**, 125–31.

Adshead, G. and Bluglass, K. (2001). Attachment representations and factitious illness by proxy: relevance for the assessment of parenting capacity in child maltreatment. *Child Abuse Review* **10**, 398–410.

Aiyegbusi, A. and Clarke-Moore, J. (2008). *Therapeutic Relationships with Offenders.* London: Jessica Kingsley Publishers.

Bakermans-Kranenburg, M. and van IJzendoorn, M.H. (2009). The first 10,000 Adult Attachment Interviews: distributions of adult attachment representations in clinical and non-clinical groups. *Attachment and Human Development* **11**, 223–64.

Bartholomew, K., Kwong, M. and Hart, S.D. (2001). Attachment. In W. John (ed.), *Handbook of Personality Disorders*, pp. 196–230. New York: John Wiley and Sons.

Bateman, A. and Fonagy, P. (2008). Co-morbid antisocial and borderline personality disorders: mentalisation based treatment. *Journal of Clinical Psychology* **64**, 181–94.

Bogaerts, S., Vanheule, S. and Declerq, F. (2005). Recalled parental bonding, adult attachment style and personality disorders in child molesters: a comparative study. *Journal of Forensic Psychiatry and Psychology* **16**, 445–58.

Bowers, L. (2002) *Dangerous and Severe Personality Disorder: response and role of the psychiatric team.* London: Routledge.

Bowlby, J. (1944). Forty-four juvenile thieves: their characters and home-life. *International Journal of Psychoanalysis* **25**, 1–57 and 207–28.

——(1969). *Attachment and Loss, Volume 1: Attachment.* London: The Tavistock Institute of Human Relations.

——(1984). Violence in the family as a disorder of the attachment and caregiving systems. *American Journal of Psychoanalysis* **44**, 9–27.

Brennan, K. and Shaver, P. (1998). Attachment styles and personality disorders. *Journal of Personality* **66**, 835–78.

Coid, J., Yang, M., Tyrer, P., Roberts, A. and Ullrich, S. (2006). Prevalence and correlates of personality disorder in Great Britain. *British Journal of Psychiatry* **188**, 423–31.

Crawford, T., Shaver, P.R., Cohen, P., Pilkonis, P., Gillath, U. and Kasen, S. (2006). Self-reported attachment, interpersonal aggression and personality disorder in a prospective case sample of adolescents and adults. *Journal of Personality Disorder* **20**, 331–51.

Crawford, T., Livesley, W.J., Lang, K.L., Shaver, P.R., Cohen, P. and Gariban, J. (2007). Insecure attachment and personality disorder: a twin study of adults. *European Journal of Personality* **21**, 191–208.

Department of Health. (1990). *Report of the Committee of Inquiry into the Personality Disorder Unit, Ashworth Special Hospital.* London: The Stationery Office.

Dozier, M., Lomax, C., Tyrrell, C. and Lee, C.S. (2001). The challenge of treatment for clients with dismissing states of mind. *Attachment and Human Development* **3**, 62–76.

Dozier, M., Stovall-McClough, K. and Albus, K. E. (2008). Attachment and psychopathology in adulthood. In J. Cassidy and P. Shaver (eds), *Handbook of Attachment*, 2nd edn, pp. 718–44. New York: Guilford Press.

Duggan, C. and Howard, R. (2009). The 'functional link' between personality disorder and violence: a critical appraisal. In M. McMurran and R.C. Howard (eds), *Personality, Personality Disorder and Violence*, pp. 19–38. Chichester: John Wiley and Sons.

Dunbar, R.I.M. (2003). The social brain: mind, language and society in evolutionary perspective. *Annual Review of Anthropology* **32**, 163–81.

Estroff, S., and Zimmer, C. (1994). Social networks, social support and violence among people with severe persistent mental illness. In J. Monahan, and H. Steadman (eds), *Violence and Mental Disorder: developments in risk assessment*, pp. 259–95. Chicago: University of Chicago Press.

Estroff, S., Swanson, J., Lachicotte, W.S., Swart, M. and Bolduc, M. (1998). Risk networks in the mentally ill. *Social Psychiatry and Psychiatric Epidemiology* **33**, 95–101.

Fallon Report (1999). *Report of the Inquiry Committee in the Personality Disorder Unit at Ashworth Hospital.* London: The Stationery Office.

Fazel, S., Gulati, G., Linsell, L., Geddes, J.R. and Grann, M. (2009). Schizophrenia and violence: systematic review and meta-analysis. *Public Library of Science Medicine* **6**(8), e1000120 doi: 10.1371.

First, M.B., Bell, C.C., Cuthbert, B., Krystal, J.H., Malison, R., Offord, D.R. and Wisner, K.L. (2002). Personality disorders and relational disorders. In D. Kupfer, M.B. First and D.A. Regier (eds), *A Research Agenda for DSM–V*, pp. 123–98. Washington DC: American Psychiatric Association.

Fonagy, P. (1998). An attachment theory approach to treatment of the difficult patient. *Bulletin of the Menninger Clinic* **62**, 147–69.

Fonagy, P. and Target, M. (1997). Attachment and reflective function: their role in self organisation. *Development and Psychopathology* **9**, 679–700.

Fonagy, P., Target, M., Steele, M. and Steele, H. (1997). The development of violence and crime as it relates to security of attachment. In J. Osojsky (ed.), *Children in a Violent Society*, pp. 150–77. New York: Guilford Press.

Frodi, A., Dernevik, M., Sepa, A., Philipson, J. and Bragesjo, M. (2001). Current attachment representations of incarcerated offenders varying in degree of psychopathy. *Attachment and Human Development* **3**, 269–83.

Gabbard, G. (ed.). (1989). *Sexual Exploitation in Professional Relationships.* Washington, DC: American Psychiatric Press.

George, C., Kaplan, J. and Main, M. (1994). *Adult Attachment Interview: unpublished rating manual.* University of California at Berkeley: Department of Psychology.

Glorney, E., Perkins, D., Adshead, G., McGauley, G., Murray, K., Noak, J. and Sichau, G. (2010). Domains of need in a high secure hospital setting: a model for streamlining care and reducing length of stay. *International Journal of Forensic Mental Health* **9**, 138–48.

Hare, R.D. (1999). Psychopathy as a risk factor for violence. *Psychiatric Quarterly* **70**, 181–97.

Hesse, E. (2008). The Adult Attachment Interview. In J. Cassidy and P. Shaver (eds). *Handbook of Attachment*, 2nd edn, pp. 552–98. New York: Guilford Press.

Holtzworth-Munroe, A., Bates, L., Smutzer, N. and Sardin, E. (1997). A brief review of the research on husband violence: Part 1, Maritally violent men versus non-violent men. *Aggression and Violent Behaviour* **2**, 65–99.

Kluft, R.P. (1990). Incest and subsequent revictimisation: the case of therapist–patient sexual exploitation with a description of Sitting Duck syndrome. In R.P. Kluft (ed.), *Incest Related Syndrome of Adult Psychopathology*, pp. 263–88. Washington DC: American Psychiatric Press.

Levinson, A. and Fonagy, P. (2006). Offending and attachment: the relationship between interpersonal awareness and offending in a prison population with psychiatric disorder. *Canadian Journal of Psychoanalysis* **12**, 225–51.

Livesley, J.W. (1993). Genetic and environmental contributions to dimensions of personality disorder. *American Journal of Psychiatry* **150**, 1826–31.

Marshall, W.L., Serran, G. and Cortoni, F. (2000). Childhood attachments, sexual abuse and their relationship to adult coping. *Sexual Abuse: Journal of Research and Treatment* **12**, 17–26.

Mikkelson, K., Kessler, R.C. and Shaver, P.R. (1997). Adult attachment in a nationally representative sample. *Journal of Personality and Social Psychology* **73**, 1092–1106.

Norton, K. (1996). Management of difficult personality disorder patients. *Advances in Psychiatric Treatment* **2**, 202–10.

Patrick, C., Fowles, D.C. and Krueger, F. (2009). Triarchic conceptualization of psychopathy: developmental origins of disinhibition, boldness and meanness. *Development and Psychopathology* **21**, 913–30.

Pfäfflin, F. and Adshead, G. (2004). *A Matter of Security: the application of attachment theory for forensic psychiatry and psychotherapy.* London: Jessica Kingsley Publishers.

Rubino, G., Barker, C., Roth, T. and Fearon, P. (2000). Therapist empathy and depth of interpretation in response to potential alliance ruptures: the role of therapist and patient attachment styles. *Psychotherapy Research* **18**, 408–20.

Sarkar, J. and Adshead, G. (2006). Personality disorder as disorders of attachment and affect regulation. *Advances in Psychiatric Treatment* **12**, 297–305.

Schore, A.N. (2001). The effect of early relational trauma on right brain development, affect regulation and infant mental health. *Infant Mental Health Journal* **22**, 201–49.

——(2003). *Affect Dysregulation and Disorders of the Self.* London: W.W. Norton and Company.

Shiner, R. and Masten, A. (2002). Transactional links between personality and adaptation from childhood to adulthood. *Journal of Research in Personality* **3**, 580–88.

Skodol, A., Bender, D.S., Morey, L.C., Clark, L.A., Oldham, J.M., Alarcon, R.D. and Siever, L.J. (2011). Personality disorder types proposed for DSM-V. *Journal of Personality Disorders* **25**, 136–69.

Smith, K. and Flatley, J. (2010). *Homicides, Firearm Offences and Intimate Violence 2008/09.* London: Home Office.

Sroufe, A., Egeland, B., Carlson, E.A. and Collins, W.A. (2005). *The Development of the Person: the Minnesota Study of risk and adaptation from birth to adulthood.* New York: Guilford Press.

Steele, H. and Steele, M. (2009). *Clinical Applications of the Adult Attachment Interview.* New York: Guilford Press.

Thomas-Peter, B. and Garrett, T. (2000). Preventing sexual contact between professionals and patients in forensic environments. *The Journal of Forensic Psychiatry* 11, 135–50.

van der Kolk, B. (1989). The compulsion to repeat the trauma. *Psychiatric Clinics of North America* 12, 38–41.

van IJzendoorn, M.H. and Bakermans-Kranenburg, M.J. (1996). Attachment representations in mothers, fathers, adolescents and clinical groups: a search for normative data. *Journal of Consulting and Clinical Psychology* 64, 8–12.

——(2003). Attachment disorders and disorganised attachment: similar and different. *Attachment and Human Development* 5, 313–20.

van IJzendoorn, M.H., Feldbruggen, J., Derks, F.C.H., de Ruiter, C., Verhagen, M., Philipse, M., van der Staak, C. and Riksen-Walraven, J. (1997). Attachment representations of personality disordered criminal offenders. *American Journal of Orthopsychiatry* 67, 449–59.

Weiss, R. (1991). The attachment bond in childhood and adulthood. In C.M. Parkes, and H.J. Stevenson (eds), *Attachment Across the Life Cycle*, pp. 66–76. London: Routledge.

Winship, G. (1995). The unconscious impact of caring for acutely disturbed patients: a perspective for supervision. *Journal of Psychiatric and Mental Health Nursing* 2, 227–31.

Zegers, M., Schuengel, C., van IJzendoorn, M.H. and Janssens, J.M. (2006). Attachment representations of institutionalised adolescents and their professional caregivers: predicting the development of therapeutic relationships. *American Journal of Orthopsychiatry* 76, 325–34.

Chapter 15

Using attachment theory to inform psychologically minded care services, systems and environments

Martin Seager

Attachment and the human condition

The first attachment relationship between a dependent infant and an adult caregiver lies at the heart of what it is to be human. Indeed, attachment appears to be one concept that most scientists of the human condition can agree about. Observing newborn babies with their caregivers shows that bodily, psychological and social development are interwoven and get started together.

For example, breast or bottle feeding at the very start of life does all of the following:

- nurtures the body, supplying the energy for physical growth
- provides a foundation for the development of a secure self and identity in the infant as the caregiver 'mirrors' the feelings and mental states that are embodied in hunger, satiation, distress and comfort
- creates an initial blueprint for social relationship.

Because human youngsters remain dependent and vulnerable for a much longer time than the young of other species, this means that the attachments formed between developing humans and those that care for them are a protracted, complex and also potentially risky affair if those attachments are disrupted or violated in any way. In 30 years of clinical practice with people experiencing severe and complex mental health problems, I cannot recall a single such case where early childhood attachments were not seriously violated or disrupted. It should be obvious that where early attachments are traumatic, abusive or neglectful, the development of a healthy adult personality cannot happen. 'Scientific' research is only belatedly looking at these issues, which have long been understood by our greatest artists and novelists, most obviously Charles Dickens, whose most famous works (e.g. *Oliver Twist*) are fascinating studies of the damage done to developing children when care-giving attachments go wrong, coupled with uplifting accounts of how emotional damage can be repaired through new and loving attachments.

If attachments go wrong, therefore, a child can grow physically into an adult form but remain emotionally damaged or undeveloped. This is not to split the brain from the mind. After all, the human brain as a biological entity has evolved mainly as a learning machine. Recognising this fact makes the nature versus nurture debate largely redundant. We now have increasingly hard evidence to show that love attachments shape our lives and even our very brain development (Gerhardt 2004; Schore 2001). From an evolutionary perspective, an 18-year childhood would indeed be pointless in a species whose essential personal characteristics (including something as vital as 'mental health') were largely pre-configured at birth.

The theory of attachment provides a powerful framework for integrating our scientific understanding of how human mental health is developed, and yet this universal concept is largely forgotten in the design of our adult mental health services, based as they are upon a default, bio-medical model where attachment and relationship processes are seen at best as vague 'facilitators' or 'stressors' that simply increase or decrease the risk of triggering underlying 'conditions'.

However, one powerful example will clearly show that it is better science to view attachment factors as fundamental building blocks of the 'human condition' in which all individuals evolve a unique personality that reflects their early care-giving environment, and that in turn helps to shape the way that future environments and relationships are experienced and managed.

In the TV documentary *Help me love my baby*[1] (Channel 4, 2007) a six-month-old girl is shown clearly, consistently and actively avoiding eye contact with her mother (whilst at other times being able to maintain eye contact with other adults). Correspondingly, the mother's face when she is holding the baby is shown to be signalling intense fear and resentment. It is clear that the attachment is going wrong. The baby has already learned to look away to protect herself from overpowering feelings that are experienced as threatening and intrusive rather than as nurturing and supportive. It emerged later that the mother herself had not been 'mothered'. Because her own mother had been unavailable emotionally and had struggled with alcohol addiction, the daughter had learned to switch off or ignore her own dependency feelings. This meant that she could not now easily relate to or 'tune in with' a child of her own that was highly dependent and in need of intensive mothering. This baby had indeed been vulnerable from birth and had required a period in a Special Care Baby Unit. However, after a period of parent–infant therapy, when both the mother's and the baby's feelings were being 'tuned into' by the therapist, the attachment between the two was repaired and developed to a point where it could be said that this mother and baby truly 'loved' each other. This difference was visible just by looking at the mother, whose eyes now seemed to twinkle when she looked at her baby. It was clear that this mother was now emotionally available, not only to her own child but also to herself. She was no longer switching off her own feelings and could now therefore more accurately identify with her child's needs and feelings.

This striking example, along with other developing research evidence (e.g. Svanberg, Mennet and Spieker 2010), raises a number of vital questions, most importantly: 'If early attachments are this powerful and formative in human personality development, why is our society so blind to attachments when designing its mental health care systems?'

This blindness to attachment is even more striking when it is considered that attachment relationships are also perhaps the core and universal ingredient of all effective psychotherapy, whatever the brand (Norcross 2002). This qualitative aspect is commonly referred to in the therapy literature as the 'therapeutic alliance', 'collaborative relationship', 'working relationship' or 'rapport'. Even lay people call it 'chemistry'. Given these universal findings and patterns, rather than seeing attachments simply as a vehicle for treatment techniques it is probably better science to see therapy models as different languages in which to deliver therapeutic and empathic attachments.

The concept of 'mentalisation' (e.g. Fonagy *et al.* 2002) has also expanded our understanding of how human attachment operates in psychological terms and how the mind of the adult caregiver impacts upon the developing mind of the dependent child. It shows that attachment is even more vital than previously thought, providing the original vehicle for empathic 'mirroring' and infant personality development. It helps us to see that it is only the accurate emotional attunement and responsiveness of caregivers to the emotional signals of infants that enables infants to build up an accurate internal map of 'self' in relation to 'other' or 'identity'.

By expanding attachment theory in this way, three robust scientific assumptions can therefore be made about the status of early attachment in human mental well-being.

1   A human being's first non-verbal attachment experiences lay down the first pattern or blueprint of 'self in relation to other' onto which subsequent language-based experience must be mapped and through which subsequent relationships are interpreted.

2   A baby cannot healthily develop an internal sense of its own feelings and its own mind (self, identity) unless an available (securely attached, emotionally invested) external adult caregiver is able accurately to empathise with, identify with, recognise, 'mirror' or 'read' the communications of the baby.

3   Adults with severe, complex and enduring mental health problems tend to have experienced insecure, damaging, neglectful or broken attachments during their earlier developmental years. This means that they will need services that can provide stable and consistent therapeutic attachments to unlock emotional defences, repair past damage and address unmet needs.

Attachment-blindness and mind-blindness[2] in adult mental health service provision

Given our implicit scientific and cultural knowledge of the centrality of the 'love bond' to the human condition, it is perhaps strange that still to this day our society organises even its mental health services in a very medicalised and un-psychosocial way, making an unquestioned assumption that people are afflicted by a range of specific illnesses that require specific 'evidence-based' treatments in specific 'doses'. Within this bio-medical framework, the age-old human activity of forming compassionate attachments and empathic relationships with our fellow human beings can itself only be viewed as another kind of 'treatment' that must be quantified as somehow being equivalent to mood-altering drugs and rated against them for comparative effectiveness. The example of parent–infant therapy described above, however, makes it clear why attempting such 'drugs versus psychotherapy' comparisons is poor science.

Perhaps inevitably, therefore, 'talking therapies' as they have come to be known are still to this day researched and marketed as distinct brands that are presumed to be quantifiable in terms of dose-effects. This framework or paradigm, by contrasting 'bio-' and 'psycho-' models, leaves very little room for genuinely integrated bio-psycho-social thinking about the human condition, and it also makes it very hard for a theory such as attachment theory, which is more developmental than clinical, however universally accepted, to gain a foothold in the shaping of wider mental health service culture. Within a paradigm that says we need to test specific treatments separately for specific conditions, attachment theory can only readily be evidenced and implemented as the basis for its own brand of 'talking therapy', and this probably explains why we do indeed now have specific 'attachment-based therapy' for specific 'attachment-based disorders'. This is a valuable development, but ignores the greater truth that nearly all serious mental health problems are attachment disorders of one kind or another.

In 2007, at the request of the Health Secretary, I set up a national advisory group on mental health and well-being (Seager *et al.* 2007). Our aim was to identify universal underlying concepts that linked all the different brands and approaches to psychological therapy and human mental well-being. The group did indeed achieve a consensus and it was agreed that secure attachment was a core and universal factor underlying well-being for all humans.

The group arrived at five universal psychological principles:

1   Human well-being depends on meeting universal psychological needs as well as physical and social needs.
2   All mental health service provision and policy – not just specialist psychological services – should be informed by psychological principles and standards.
3   Attachment theory provides a universal evidence base that has not yet been fully recognised or utilised in general mental health policy and service design.

4   In mental health, it is misleading to claim that relationships merely provide a setting or a set of values within which treatment is delivered. Relationships are the essence of the treatment and are the 'baby, not the bath water'.

5   Choosing between medical and psychological approaches to mental health is bad science and based on a Cartesian body–mind split – there is always a psychological aspect and a psychological impact arising from every human intervention, even so called 'pure' medical treatments; there is no such thing as a psychological or relational vacuum.

Whilst principle 3 is clearly the most relevant for our present purposes, the central implication of all five principles is that care-giving attachments directly shape and dynamically maintain the health and well-being of the human personality. Under principle 1, the primary universal psychological need was also defined as follows: To have a secure and stable attachment to at least one significant other person who knows us well and whom we can trust.

According to these principles, attachments and other relationship factors are always vitally operative in any human care situation and should therefore inform the overall design of all mental health services, systems and cultures. However, what is striking about our adult mental health services to this day is that they are run in ways that remain blind even to the basic concept of attachment. This contrasts with the fact that there is at least some implicit acknowledgement of attachment in the design and delivery of child and family mental health services, if only because children are by definition still dependent on adult caregivers.

In our current mental health service culture we generally think of drugs as a last resort for children but a first resort for adults. This 'apartheid' between our service cultures for adults and children cannot be explained in terms of biological science. After all, we do not deny life-saving drugs to children with cancers and other life-threatening physical diseases.

What this massive difference in the cultures of our mental health services for children and adults truly shows us, therefore, is a failure of a coherent scientific hypothesis relating to the real nature and causes of mental well-being. We know implicitly that children need love bonds for their well-being but we somehow forget or 'turn a blind eye' to this in our services for adults.

When faced with an unhappy child, it is usually impossible to medicalise the issues. Children are more transparent in their distress and their dependency on care-giving relationships is all too obvious. In trying to achieve scientific coherence in our approach to mental health services, therefore, the real question must be:

> Should we change our child mental health service culture to be more medical or make our adult service culture more developmental and psychosocial?

The answer to this question is surely self-evident. In a medical service culture, however, where psychological approaches are seen merely as an alternative treatment 'technique' rather than as tapping into a universal human need for love, relationships and psychological nutrition, the possibility of establishing effective therapeutic attachments is severely restricted by:

1   a false assumption that psychological approaches are only relevant to selected 'conditions';
2   prescribing relationships in predetermined 'doses' and 'courses' like drugs;
3   discharging and transferring patients based on symptom counts rather than relationship and personality developments;
4   staff rotations and changes to staff availability that are based on organisational considerations rather than the attachment needs of service users;
5   a lack of recognition that a psychologically-informed stance is the business of all care professionals and that all care should meet fundamental psychological standards (particularly relating to care-giving attachments);
6   a failure to recognise that all attachments, including those formed with families, friends, colleagues, other service users or non-clinical staff (e.g. domestics, receptionists), can have a critical value and a therapeutic (or negative) impact on a person's mental health.

Given that attachment and empathy are intertwined at the root of the health of the human mind, this ongoing 'mind-blindness' in our adult mental health services is, therefore, potentially quite harmful, especially when it is considered that these services are dealing with the very people for whom early attachments have already gone badly wrong.

From mind-blind to psychologically minded services

How then can the concept of attachment be introduced into the design and culture of adult mental health services to render them more psychologically-minded and to improve their safety and effectiveness? The following list is not exhaustive, but provides some obvious examples.

Reducing the risk of attachment breakdown for in-patients

There is strong evidence that a time of significantly heightened risk for suicide is the period immediately following discharge from psychiatric hospital (e.g. King *et al.* 2001). Such a finding defies medical explanation. After all, aren't people discharged because they're better? However, this evidence can readily be explained in terms of attachment theory (Seager 2006). Vulnerable in-patients at a time of distress can feel more secure as they start to build certain attachments to individual staff, to fellow patients and even to the system as a kind of 'professional family'. Discharge from hospital, which might seem a positive move in medical terms, can therefore represent a major rupture of attachments, prompting feelings of rejection, abandonment and intense emotional insecurity (ironically provoking what in medical terms would look like a 'relapse'). Even a basic application of attachment theory, therefore, would mean that the medical concept of 'discharge' from in-patient units is at best misleading and should perhaps be replaced by a more developmental concept of 'transition'. Such transitions would be safer if some measure of attachment was factored into the care planning. If a significant drop in available attachments would result from leaving hospital, then the timing would not be right for such a transfer. Using attachment theory in this way would constitute safer practice and potentially save lives. Of course, this sort of thinking and practice can and does take place in our mental health services already, but it is sporadic, precisely because it is not explicitly part of the service model.

The explicit use of attachment theory would of course clearly demand a change in the whole culture of in-patient care. In-patient units would be designed to promote consistent and therapeutic relationships between staff and service users. The recruitment, deployment and training of all mental health professionals would need to be informed by some knowledge and understanding of attachment issues. Longer and more therapeutic stays involving the explicit and systemic use of attachment principles, with better planned transitions to community care, would improve outcomes, save lives and in the longer term save money through a reduction both in the suicide rate and in the all too familiar 'revolving door syndrome'.

Attachment theory as a basis for personalisation of services

The term 'personalisation' (e.g. Mind 2009) is becoming fashionable in mental health circles but it lacks an underlying theory. Attachment theory is well placed to provide such a theory along with clear service standards such as:

- Who is there in the care system with a consistent and stable emotional investment in the service user?
- Who is there in the system that knows who the service user is, remembers their individual life story and 'holds them in mind'?
- Who is there in the system that the service user can trust and get hold of quickly?
- How many different people in the system are relating to the service user? Is this pattern insecure because there are too many to really get to know the person or too few to cope with their needs?

One obvious and simple application of these standards is to appointment systems. To this day, psychiatric appointment systems remain relatively impersonal. It is still common practice to give outpatient appointments to adults on a 'clinic' basis, where the identity of the clinician is not consistent or even predictable. The same applies to 'ward reviews' in psychiatric hospitals, where it is also routine for different professionals to come and go on the basis of organisational needs rather than relationship considerations. Because the system is built on the assumption that it is 'conditions' that need to be reviewed and treated, not people in relationships, little or no primary consideration is given to personal attachments formed between the patient and caregivers either as individuals or as an overall professional 'family' system. This means that it is often a 'hit and miss' affair whether stable and continuous attachments do ultimately get formed within our adult psychiatric care culture.

Whilst service brochures and mission statements often aspire to 'personalised' or 'client-centred' services, this failure to take account of attachment theory in something as basic as the appointment system speaks for itself. This indeed is the theme of many complaints that services receive: 'I never saw the same person twice and I had to keep telling my story over and over again'.

Depersonalisation is, of course, one of the key causes and symptoms of poor mental health in the first place. It can, therefore, be argued that the traditional mental health care culture risks reinforcing rather than reducing problems. Factoring attachment into the appointment system is therefore one obvious step that would help to create genuine personalisation in practice by ensuring a standard of continuity of relationship in the booking of appointments. Similarly, whilst service users are increasingly offered 'key workers' or 'care co-ordinators' in our adult mental health system, this is not based on attachment theory or indeed on any relationship model so much as a 'pragmatic' belief in the value of co-ordinated care. This means that much of the potential therapeutic benefit of 'key working' may be lost or even violated when key-workers and care co-ordinators are blindly transferred, replaced or substituted for 'pragmatic' reasons. Informing key working and care co-ordination with even the most basic understanding of attachment theory, therefore, could help to make mental health services significantly safer.

From physical safety to 'psychological safety'

Our 'health and safety' culture even in mental health care remains heavily focused upon the physical environment. I have elsewhere (Seager 2006) described a concept of 'psychological safety', rooted in the science both of attachment theory and of psychodynamics. Putting this simply, psychological safety means that people are much more at risk from failures of relationship than they are from deficiencies in the physical environment, in the sense that an environment can be seen to be only as safe as the security of emotional attachments that it can provide for service users.

Attachment theory can therefore provide a framework for defining and measuring the psychological safety of care environments. Goodwin and colleagues (2003) have developed the Service Attachment Questionnaire (SAQ), which assesses the extent to which services meet the attachments needs of service users. Questions cover six key areas: being listened to; consistency and continuity; being given time – ending and leaving; safe environment; enabling relationships; contact and comfort. This information, along with measures of service users' individual attachment styles, could create an audit tool for service safety (Berry and Drake 2010).

One other obvious application of this idea is to the prevention of suicide in psychiatric units. When suicides and other 'serious untoward incidents' (SUIs) occur, psychiatric units are frequently investigated in terms of physical safety for the presence of 'ligature points', but no real attempt is made to investigate breaks in the security of the attachments between service users, professionals and others, especially at times of transition (e.g. discharge from hospital, see above). The relevant emotional attachments of those involved are not measured or even considered, and therefore psychological lessons are rarely learned. Creating even the crudest of attachment measures for use at key points in the care pathway could therefore potentially save lives.

Availability and accessibility of the service system as an attachment issue

The failure of early care-giving attachments is inevitably one of the greatest sources of emotional damage. It follows from this that emotionally vulnerable people will ideally need a mental health system that can provide stable, consistent and accessible attachments if this emotional damage is ever to be repaired. Putting it crudely, services need to provide some experience of healthy 're-parenting'.

However, even the working hours of traditional mental health services in the UK still follow the normal 'business' hours of 9.00 am to 5.00 pm. Some 'out of hours' services are provided but these are limited. Again, even the most basic application of attachment theory indicates that care-giving relationships do not work in this way. With vulnerable, insecurely attached and emotionally damaged service users, it should be evident that there is a need for a flexible, accessible and available care-giving system based on psychological time rather than physical time. It is precisely 'in the wee small hours', at those very times when normal facilities are shut down, that vulnerable people would be predicted to feel most alone, most in need of help and most at risk.

The very design of statutory community mental health services can therefore be experienced as alienating and this partly explains the popularity and value of 24-hour alternatives in the voluntary sector, particularly the Samaritans. Within statutory services the only routinely available 24-hour access-point for mental health service users is 'A and E', which is primarily geared for physical emergencies and is certainly not informed by attachment theory or by any psychological model. Using attachment theory, all mental health services would need to be designed in such a way that attachment figures did not conspicuously fade away after 5.00 pm. To avoid creating a culture of neglect, statutory services need some redesign, using the concept of attachment, to ensure that there is at least one accessible professional caregiver at any time of the day. This might involve closer collaboration with the voluntary sector.

Honouring human dependency needs rather than stigmatising them

Attachment theory helps to explain why children need a critical period of dependency within a stable home environment if they are to develop into healthy, independent adults. To become self-reliant a human being has first of all to be able to rely on at least one external caregiver.

Dependency, including the basic human need for love and attention, is all too often stigmatised as a problem ('attention-seeking') or as a symptom to be eradicated rather than as a need to be understood and met. Public mental health services are also increasingly focused on low cost, time limited 'quick fixes' rather than on wider notions of human attachment and development. An attachment-blind system therefore can become self-defeating, creating a 'revolving door' culture of dependency, rejection and abandonment. This is perhaps most obvious within the homelessness sector where, ironically, service users are provided only with housing, hostels and brief hospital admissions rather than genuine homes. Even the simplest application of attachment theory, however, should lead us towards designing more homely environments based on 'family' relationships, so that such damaged people could begin to let down their defences and address their unmet universal needs. After all, no human being can ever grow up, move out or move on from a home that they have never had (Seager 2011).

Creating a secure family atmosphere and environment

Attachment theory supports the common-sense view that where a mental health service (like any other human system) is organised in ways that support a healthy 'family atmosphere', the well-being of both staff and service users is promoted. The recent notion of a 'psychologically informed environment' (PIE) (Johnson and Haigh 2010) represents some movement in this direction and is perhaps a revival of the older concept of the 'therapeutic community'. I have referred elsewhere (Seager 2006) to the concept of a 'professional family' (as distinct from the concept of treating the family system). Implicit in such a model is the idea that mental health is promoted by a containing framework of secure attachments to a limited and consistent number of professionals who work together and who get to know their clients and help them develop over time. In a recent paper (Seager 2011) I argued for the concept of 're-parenting' to be expanded to that of 're-homing'. Essentially, this highlights that no human being can develop without a sense of roots and of 'home'. The core part of any home is the attachment relationships within it. If our mental health services were designed on this personalised principle, they could only work better.

Caring for the mind of the care-giver

Attachments between staff and their own caregivers (supervisors, managers) are also vital in creating therapeutic conditions. If care professionals are not securely attached to their place of work then they cannot transmit that security and stability to the service users, in the same way that a chaotic family will undermine the healthy development of its children. If our service users are forming attachments to professionals who are themselves not feeling a sense of secure attachment and belonging to their place of work, a culture of deprivation will be created. Attachment theory, extended by the more recent concept of mentalisation, makes it clear that an attachment is only as good as the mental state of the caregiver. It is equally clear therefore that the mental state of the caregiver must in turn rely upon empathic back-up and support.

Leaving aside issues of psychological training, aptitude and skill, caregivers can lose their empathic stance through fatigue, burnout, 'vicarious trauma', negative counter-transference, stress, overload, poor managerial support, limited supervision, bureaucracy and other distractions (see Figley 1995; Seager 2006). 'Minding the baby' is the essential task of any caregiver but so many things can get in the way. An organisational culture can foster empathy in its staff or impair it. Supervision, for example, is not just a skills issue but a necessary way of detoxifying the emotional impact on professionals of caring for society's most vulnerable individuals. A fatigued and stressed General Practitioner (GP) or psychiatric nurse (however highly trained and motivated), who is coming to their twelfth clinical encounter of the day but who has not had the chance to reflect on and process the impact of the previous eleven, is unlikely to be in any state of mind to listen. Good supervision, therefore, (whatever the model: group/ individual, peer/expert, face to face/telephone) can be a vital emotional 'reviver' that can prevent emotional neglect and potentially save lives. In healthier service cultures, informal conversations can also often fulfil this function. Given that all human beings have a limited emotional capacity to listen and engage with their fellow human beings, perhaps the single most simple and vital safety test that could be applied across the care system is 'How many attachments of a given intensity can any one professional caregiver hold in mind at any time before empathy breaks down?' Such an attachment-informed approach to caseload management could in itself and at a stroke improve the safety of our adult mental health services for the future.

Conclusion

Attachment theory is widely recognised and there is implicit acceptance that attachment is a fundamental factor underlying human well-being. And yet the attachments formed between service users and their professional caregivers remain almost totally neglected in the design of our adult mental health services. In this chapter it has therefore been argued that this continued neglect of attachment amounts to a kind of 'mind-blindness' that can only increase risk and impair therapeutic effectiveness. Practical ideas for introducing attachment theory into the future culture and design of adult mental health services have been proposed.

Notes

1   Broadcast on Channel 4, 3 December 2007.
2   Broadening Simon Baron-Cohen's autism-related concept.

References

Berry, K. and Drake, R. (2010). The relevance of attachment theory for psychiatric rehabilitation and implications for practice. *Advances in Psychiatric Treatment* **16**, 308–15.

Figley, C.R. (ed.) (1995). *Compassion Fatigue: coping with secondary traumatic stress disorder in those who treat the traumatized.* New York: Brunner/Mazel.

Fonagy, P., Gergely, G., Jurist, E.L. and Target, M. (2002). *Affect Regulation, Mentalization and the Development of the Self.* New York: Other Press.

Gerhardt, S. (2004). *Why Love Matters: how affection shapes a baby's brain.* Hove: Routledge.

Goodwin, I., Holmes, G., Cochrane, R. and Mason, O. (2003). The ability of adult mental health services to meet clients' attachment needs: the development and implementation of the Service Attachment Questionnaire. *Psychology and Psychotherapy: Theory, Research and Practice* **76**, 145–61.

Johnson, R. and Haigh, R. (2010). Social psychiatry and social policy for the 21st century – new concepts for new needs: the 'psychologically-informed environment'. *Mental Health and Social Inclusion* **14**, 30–5.

King, E.A., Baldwin, D.S., Sinclair, M.A., Baker, N.G., Campbell, M. and Thompson, C. (2001). The Wessex Recent In-Patient Suicide Study 1. *British Journal of Psychiatry* **178**, 531–6.

Mind (2009). *Personalisation in Mental Health: a review of the evidence.* London: Mind Publications.

Norcross, J.C. (ed.) (2002). *Psychotherapy Relationships that Work: therapist contributions and responsiveness to patients.* New York: Oxford University Press.

Schore, A. (2001). The effects of secure attachment relationship on right brain development, affect regulation and infant mental health. *Infant Mental Health Journal* **22**, 7–66.

Seager, M. (2006). The concept of 'psychological safety' – A psychoanalytically-informed contribution towards 'safe, sound and supportive' mental health services. *Psychoanalytic Psychotherapy* **20**, 266–80.

——(2011). Homelessness is not houselessness: a psychologically-minded approach to inclusion and rough sleeping. *Journal of Mental Health and Social Inclusion* **15**, 183–9.

Seager, M., Orbach, S., Sinason, V., Samuels, A., Johnstone, L., Fredman, G., Antrican, J. and Hughes, R. (2007). National advisory group on mental health, safety and well being – towards proactive policy: five psychological principles. (Unpublished paper commissioned by the Health Secretary, Patricia Hewitt.)

Svanberg, P.O., Mennet, L. and Spieker, S. (2010). Promoting a secure attachment: a primary prevention practice model. *Clinical Child Psychology and Psychiatry* **15**, 363–78.

Chapter 16

We are the tools of our trade

The therapist's attachment history as a source of impasse, inspiration and change

David Wallin

Please note that an earlier version of this chapter was published in the book Clinical Pearls of Wisdom *edited by Michael Kerman.*

For the past fifteen years, my work – practising, teaching and writing about psychotherapy – has been inspired by a mixture of curiosity and conviction about the power of attachment theory to enhance clinical practice. That work culminated in a book, *Attachment in Psychotherapy* (2007), in which I identified three research findings that appeared to have the most profound and fertile implications for treatment: first, that co-created relationships of attachment are the key context for development; second, that preverbal experience makes up the core of the developing self; and third, that the stance of the self toward experience is a better predictor of attachment security than the remembered facts of personal history themselves. Accordingly, my approach as a clinician has focused on the therapeutic relationship as a developmental crucible, the centrality of the nonverbal dimension, and the transformative influence of reflection and mindfulness. Within this framework, attending to the attachment history and patterning of the therapist is of vital importance.

In the pages that follow, I will discuss the advantages and vulnerabilities that arise from the therapist's characteristic career trajectory, with its roots in a history of trauma and adaptation to trauma. I will go on to explore how, as therapists, we can identify our own states of mind with respect to attachment and the implications that flow from recognising that our state of mind is presently secure, dismissing, preoccupied, and/or unresolved. Then I will describe how mindfulness and mentalising can be enlisted to help us recognise and work with the enactments of transference/countertransference that take shape where our own attachment patterns interlock with those of the patient. Finally, I will present an illustrative clinical vignette.

Attachment and the therapist

Despite the reality that 'we are the tools of our trade' (Pearlman and Saakvitne 1995), the impact of the therapist's own psychology upon his or her clinical effectiveness is a topic the psychotherapy literature has largely ignored. From the attachment perspective within which I work, this omission appears very problematic. At the heart of the matter is my assumption that, in childhood and psychotherapy alike, the relationship is where the developmental action is. Just as the child's original attachment relationships make development possible, it is ultimately the new relationship of attachment with the therapist that allows the patient to change. But development, of course, takes (at least) two. For this reason, the finding of attachment research that the parent's security, insecurity or trauma is regularly transmitted to the child must surely catch our attention. For it suggests that not only as parents but also perhaps as therapists, our ability to generate a secure attachment relationship will be profoundly affected by the legacy of our own attachment relationships – a legacy that is, for many of us who choose this work, marked by trauma. Regardless of our theoretical orientation, then, our own attachment patterns may well be the single most influential factor in shaping – that is, enhancing but also constraining – our capacity to create with the patient a genuinely therapeutic relationship.

Let me be more specific. Attachment history is 'engraved' in the psyche. It takes the form of internal representations and rules for processing information that derive from our experiences of what has and has not 'worked' in relation to particular attachment figures. These 'rules of attachment' are quite literally rules to live by, given that they initially emerge from interactions with caregivers upon whom we depend for our very survival. The key issue here is what has been ruled in and what has been ruled out in the relationship with our original attachment figures. Put differently, the question is: What have we been able to integrate (because it elicited an attuned response from attachment figures) and what have we needed to defensively dissociate (because it threatened the survival-critical attachment bond)? The answers to this question shape our attachment patterns, determining not only how we relate to ourselves and to others, but also what we allow ourselves to know. For what in infancy began as behavioural 'strategies' for optimising the relationship to attachment figures soon become emotional, cognitive and attentional strategies that determine how freely we can feel, think, sense and remember. As therapists, then, our own (more or less troubled) attachment history – marked by the dissociations it has imposed and the integration we have managed to achieve, often with the help of personal therapy – is always both an asset and a liability.

On the one hand, we know others most profoundly on the basis of what we know about ourselves. Such self-knowledge can be a therapeutic resource to the extent that we have been able to recognise, tolerate and make meaningful sense of the painful aspects of our own history – that is, to integrate them. Then our personal experience may confer a heightened capacity for empathic understanding grounded in our partial identification with the patient's own difficult experience. Moreover, the freedom we have won to think deeply and feel fully can equip us well to kindle or strengthen the patient's capacities for reflection and emotion regulation. Finally – because of the mutual reciprocal influence therapists and patients inevitably exert upon one another – our real-time awareness of the ways our attachment patterns are presently being enacted with the patient can help to illuminate the patient's own attachment patterns.

On the other hand, the impact of the therapist's history – particularly experiences that have yet to be integrated – can have adverse effects on treatment. To begin with, our view of the patient can be clouded by what we are unable or unwilling to know about ourselves. Additionally, our own attachment-derived skew toward thinking at the expense of feeling – or vice versa – can undermine our ability to upgrade the patient's ability to think and feel in an integrated fashion. Most problematically, impasses in treatment can arise out of the need to keep at bay our own unbearable, and hence dissociated, experiences of self or other. These impasses can take the form of collusions or collisions (Goldbart and Wallin 1996). In keeping with our own attachment rules and patterns, we may find ourselves colluding with the patient to avoid experiences that are troubling to us and, not infrequently, to the patient as well. Alternatively, disowned aspects of ourselves – not only our dissociated experiences and our dread of them, but also our wish to work them through – can be defensively 'relocated' in the patient. Then we may find ourselves caught in collisions with patients who evoke reactions in us that initially arose (but often had to be suppressed) in response to our original attachment figures. Or we may find ourselves embroiled in conflict when we unconsciously push our patients to take on developmental challenges that we have only ambivalently or incompletely addressed ourselves. As therapists, in short, we need to be aware of the ambiguous relationship between what we recognise in the patient on the basis of overlapping experience and what we project onto the patient on the basis of what we have yet to fully integrate in ourselves.

For many therapists, I would propose, this unfinished work of integration involves a history of early trauma to which we have adapted with what attachment researchers call a 'controlling-caregiving strategy.' Longitudinal studies (Main and Cassidy 1988; Wartner et al. 1994) show that many infants assessed at twelve months as 'disorganised' – presumably as a result of growing up with attachment figures whose own unresolved trauma made them frightening to their babies – have by age six developed a distinctly solicitous role-inverting strategy. Like these children, I would suggest, many future therapists have learned to take control of scary parents by taking care of them. Put differently, many of us are 'wounded healers' who in the role of 'parentified' children first acquired many of the skills – but also the constraints – we now bring to our clinical work.

Identifying and working with the therapist's attachment patterns

From an attachment perspective, therapy heals when the quality of the therapist's presence and interventions can help patients both to deconstruct the attachment patterns of the past and to construct fresh ones in the present. From a slightly different angle, the therapist aims to create a relationship within which the patient may be able to integrate experiences that have previously had to remain dissociated. But our deliberate efforts to offer the patient a new and healing attachment relationship are invariably complicated, if not undermined outright, by the hidden pressures and constraints of our own attachment patterns.

For research purposes, identifying the attachment patterns of adults with singular descriptors (secure-autonomous, dismissing, preoccupied and unresolved) has been shown to have enormous value. For clinical purposes, however, it may be both more useful and true to the facts to assume that therapists in the course of their work can inhabit more than a single 'state of mind with respect to attachment'. In particular, therapists who have had a lot of therapy – and consequently a breadth and depth of self-knowledge and experience – will likely be well acquainted with a multiplicity of such states of mind in themselves. These states of mind are developmentally determined, to be sure, but they are also context-dependent. By this I mean that the therapist in the clinical setting may find herself or himself in a secure, dismissing, preoccupied or unresolved state of mind depending on the particular moment in the particular therapy of the particular patient.

Recognising the state of mind in which, as therapists, we are presently lodged can be especially important when that state of mind is dismissing, preoccupied or unresolved – and thus imposes limits on our awareness and effectiveness. Advantageously our very effort to notice and identify our state of mind can begin to loosen its grip – for then that state of mind may become an experience that needs to be understood rather than a fact that defines (and confines) us. Through such a process of attention and reflection, the constraints associated with particular states of mind can be transformed into therapeutically productive questions. For example, having noticed that we seem to be in a dismissing state that leaves us cut off from our feelings, we can ask ourselves, 'What might be the feelings we don't now wish to feel?' Scrutinising our experience in this fashion helps us to get out of our own way. And because our state of mind is always determined in part by the relational context, our efforts to grasp the nature of our own experience often wind up illuminating aspects of the patient's experience as well.

The therapist in a secure state of mind

Two key words describe our experience when we can inhabit this much-to-be-desired state of mind: freedom and flexibility. We have the freedom here to reflect, to feel, and to be aware of bodily sensations. We also have a kind of 'binocular vision' which permits flexible access to a wide range of experience both in ourselves and in our patients. Consequently, we are able to value, recognise and manifest in our conduct the balanced capacity for attachment and exploration that is the hallmark of secure attachment. Put differently, we are able in a secure state of mind to experience our relationship with the patient as a context in which there is room for two – two voices, two perspectives, two centres of desire and initiative. In an insecure state of mind, by contrast, we tend to experience the therapeutic relationship as a setting in which there is only room for one. In a dismissing state of mind, as I will explain, that one is the self; in a preoccupied state of mind that one is the other.

The therapist in a dismissing state of mind

The key word here is isolation. As therapists in a dismissing state of mind, we tend to be isolated both from the patient and from our own internal experience. 'Compulsive self-reliance' was Bowlby's shorthand to describe this drift toward disconnection and emotional shutdown. Sustaining such a stance may require us to think too well of ourselves and too little of the patient. It may lead us to be more involved with conveying our own perspective than in empathising with the patient, or deepening the patient's experience. In such a state we are gripped by the 'deactivating' attachment strategy characteristic of avoidant infants and dismissing adults alike. This means that rather than feeling comfortable with the primary biological attachment strategy – which is to turn to others when in distress – we are prone to tune out, in ourselves and from the patient, whatever cues might activate the attachment behavioural system. Clues to the therapist's deactivating strategy may be found in the research showing that infants classified as avoidant have usually been raised by controlling attachment figures who reject their overtures for closeness. In other words, therapists who become distant from their feelings and from their patients may unconsciously be protecting themselves from the threat of being rejected and/or controlled – which threats may also carry the potential to activate the therapist's feelings of shame.

Against this backdrop, it should come as no surprise that in a dismissing state of mind we tend to be dissociated from attachment-related emotions, impulses, memories and vulnerabilities. In particular, we may be 'allergic' to experiences of need and shame. More broadly, we may be cut off altogether from the world of feelings and bodily sensations – especially in ourselves, but often in our patients as well. From a certain angle and with certain patients – especially, perhaps, those in a preoccupied state of mind – these liabilities can be seen as assets (see Dozier, Cue and Barnett 1994), in that they allow the therapist to focus in a disciplined fashion, to analyse (albeit with limited empathy), to establish boundaries and, ultimately, to cope.

Primarily, of course, we need to be aware of the constraints to which we are vulnerable when we find ourselves in a dismissing state of mind. In the overview, we are likely to pay inadequate attention to attachment-related experience, may analyse the patient's experience rather than deepen it, may think rather than feel, and may focus too much on behaviour and too little on internal states. 'Merger wariness' (Goldbart and Wallin 1996) in the dismissing state of mind can lead to withdrawal rather than intimacy. There may also be a tendency to externalise, so that the patient rather than the therapist is regularly felt to be responsible for whatever problems arise in the relationship.

Rather than wear these constraints like an invisible straitjacket, we can, ideally, use our awareness of them as information that may allow us to correct our course.

Whenever I find myself in a dismissing state of mind – isolated from my feelings and distant from the patient, engaged in a conversation between 'talking heads', bored and sometimes drowsy – I try to take a step forward in the direction of the patient and my own internal experience. I also try to remember to ask myself, 'What is it that I don't want to experience now?' Or alternatively, 'What is it in myself and/or in the patient that I have needed to isolate myself from?' Finally, I tend to wonder if I may be involved in a collusion with the patient to avoid emotional experience that is troubling not only to me, but to the patient as well.

The therapist in a preoccupied state of mind

The preoccupied is in many ways the polar opposite of the dismissing state of mind. In the latter, we inhabit a 'left-brain' world in which thinking prevails over feeling and the self, rather than the other, is the centre of gravity. In the former, we are in a 'right-brain' world in which strong feelings can drown out thought, and the other is the centre of gravity – the partner in the relationship with influence and importance. To capture our experience as therapists in a preoccupied state of mind, the key word is accommodation. We accommodate to the patient, or try very hard to, out of the fear that if we do not, the patient will leave us. While we may feel very connected to the patient, we have little solid sense here of our own value, our ability to be of real help, or our potential significance to the patient. As a consequence, we can find ourselves reflexively attempting to please and reassure the patient in any number of ways. We may bend over backwards to communicate our empathy. We may disclose our identification with the patient's experience. Or we may yield to the temptation simply to say what we think the patient wishes to hear.

Our surplus insecurity and fear of losing the patient, as well as our compulsive accommodation, can be understood in the light of certain aspects of the 'hyperactivating' strategy common to ambivalent infants and, of course, preoccupied adults. This strategy arises out of repeated experiences of abandonment by unpredictably responsive attachment figures (now you see them, now you don't) upon whom we are dependent and from whom we learn that our best hope for securing the support and attention of others is to make our distress too conspicuous to ignore. In the context of this strategy, our helplessness and vulnerability are felt to foster connection, while our strength and autonomy are felt to threaten it. The problem with this solution is that our need to keep the attachment system chronically activated can undermine our potential to feel emotionally balanced, confident about ourselves, and trusting in relation to others.

As therapists, this preoccupied approach is clearly constraining. On the other hand, it also enables us to resonate with the experience of our patients and to offer them the experience of 'feeling felt' (Siegel 2001) that is critical to forming a therapeutic relationship. We have valuable resources here – particularly our access to our emotions and intuition – but they can be hard to capitalise on because of our fears that link autonomy to abandonment. When we have trouble experiencing a relationship as a setting that has room for two, how are we to have a mind of our own?

Among the consequences of this quandary for the therapist in a preoccupied state are the following: expressions of our authentic autonomous self can too easily be suppressed or dissociated, in which case it will be hard to have – and still harder to convey – views that differ from the patient's. This means that as we relate to the patient our freedom to interpret – that is, to recognise and articulate alternative perspectives – can be very constrained. Much the same is likely to be true when it comes to appropriately asserting, as therapists, our influence upon the patient, our needs and our desires. Instead we are vulnerable to a kind of boundary loss or merging in which our independent experience of ourselves seems to evaporate as we are absorbed in the experience of the patient. The other side of the same coin may be our tendency to attribute traits of our own to the patient. Recall in this connection the social psychological research showing that 'anxious' (aka preoccupied) subjects are prone to over-identify with others through a bias toward 'false consensus' (Mikulincer and Shaver 2003). Thus we need to be cautious about assuming that our own psychology and that of the patient are the same. Needless to say, perhaps, we also need to be wary of our tendency to drift towards conflict avoidance, submission, self-blame and shame.

Noticing that we are caught in these kinds of undercurrents can be informative. I can identify my state of mind as preoccupied when I feel that I am losing myself in the patient's experience while becoming out of touch with my own – or that I am full of feelings but unwilling or unable to consider what these feelings might mean. When I observe, in short, that I am too gripped by the impulse to accommodate, then I realise that I may need to take a step back both from the patient and from the 'literalness' of my own emotional experience. To this end, I often find it helpful to ask myself questions such as these: 'How am I accommodating to the patient in ways that may not be useful?'; 'What is it that I have been afraid to say or do, out of a fear of losing or hurting the patient?'; and 'What is it in myself, in the patient, and/or in the nature of our relationship that might help explain my fearful inhibition?'

The therapist in an unresolved state of mind

As suggested earlier, therapists are often 'wounded healers' with our own history of attachment-related trauma to which we have adapted with a 'controlling–caregiving' strategy. Despite all the work we have done on ourselves – and the 'earned security' we hope for as the result – most of us still have elements of this traumatic history that remain unresolved. Thus we are usually vulnerable to four distinct experiences of ourselves in relation to others that Liotti (1995, 1999) describes as features of an unresolved state of mind. Having been on the receiving end of trauma, we can experience ourselves as victims. Having experienced ourselves as both angry and responsible in response to trauma – and also perhaps identifying with the aggressor – we can experience ourselves as persecutors.

Having experienced with attachment figures the role reversal involved in being 'parentified' (recall that disorganised infants often become care-giving – i.e. controlling – children), we can experience ourselves as rescuers. And finally, because as victims of trauma we have had recourse to the defence of dissociation, we can experience ourselves as cognitively incompetent or confused. Like the dismissing and preoccupied states of mind, an unresolved state in the therapist confers both strengths and vulnerabilities. The strengths associated with this state of mind include a sensitivity to the patient's experience of trauma as well as the potential to understand it on the basis of partial identification. On the downside, therapists in an unresolved state of mind can tend to become too rigidly lodged in one or more of the roles I described above – victim, persecutor, rescuer, or cognitive incompetent.

The other day I found myself feeling apprehensive as I waited in my office for a particular patient to arrive. I was aware of feeling anxious at the possibility that I might be attacked by the patient or that she might experience me as attacking her. Worried about being a victim or a persecutor, I saw that I was standing at the edge, so to speak, of my own unresolved state of mind with respect to attachment. Unsurprisingly, I saw this patient, too, as inhabiting (much of the time) an unresolved state of mind. As mentioned earlier, the states of mind we experience with our patients are both developmentally determined and context-dependent. Thus while our potential to occupy an unresolved state is established by our history, it is activated in a specific relational context – and usually that context is our relationship with a patient who is unresolved with respect to trauma.

Of the various states of mind with respect to attachment, it is the unresolved state in ourselves that is usually the most difficult to manage and make use of. Our fears of being victims or persecutors can be very threatening indeed. And our default options here – the roles of 'space case' and rescuer – may afford us some protection but at the price of undermining our ability to help our patients. The conscious and unconscious threats that hover around us in an unresolved state can make it hard to think straight as we find ourselves becoming defensively drowsy or spaced-out. Alternatively, we may find a modicum of security as we take charge of scary patients by taking care of them – thus repeating in the context of clinical work the 'controlling/care-giving' strategy we learned in childhood. The problem, of course, is that consoling, soothing and/or giving advice to patients is an inadequate substitute for the genuine empathy, limit-setting and activation/ regulation of intense trauma-related emotions and memories that are essential to the integration of unresolved states of mind.

My advice to myself when working with such states is not to avoid them – neither in myself nor in the patient – but instead to recognise, describe, understand and discuss them with the patient. Of course, this advice is often easier to offer than to implement, because the threatening roles of victim and victimiser evoke fear and shame of an intensity that is sometimes hard to manage. But this is exactly what we must try to do in whatever ways we can. And in this effort, as I will shortly explain, our own mindfulness and mentalising have key roles to play.

Mindfulness, mentalising and the therapist's self-enquiry

Identifying the state of mind – secure, dismissing, preoccupied, or unresolved – in which we are lodged at a specific moment with a specific patient enlists a particular 'map' to orient ourselves as we attempt to generate a new and developmentally facilitative attachment relationship with the patient. But such a map is not the territory, and certainly not the whole territory, for it may leave out the specific and personal details of our here-and-now participation in what we hope will be a healing relationship. Scrupulously examining what in fact we are doing as we relate to the patient can help us to access the nonverbal subtext of the therapeutic conversation, which may in turn reveal the impact of our own attachment patterns as they interact with those of the patient. Such self-scrutiny also has the invaluable potential to illuminate the perceptible edge of dissociated experience in both partners in the therapeutic couple – which is vital because accessing dissociated experience is a precondition for its eventual integration. To make all this clearer requires a brief turn to the realm of nonverbal experience.

All of us are profoundly affected by experiences that are difficult to put into words. Such experiences can be hard to articulate for different reasons: their origins may be preverbal, they may be defensively dissociated, or they may have occurred in the shadow of trauma that disabled the brain structures that underpin speech and autobiographical memory. Though unspoken or unspeakable, these implicit experiences – Bollas (1987) called them the 'unthought known' – are nonetheless communicated. How so? In treatment, therapists and patients regularly evoke in each other and enact with each other aspects of themselves (memories, feelings, conflicts, internalised images of self and other) that they are unable to put into words. Both for better and for worse, these nonverbal communications generate the web of transference-countertransference enactments that arises as the attachment patterns of therapist and patient interlock. And given the inescapable reciprocal influence that helps shape such enactments, the therapist's attachment patterns are nearly always manifest in ways that are meaningfully, rather than adventitiously, related to those of the patient.

Repeatedly asking ourselves what we are actually doing with the patient can thus help us both to identify our role in these ongoing enactments and to access the dissociated experience that psychotherapy aims to integrate. To be most effective, the self-inquiry I advocate should pose not only the key question – 'What am I actually doing with this patient?' – but also two others aimed at deepening our understanding: 'What are the implicit relational meanings of what I'm doing?' and 'What might be my motivations for doing what I'm doing?' As I'll explain shortly, the first question can best be answered when the therapist mobilises a mindful stance, the next two when the therapist mobilises a reflective or mentalising stance.

Recognising our role in enactments can be a considerable challenge because we are never altogether transparent to ourselves. We remain ignorant of much of what we do, partly because it is simply an automatic, unreflective expression of who we are, and partly because we tend to suppress awareness of what might trouble or unsettle us. The latter can be a particular problem for therapists whose history of trauma has imposed dissociations, including – almost universally – dissociated feelings of shame.

Adopting a stance of mindfulness – the centrepiece of a 2,500-year-old Buddhist tradition – can help to overcome these barriers, because it breaks the trance of conducting treatment as if we were on autopilot. When we aim to be mindful, it is as if we 'snap out of it' by deliberately choosing to pay attention to our here-and-now experience with the patient as, moment by moment, this experience unfolds – neither judging nor evaluating it, but simply pausing to notice what we are doing while we are doing it. Moreover, cultivating mindfulness promotes acceptance, so mindfulness can function as an antidote to the shame that constricts self-awareness. Finally, a mindful stance not only facilitates the recognition of our role in enactments, but may also help to loosen their grip.

Simply asking ourselves what we're doing with the patient is a kind of 'mindfulness in action' (Safran and Muran 2003) that allows us to grasp – at a literal, explicit, 'facts of the case' level – the details of our participation in the ongoing enactment. Then, having explicitly identified the nature of our action (empathising, interpreting, offering advice, making a joke), we need to understand its implicit meaning – particularly in the light of the relationship between our own psychology and that of the patient. For again, the clinician's attachment patterns as played out in the therapeutic interaction are nearly always meaningfully related to the attachment patterns of the patient. In trying to understand our conduct both in terms of its implicit relational meanings and in terms of our motivations, our key resource is our ability to mentalise – that is, to make sense of behaviour by inferring the mental states (feelings, beliefs, desires) that underlie it.

With one rather prickly patient, for example, my initial self-inquiry – mindfulness in action – allowed me to see that what I was actually doing early in the session was . . . nothing. At the explicit behavioural level, I was making room for the free flow of the patient's spoken thoughts by making sure to share none of my own. Privately exploring the implicit relational meanings of my silence, I recognised my fear that whatever words I spoke, my patient would experience them as intrusive and hurtful – and would probably become angry. Yet I felt in a bind, for if I could not speak, I could not help. And as for the question of my motivation? I realised that with this particular patient (and no doubt with others as well) I was bending over backwards to avoid experiencing myself as destructive.

Eventually I broke my silence by sharing my dilemma about speaking – wanting to say something useful, but fearing his anger in response to words of mine that he was likely to experience as disruptive incursions on his own thoughts. This disclosure allowed him to share with me a related dilemma of his own: Should he risk 'letting me in' when his history had proven that his only safety lay in mobilising an off-putting 'force field' of ever-ready anger? As he went on to describe the 'three-headed monster' (narcissistic father, seductive mother, sadistic brother) against which his force field had originally been deployed, it suddenly occurred to me that the fear of destructiveness that had shut me up was linked with another kind of monster: a dreaded, shame-ridden facet of myself that I had recently come to call the 'Bug'.

Case Example: Jacob, the 'Bug' and me

To begin at the middle of this story, I will say that one memorable day I was sitting with a patient who, despite a history replete with horrific trauma, seemed to bear no visible scars. Apart from some discontent with the quality of his intimate relationships, Jacob was apparently a very happy man who lived a charmed life. Yet he lived, I felt, on the surface. To keep safely distant from the neglect, loss and abuse of his traumatic past, he was distant from himself while letting no one fully know him. To offset this distance and compensate for what (I felt) was missing in his life – the experience of being known and deeply cared for as a whole person – he indulged in various forms of 'acting out' that put him at considerable risk.

On the day in question, Jacob was telling me with pleasure about still another stroke of good fortune that had recently come his way; he followed this with some uncurious words about his risky behaviour, a little as if he were confessing. Such communications from Jacob were all too familiar to me, as were my responses to them. To today's good news, I responded as if I shared in his pleasure; to the confession, as if his conduct were worth exploring in an effort to better understand its meaning and allure. Then, rather suddenly, it struck me that the words I was speaking to Jacob had begun to have a hollow sound and that his face in response to them was unexpressive. Plainly something was off. Deliberately attempting now to land in the present moment, I paused to silently inquire of myself, 'What was it that I was actually doing as I related to Jacob?' I became aware of the effort I was expending in order to be there for him, for it certainly was not coming naturally. I realised that I had been operating as if on autopilot, without thoughtful intention, almost compulsively offering Jacob what amounted to a kind of pseudo-therapy. If I were to talk about what was really going on inside myself, I would have to say something about my anger and my envy that Jacob seemed to be able to do whatever he wanted whenever he wanted to do it – with no repercussions or even pangs of conscience! I was extremely distressed at the intensity of what I was feeling and tried, silently and privately, with little success, to make sense of what I was experiencing. I felt immobilised and realised that, in fact, I had been effectively immobilised for some time. I recognised that my patient and I were at an impasse.

Taking a step back for a moment, I would say that sometimes as therapists we are capable – having recognised the impasses in which we are lodged – of understanding and resolving those impasses through diligent self-analysis and dialogue, negotiation and exploration with the patient. On the other hand, there is often truth to the old joke that the problem with self-analysis is the countertransference. As I have mentioned, we are never completely transparent to ourselves, in part because we are compelled to remain blind to sights that deeply trouble us. Moreover, our capacity for useful reflection is always compromised when we find ourselves gripped by intensely disturbing feelings. Hence the necessity at times for the 'two-person mentalising' available in the form of consultation and the therapist's own therapy, both of which I made use of in attempting to resolve the impasse with Jacob.

In a small group consultation with colleagues Susan Sands and David Shaddock, I talked about my experiences with Jacob – and specifically the problem of doing therapy with someone who communicates as if he has no problems. With an obvious surplus of emotion I discussed the anger and envy I had recently become aware I felt in the presence of this man who seemed to possess the psychological and practical wherewithal to live with nearly perfect freedom. I also discussed the repetitious and frustrating sequence of the work with Jacob's high-risk behaviour: how we would approach it, seem to get somewhere, then find it slipping off the radar screen, only to have it reappear again – and again. The patient I sketched seemed large and strong, capable of being intimidating – though I was not aware of feeling intimidated. What I did often feel with Jacob was a sense of lack, as if I had much less to offer than I usually feel I do. Sometimes it was hard to think clearly or feel fully in his presence. At worst I could feel deadened or invisible. Rarely did I feel needed.

About all this my colleagues had many useful things to say. But what opened my eyes and my heart was Susan saying, 'We now know about what it's like for you to be with him, but can you tell us something about how he got to be the way he is? Something about his childhood?' I literally felt stunned to realise that I had not said a single word about Jacob's experiences growing up, which were largely experiences of coping with trauma. As I began to describe this lonely story of constant squalor and intermittent horror, I had two nearly simultaneous images so vivid that they were like living presences: The first was of Jacob as a helpless and humiliated little boy; the second was of myself as a similar kind of little boy. And what felt like the superimposition of our related – though certainly not identical – experiences, one upon the other, brought me to tears. As I sobbed, the meaning of the impasse with Jacob crystallised for me, virtually in an instant.

In my own therapy I had recently been struggling with a profound and disturbing set of feelings that I had come to refer to as the 'Bug' (think: Kafka's *Metamorphosis*). I initially experienced these utterly excruciating emotional sensations as nearly impossible to bear and no easier to name, though the visceral sense they carried was that I was disgusting, destructive, dangerous. Because they were inside me, or because I felt at some primal level that they simply were me, there seemed no escape from them save through self-destruction. Perhaps needless to say, I never believed that the Bug was all of me, so I could feel the self-destructive impulses without feeling compelled to act on them. What I have come to believe is that the Bug is a residue of my preverbal experiences with a mother who found her baby's needs (and undoubtedly her own needs) disgusting and dangerous.

The emotional response to being treated as a bug is probably best summed up with the word shame – the nearly intolerable pain of feeling not just that one has done something bad, but that one is bad. In my own therapy I had stumbled upon this dissociated pain and I was apparently averse to dragging Jacob – who I 'knew' intuitively was as vulnerable to it as I was – into that particular torture chamber. Nor, evidently, did I wish to spend any more time there myself, even vicariously, if I could somehow avoid it.

And so I had avoided it – by colluding with Jacob in living out a relationship between the two of us in a safer realm where need, vulnerability and shame were relegated to the sidelines. At centre stage in that psychological Green Zone were variations on the theme of omnipotence (and, perhaps, impotence). Rather than experience the danger of seeing or feeling in Jacob the shamed and fearful boy (or baby) with whom I might painfully identify, I had been focused self-protectively – if angrily, enviously and somewhat impotently – on the man who could do anything.

Perhaps unremarkably, when I next met with Jacob our relationship had a profoundly different and deeper 'feel' – I presume because, through Jacob in a sense, I had further integrated a disowned part of myself. This allowed me both to be more of a whole person when I was with him and to experience him as more of a whole person. Of course, there was no 'miracle cure'. But shortly after the session we agreed to meet more frequently and to address in a more deliberate and head-on fashion the 'acting out' with which we had previously grappled superficially, only to let it slip away. In the sessions following that pivotal meeting, Jacob also began to talk – often pointing with his hand in the direction of his belly – about his vague, shameful sense of inferiority and its origin in the troubling experience of his early years.

Concluding comments

My choice to concentrate in these pages on the impact of the therapist's own troubling origins and attachment patterns has to do, in part, with the fact that this important matter tends to be slighted in most of the clinical literature – as it does, I suspect, in much of our clinical practice – despite the fact that the primary creative instrument of the therapist is a self whose resources and liabilities are originally forged in the crucible of personal history. And as I have mentioned, the therapist's personal history is liable to be one that bears the scars of trauma.

In suggesting that the therapist's attachment patterns are often shaped by trauma, I am departing from a conventional view that patients and therapists alike may be tempted to embrace – namely, that the vulnerabilities in the therapeutic couple reside primarily if not exclusively in the patient. This view is a fiction that may serve the hopes of the patient and the self-protective needs of the therapist. But it is a fiction that diverts attention from the important reality that it is actually the interaction of the attachment patterns of both partners – their strengths and vulnerabilities, their integrations and dissociations – that ultimately determines the extent to which a new and healing attachment relationship will develop in psychotherapy.

I am proposing that we regard the therapist's vulnerabilities, like those of the patient, as integral and inevitable facts of life in psychotherapy. They are not necessarily best understood as psychopathological. Instead they may be seen as evidence of human imperfection. These vulnerabilities – in interaction with those of the patient – can generate difficulties in therapy that present obstacles, but also opportunities. When enactments engage the core vulnerabilities of the patient and the therapist, there is a risk of rupture, to be sure, but there is also the potential to provide the patient with a corrective relational experience and the therapist with a chance to further his or her own ever-unfinished psychological work.

In concluding, let me return to the point I asserted in the title of this chapter. The therapist's attachment history can indeed be a source not only of impasse but also of inspiration – for there are unique advantages potentially bestowed upon the clinician by the experience of an unhappy or traumatic childhood. Of course, realising these potential advantages depends upon the clinician's working through and integrating much (though probably never all) of the pain and difficulty imposed by such a childhood. It is the 'earned security' achieved through subsequent attachment relationships in therapy, analysis and elsewhere that eventually allows 'the clinician's wounds to serve as tools' (paraphrasing Harris 2009). As wounded healers many of us know the patient's struggles at first hand. And having made the journey ourselves – at least part way from dissociation to wholeness – we may be exceptionally well equipped to help patients undertake their own healing journey.

References

Bollas, C. (1987). *The Shadow of the Object: psychoanalysis of the unthought known*. New York: Columbia University Press.

Dozier, M., Cue, A. and Barnett, L. (1994). Clinicians as caregivers: role of attachment organization in treatment. *Journal of Consulting and Clinical Psychology* **62**, 793–800.

Goldbart, S. and Wallin, D.J. (1996). *Mapping the Terrain of the Heart: passion, tenderness, and the capacity to love*. Lanham, MD: Jason Aronson.

Harris, A. (2009). You must remember this. *Psychoanalytic Dialogues* **19**, 2–21.

Liotti, G. (1995). Disorganized/disoriented attachment in the psychotherapy of the dissociative disorders. In S. Goldberg, R. Muir and J. Kerr (eds), *Attachment Theory: social, developmental and clinical perspectives*, pp. 343–67. Hillsdale, NJ: Analytic Press.

——(1999). Disorganization of attachment as a model for understanding dissociative psychopathology. In J. Solomon and C. George (eds), *Attachment Disorganization*, pp. 291–317. New York: Guilford Press.

Main, M. and Cassidy, J. (1988). Categories of response to reunion with the parent at age 6: Predicted from infant attachment classifications and stable over a 1-month period. *Developmental Psychology* **24**, 415–26.

Mikulincer, M. and Shaver, P.R. (2003). The attachment behavioral system in adulthood: activation, psychodynamics, and interpersonal processes. In M.P. Zanna (ed.), *Advances in Experimental Social Psychology*, vol. 35, pp. 53–152. New York: Academic Press.

Pearlman, L.A. and Saakvitne, K.W. (1995). *Trauma and the Therapist: countertransference and vicarious traumatization in psychotherapy with incest survivors.* New York: Norton.

Safran, J. and Muran, C. (2003). *Negotiating the Therapeutic Alliance: a relational treatment guide.* New York: Guilford Press.

Siegel, D.J. (2001). *The Developing Mind: how relationships and the brain interact to shape who we are.* New York: Guilford Press.

Wallin, D.J. (2007). *Attachment in Psychotherapy.* New York: Guilford Press.

Wartner, U.G., Grossmann, K., Fremmer-Bombik, E. and Suess, G. (1994). Attachment patterns at age six in south Germany: Predictability from infancy and implications for preschool behavior. *Child Development* **65**, 1014–27.

Index